CW00431109

Advanced Introduction to Private E

Elgar Advanced Introductions are stimulating and thoughtful introductions to major fields in the social sciences, business and law, expertly written by the world's leading scholars. Designed to be accessible yet rigorous, they offer concise and lucid surveys of the substantive and policy issues associated with discrete subject areas.

The aims of the series are two-fold: to pinpoint essential principles of a particular field, and to offer insights that stimulate critical thinking. By distilling the vast and often technical corpus of information on the subject into a concise and meaningful form, the books serve as accessible introductions for undergraduate and graduate students coming to the subject for the first time. Importantly, they also develop well-informed, nuanced critiques of the field that will challenge and extend the understanding of advanced students, scholars and policy-makers.

For a full list of titles in the series please see the back of the book. Recent titles in the series include:

Business and Human Rights
Peter T. Muchlinski

Spatial Statistics
Daniel A. Griffith and Bin Li

The Sociology of the Self
Shanyang Zhao

Artificial Intelligence in Healthcare
Tom Davenport, John Glaser and Elizabeth Gardner

Central Banks and Monetary Policy
Jakob de Haan and Christiaan Pattipeilohy

Megaprojects
Nathalie Drouin and Rodney Turner

Social Capital
Karen S. Cook

Elections and Voting
Ian McAllister

Youth Studies
Howard Williamson and James E. Côté

Private Equity
Paul A. Gompers and Steven N. Kaplan

Advanced Introduction to

Private Equity

PAUL A. GOMPERS

Eugene Holman Professor of Business Administration, Harvard Business School, USA

STEVEN N. KAPLAN

Neubauer Family Distinguished Service Professor of Entrepreneurship and Finance, Booth School of Business, University of Chicago, USA

Elgar Advanced Introductions

 Edward Elgar
PUBLISHING

Cheltenham, UK • Northampton, MA, USA

Published by
Edward Elgar Publishing Limited
The Lypiatts
15 Lansdown Road
Cheltenham
Glos GL50 2JA
UK

Edward Elgar Publishing, Inc.
William Pratt House
9 Dewey Court
Northampton
Massachusetts 01060
USA

A catalogue record for this book
is available from the British Library

Library of Congress Control Number: 2022939161

ISBN 978 1 80037 217 7 (cased)
ISBN 978 1 80037 219 1 (paperback)
ISBN 978 1 80037 218 4 (eBook)

Printed and bound in Great Britain by TJ Books Limited, Padstow, Cornwall

Contents

About the authors

Paul A. Gompers is the Eugene Holman Professor of Business Administration at the Harvard Business School and specializes in research on startup, high growth and newly public companies as well as venture capital and private equity investors. He has published six books, dozens of refereed journal articles and more than 100 business case studies. He received his A.B. summa cum laude in biology from Harvard College in 1987. He attended Oxford University on a Marshall Fellowship where he received an M.Sc. in economics. He completed his Ph.D. in Business Economics at Harvard University in 1993. Professor Gompers is co-founder and non-executive director of Spur Capital Partner, a venture capital fund-of-funds. He is also a board member of the Boston Symphony Orchestra, the Beth-Israel Deaconess Hospital and USA Triathlon Foundation.

Steven N. Kaplan is the Neubauer Family Distinguished Service Professor of Entrepreneurship and Finance at the University of Chicago Booth School of Business. He is a Research Associate at the National Bureau of Economic Research. A *Fortune* magazine article referred to Professor Kaplan as "probably the foremost private equity scholar in the galaxy." He co-created the Kaplan-Schoar Public Market Equivalent (PME) private equity benchmarking approach. He also co-created the Lincoln Middle Market Index. *Business Week* named him one of the top 12 business school teachers and one of the top four entrepreneurship teachers. He is an investor in several private equity funds.

Preface

This book represents the integration of several streams of professional activities that we have been involved in over the past several decades. Both of us have been active in researching, teaching, advising and investing in the private equity industry for more than 30 years.

We've often been asked by private equity professionals, MBA students and investors to recommend a book that explains both what private equity does and how to do it. We usually make a couple of recommendations, but reply that there is no one book that integrates the insights from academic research with practical recommendations and examples. The best thing they can do is to take one of our courses. Until now. We decided that it was time to take the material from our courses and turn the material into this book.

Over the three-plus decades of our careers, the private equity industry has grown dramatically in assets under management, diversity of investment strategies and breadth of geographies. The number of private equity professionals has similarly exploded. The huge demand for courses addressing these issues from our MBA students is another indication of these changes. The high level of compensation of private equity investors has received a great deal of attention as well, much of it highly politicized.

The demand from students, practitioners and academics for actionable insights has grown commensurately. Most top business schools have scholars researching and teaching private equity. Those academics have contributed to a significant body of academic research that describes and evaluates a number of important facets of the private equity industry. That work has explored how PE funds and investments perform, how various stakeholders are affected, the levers that PE firms employ to effect those changes and how PE firms are organized and compensated.

We have organized this book around these major research streams, integrated that research with a large number of detailed examples and attempted to provide useful frameworks and actionable insights. Many of these examples are derived from detailed case studies that are among the many case studies we have written on private equity firms and investments. Other examples come from our relationships with private equity professionals and our own investing experience in private equity.

At the end of the day, the business of investing depends on decision making under uncertainty. No decision can be made with perfect foresight. But investment decisions made that are based upon insights from data, buttressed by well-reasoned examples and logically articulated, have a much better chance to generate attractive returns. We hope that this book can serve as a source of these insights and that everyone who has an interest in private equity – academics, students, young professionals and industry veterans – finds this book to be a useful reference.

Acknowledgments

Paul A. Gompers

This book would not have been possible without so many people who have been a part of my professional career. I have had the privilege to have amazing mentors from the very beginning of my academic career. Andrei Shleifer, Richard Ruback and Bill Sahlman have continued to provide tremendous opportunities to grow as a scholar and have given me critical advice over the years. Andrei has always focused on the importance and rigor of the research and ideas. Rick provided early encouragement to dive into the private equity space and continues to be a sounding board in many areas. And Bill always made sure that my research had a lens towards ideas that mattered in practice. My co-author in this book, Steven Kaplan, deserves a special shout-out. Thirty-five years ago as I toiled doing a biochemistry D.Phil., Steve helped guide me to pursue my Ph.D. in business economics and started me on the path to this career. His friendship and counsel for nearly 40 years have been pivotal, making the writing of this book that much more meaningful.

I have also benefited from having tremendous co-authors over the years. Andrew Metrick, Josh Lerner, David Scharfstein, Alon Brav, Yuhai Xuan, Vladimir Muhkarlyamov and Sophie Calder-Wang, in particular, have contributed to my intellectual growth in numerous ways. Each has helped me see finance and research in new ways and deepened my understanding of private equity.

My research and insights for this book have been deepened by my teaching at Harvard Business School. Over my 27 years at the school, I have written more than a hundred case studies. Each of those companies and protagonists was willing to share their stories and provided faces and texture to insights from the academic research. Many of the frameworks for this book have come out of knitting the case insights together. I am also indebted to the thousands of students who have helped shape the discussion around those cases.

My colleagues at Spur Capital Partners also deserve special note. While it was never my intention to found an investment management company, when circumstances presented themselves to put insights from my work into practice, I eagerly joined Paul Fetsch, Joan Heidorn and Brad Kelly to start on a 21-year adventure in the private equity space. We have been joined on this journey by Teri Hightower, Matt Horten and Kevin Moore. Having to meet with investors and vote on investments has forced me to think practically about the research and teaching that are at the core of my career. Senior professionals at the underlying funds in which we invest have also given me a greater appreciation for how great investors operate.

Finally, my family has been a source of support and inspiration. Jody, Sivan, Annika and Zoe have always been willing to challenge conventional wisdom. Through their own efforts to achieve in their own domains, I have continued to find motivation to plow new fields.

Acknowledgments

Steven N. Kaplan

I began studying leveraged buyouts and private equity almost 40 years ago. At that time, the asset class was new, relatively small and not well understood. I have been lucky to be able to research and teach in an area that has grown spectacularly. I have many people to thank for their help and interest.

I first started thinking about leveraged buyouts and private equity sometime in the mid-1980s with the encouragement of Bob Glauber at Harvard Business School. Mike Jensen continued that encouragement as the chair of my dissertation committee. He is a Nobel Prize–caliber economist and an amazing mentor.

I also have had a wonderful set of co-authors on private equity research from whom I have learned and continue to learn. They include Greg Brown, Paul Gompers, Will Gornall, Oleg Gredil, Bob Harris, Wendy Hu, Tim Jenkinson, Josh Lerner, Vladimir Mukharlyamov, David Robinson, Antoinette Schoar, Berk Sensoy, Morten Sorensen, Ilya Strebulaev, Per Stromberg and Rudi Stucke.

Bob Hamada suggested I teach entrepreneurial finance and private equity when Paul Gompers left the University of Chicago to return to Harvard Business School. Since 1996, I have learned about private equity and how to teach it from thousands of students. A number of those students have gone on to be successful private equity investors as well as friends. One of the few good things about getting older is that you get to see your former students become more and more successful.

I also want to thank Paul Gompers. He has been a terrific co-author and friend. He suggested we write this book and was the driving force behind getting it done.

Finally, and most importantly, my wife – Carol Rubin – and my sons – Sam and Alec – have provided support, motivation and encouragement for everything I have done.

1   Introduction to private equity

Why this book?

This book explores and provides a guide to private equity. This guide has four components. The first provides a brief history of private equity. The second describes the effects of private equity at both the portfolio company level and the fund level, particularly whether and how private equity creates economic value. The third provides a set of frameworks and considerations for making successful private equity investments. The fourth provides frameworks and considerations for setting up and running a successful private equity firm.

We have written this book because we think it will be useful for a book to put all four components succinctly in one place. The book should be useful to a number of different types of people: anyone who is interested in working for a private equity firm; anyone who is interested in selling their business to a private equity firm; and anyone who is interested in investing in a private equity fund.

In this introduction, we do four things. First, we describe the private equity industry, focusing on different sub-sectors and geographies. Second, we offer a brief history of the development of the private equity industry. Third, we present a framework for understanding the creation of value by private equity investors. Fourth, as we discuss the first three, we describe the contents of the rest of the book.

What is private equity?

The term *private equity investment* in the most general sense means investments in equity (stock) of companies that are not traded on stock exchanges and, therefore, are not available for investment by the general public. *Private equity firms* are financial intermediaries that help investors (usually large institutional investors and often referred to as limited partners or "LPs") make private equity investments by contributing capital to "funds" established by the private equity firms. Successful private equity investing relies on *careful evaluation of investments,* structuring the investments or *deals, financial engineering, governance engineering* and *operational engineering.* Each of those activities creates value for private equity investors and their operating companies.

In this book, we draw a distinction between venture capital and private equity. Private equity grew out of the venture capital industry, but the typical definition of private equity generally refers to investments in *leveraged buyouts* (LBOs, discussed below), *growth capital* (large, but usually minority investments in stock of growing or scaling companies), *distressed investments* (investing in company securities in bankruptcy or close to it) and, sometimes, *mezzanine capital* (preferred equity investments senior to common stock, typically raised by smaller companies).

The private equity industry became established during the leveraged buyout boom of the 1980s, but was preceded by the first venture capital funds which were formed in the 1940s. Although they emerged later, buyout funds share a common structure, compensation and investor base with venture capital funds. The industry practices in buyout funds, in many respects, stem from the venture capital industry's practices that developed during the early stages of its evolution.

As discussed above, private equity investors often have various strategies that target companies at different stages of their life cycle or different states of financial health. The earliest private equity investments were leveraged buyouts, which emerged and became important in the first half of the 1980s. In a typical leveraged buyout transaction, a private equity firm buys majority control of an existing company – whether, public, private or the division of another company – hence, the "buyout." Target companies are generally sought for identifiable opportunities for private equity investors to create value. Many of the early targets of LBO firms were underperforming or undermanaged public companies in which the incentives of management were misaligned with outside shareholders. Some of those targets were firms that engaged in conglomerate mergers in the 1960s and 1970s. Private equity investors would *take private* these companies by raising a significant amount of debt and delisting their stock from the public market.

The rise in leveraged buyouts in the 1980s was fueled by the rapid development of the "junk bond" market that allowed firms with less than an investment-grade rating to raise significant amounts of debt capital. With a source of debt, LBO investors could target underperforming firms and put in place financial, governance and, later, operational levers that improved performance.

Michael Jensen in a variety of seminal papers argued that LBOs were a superior organizational form for many companies. Managers, who typically owned little in the way of company stock, had a much larger ownership of the firm after the LBO, providing incentives to increase cash flows and value. The large, fixed interest and principal repayment schedules on debt enforced discipline on these managers as well.

LBOs are typically financed by equity capital from the private equity firm and debt capital provided by banks, private investors and the public markets. The fraction of deal value provided by equity capital has varied markedly over time from a low of roughly 10% in the late 1980s to roughly 50% today. In Chapter 5, we discuss financial engineering and explore the firm- and market-specific factors that influence the amount of debt that is raised when a transaction is completed. We highlight the important intermediaries and contractual terms that are typically used in these deals. Private equity investors usually look to firms with strong stable cash flows to pay the fixed interest and principal payments. Similarly, firms that are underleveraged, having relatively modest amounts of debt, create the opportunity to enhance value through increased interest tax shields.

LBO transactions occur across the size spectrum. Many of the transactions that receive public attention are the large, take private transactions in which large public companies are taken private. These transactions can be in the tens of billions of dollars. On the other end of the spectrum, lower middle-market private equity investors target smaller companies, most of which are already private. In these transactions, convincing the owners to sell their stake is often the critical element of the deal process. Some of these lower middle-market private equity firms specialize in buy-and-build transactions, often purchasing multiple players in an industry in the hopes of building a larger company that can be sold at a higher price.

A second important sub-sector of private equity is growth capital or growth equity. Growth equity investors look for companies that have established business models but require large amounts of capital to scale. Some of these companies may have started as venture capital-backed startups but have grown to the point at which growth equity is required. In these cases, growth equity often partially cashes out the venture capitalists and founders. Many other growth equity investments have been bootstrapped or grown as private companies and are looking to transition to the next stage of their development. An example would be a company with a restaurant concept that is established with five or ten sites in a region, but needs capital to expand nationally. Many growth equity investors specialize by industry and bring strategic/operational knowledge to the deal.

Distressed investing represents a third sub-sector within private equity. Distressed investors often look to acquire their ownership through the purchase of debt instruments. Typically, the debt of a distressed company trades at a discount, i.e., below par value, in anticipation of a potential default and bankruptcy restructuring. Distressed investors typically have a strategy that either entails having the debt repaid at par value or exchanging their debt holdings for equity in some type of debt for equity swap. Given the complex contractual and legal aspects of these investments, private equity firms that focus on distress typically have significant knowledge and capabilities around the reorganization and bankruptcy process. Deal execution often entails coordination of multiple parties as the restructuring progresses.

Finally, some private equity investors opportunistically target private investments in public equity (PIPEs). In a PIPE transaction, the private equity firm invests a substantial amount of equity in a public company, but does not take the company private. The company may need liquidity or may want access to the private equity investors' expertise. Terms of the PIPE typically provide the private equity investors with favorable terms and conditions in return for providing needed capital. PIPE investments tend to be somewhat counter-cyclical to debt markets, i.e., when it is more difficult to raise debt capital for LBOs, private equity investors often look to invest in PIPE transactions. Two examples would be Silver Lake Partners investing in Airbnb and Expedia in the midst of the COVID-19 pandemic in the spring of 2020.

One other class of funds, secondary private equity funds, is worth mentioning. In the last twenty years, these funds have emerged to provide liquidity for investors (in all types of private equity funds) who need to sell their fund positions for liquidity, regulatory or strategic reasons.

Whatever the sector, a critical element of the private equity investment process is identifying potential targets, evaluating them and negotiating transactions. In Chapter 4, we explore the deal sourcing, selection and structuring of private equity investments. Importantly, we present both qualitative and quantitative frameworks for evaluating investments.

As the private equity industry has grown, deals have become more competitive and driven up purchase multiples. Some private equity firms, particularly those that target smaller deals, claim that they have proprietary deal flow and are able to purchase companies at attractive prices. As the market for private equity deals has become more competitive, however, this has become increasingly difficult to do. Most private equity firms, if not all, need to focus on generating value through other means.

Accordingly, most private equity firms seek to identify companies that need operational improvements. Improving operating performance is critical to consistently generating attractive returns. Private equity investors do this by picking targets in attractive industry segments and then improving governance and operations. In fact, investors often specialize in a sector and/or have sector-focused operating partners within their firms. In Chapter 6, we discuss governance engineering in more detail, and in Chapter 7, we discuss operational engineering in more detail.

Before purchasing a company, private equity firms conduct extensive due diligence; i.e., research and analysis of the company's strategy, business plans, financial information, products, relationships with customers, suppliers and employees, positioning in the industry, etc. Effective due diligence does at least two things. First, it reduces the general uncertainty about the transaction. This allows the private equity investor to better forecast cash flows and outcomes. That, in turn, allows the investors to better decide whether a transaction is desirable, at what price and whether it can support leverage.

Second, due diligence reduces the asymmetry of information between the private equity investor and the seller of the portfolio company. This is important because the seller will typically know more about what it is selling than the buyer does. When the buyer is at such an information disadvantage, the buyer is afraid of getting a "lemon" and will tend to offer a lower price. When a buyer gets access to better and more detailed information, information asymmetry is reduced. If the information is favorable, the buyer will be willing to bid higher. Acquirers who are strongly aligned with the target's management generally have access to better information and also are able to interpret that information through the eyes of key senior management.

In addition to being skilled themselves in analyzing targets and managing their portfolio companies, private equity firms, particularly the larger ones, often retain leading consulting firms that have specific expertise in a particular industry or area of operations – both during the due diligence period and after the purchase. Typical operating improvements that private equity firms introduce include retaining experienced professional management, finding new areas of growth, reducing costs, spinning off non-core activities and achieving synergies with other portfolio companies of the same funds of private equity firms.

Private equity investors do not intend to own and operate portfolio companies indefinitely. Because the funds from which investments are made have predetermined lives, usually between 10 and 13 years, private equity investors target an exit within that time frame. Most deals are modeled with a five-year time horizon. Typical realized holding periods are between three and eight years.

Private equity investors look to exit by taking the company public through an initial public offering ("IPO"), selling the company to a strategic acquirer or another private equity investor, performing a leveraged recapitalization in which debt is raised to buyback the private equity firm's equity and, most recently, by selling to a special purpose acquisition corporation or SPAC. By forcing private equity firms to seek an exit, limited partners ensure that private equity managers do not retain investors' cash and are forced to raise new funds if they desire to continue making new investments. In Chapter 8, we discuss exit in greater detail.

Private equity organizations

Private equity firms typically raise dedicated funds in the form of limited partnerships. Investors in these limited partnerships (referred to as

LPs) are large institutional investors like pension funds, endowments, sovereign wealth funds and family offices or high net worth individuals. Private equity, as an asset class, has grown substantially over the past 20 years. This growth has been accelerated by the increased allocation to the asset class by large institutions. This desire to increase allocation has been driven, in part, by the substantial outperformance of large university endowments like Yale University (and its longtime chief investment officer, David Swensen) which were early investors in these types of funds.

Some private equity firms raise multiple funds with distinct investment strategies (growth, buyout, distress) or distinct geographies (e.g., US, Europe, Asia). Other private equity firms with more narrow strategies may raise only one fund at a time. All of these funds typically have 10- to 13-year lives with an investment period that is usually on the order of five years. Private equity firms typically raise a new fund every two to five years depending upon how quickly they invest the capital from their current existing fund.

Limited partnership agreements govern the relationship between GPs (the private equity investors) and LPs. The limited partnership agreement explicitly specifies the terms that govern the private equity firm's compensation during the fund's lifetime. It is rare for terms to be renegotiated. In addition, the specified compensation has a simple form that governs the relationship over the entire 10- to 13-year life of the fund. The private equity investor typically receives an annual fixed fee based on committed capital or net asset value (1–2%) plus variable compensation, or carried interest, that is a specified fraction of the fund's profits (usually about 20%).

Among other terms, these contracts contain a variety of restrictions on the GPs in terms of their investment activities. There are often limits on portfolio concentration or on which types of investments can be made. From a governance perspective, LPs typically do not become involved in oversight of the GPs and rely on the limited partnership contract to define the relationship between investors and the fund managers.

Private equity firms' fundraising comes in the form of commitments from LPs rather than actual cash. The private equity firm calls the funds from investors when an investment has been located and closed or when management fees need to be paid. The LPs then contribute a proportional share of their commitments. This "just in time" funding of investments and fees ensures that cash is put to use as needed while generally maximizing the rate of return on investment. In Chapter 9, we discuss fundraising and how funds are structured in greater detail.

The history of private equity

The evolution of the modern private equity firm begins with the history of venture capital in the US. Venture capital first developed in the late nineteenth and early twentieth centuries. Wealthy families began to look for ways to invest in potentially high-return, high-tech undertakings. The market for venture capital remained largely unorganized and fragmented throughout the late nineteenth and early twentieth centuries. The first impetus to organize investing came from wealthy Americans. In the 1930s and 1940s, members of the Rockefeller, Bessemer and Whitney families hired professional managers to seek out investments in promising young companies.

The first modern venture capital firm was formed in 1946, when MIT president Karl Compton, Massachusetts Investors Trust chairman Merrill Griswold, Federal Reserve Bank of Boston president Ralph Flanders and Harvard Business School Professor General Georges F. Doriot started American Research and Development (ARD). The goal of the company was to finance commercial applications of technologies that were developed during World War II.

These earliest venture capital firms were organized in the Northeast, centered both in Boston and New York. It was not until 1957 that West Coast venture capital came into existence. Arthur Rock, then an investment banker at Hayden, Stone & Co. in New York City, was sent to investigate a potential project in California. Rock called various individual and institutional investors to secure financing for Eugene Kleiner and a group of Shockley Laboratory employees.

A key event in the history of venture capital, and hence private equity funds, was the rise of the limited partnership. The early venture capital firms were structured as publicly traded closed-end funds. This structure created a number of problems, particularly the difficulty of raising additional capital when the fund's share price was depressed. The intro-duction of the limited partnership, by Draper, Gaither and Anderson in 1959, heralded a critical innovation for the industry that would serve as the nearly universal organizational form for private equity funds.

Private equity, as distinct from venture capital, begins in the late 1970s when the private equity firm Kohlberg Kravis & Roberts (KKR) began financing and, likely, invented the first meaningful LBOs. LBOs increased in size and frequency in the 1980s, a decade when hostile takeovers and other often highly leveraged transactions also became common. The growth in the junk bond market, created by Michael Milken and Drexel Burnham Lambert, fueled both the LBO and hostile takeover wave. Many of these transactions purchased companies with ever higher levels of debt to total capital and came under public scrutiny. Perhaps no deal better captures this time period than KKR's purchase in 1988 of RJR-Nabisco, a large public company. KKR, which has gone on to become one of the largest global managers of private equity, paid a large premium – roughly 100% – to take control of RJR-Nabisco. The deal became the stuff of legend when *Barbarians at the Gate*, a best-selling account of the deal, was pub-lished. The deal also inspired movies like *Wall Street*, which demonized LBO investors. The rise of the LBO led to scrutiny among regulators and lawmakers as the transactions gained a reputation for drastically reduc-ing costs, including employment. In 1989, the US Senate and House con-ducted hearings on "LBOs and Corporate Debt."

Private equity today

The private equity industry has grown substantially over the decades. Table 1.1 shows the amount of money committed to private equity funds globally each year from 2006 through 2019. Fundraising from 2006 to 2008 was strong, at roughly $300 billion annually. It declined markedly with the global financial crisis in 2009 and 2010, bottoming out at $130 billion raised globally in 2010. Since then, robust global economic growth likely has fueled rapid growth of the industry. Fundraising has increased steadily and reached a record of $733 billion in 2021.[1]

One of the more dramatic changes in the private equity industry over the past 30 years has been its expansion outside of the US as shown in Table 1.2 which tabulates global fundraising by region. Not surprisingly,

Table 1.1   Private Equity Fundraising Activity

	Capital Raised (USD bn)	Number of Funds
2006	$280.17	540
2007	$387.41	614
2008	$301.72	551
2009	$170.16	362
2010	$129.95	408
2011	$176.78	481
2012	$183.88	493
2013	$276.51	564
2014	$322.74	682
2015	$259.07	632
2016	$350.59	656
2017	$397.02	702
2018	$476.38	610
2019	$505.40	529

Source: Pitchbook

North America has been the top region in every year, accounting for $162.6 billion in capital in 2006 and $322.3 billion in 2019. Europe has generally been the second most active region, raising $90.2 billion in 2006 and increasing to $108.3 billion in 2019. The most significant growth in recent years has occurred in Asia. At the beginning of the period, Asian private equity firms raised only $16.7 billion. In 2018, Asian funds raised $169.4 billion. Oceania, the Middle East and Africa have generally been substantially smaller private equity markets, usually only several billion dollars per year.

To get a sense of magnitudes, PE funds raised almost $1.2 trillion in North America from 2015 to 2019. PE funds generally hold their investments for five years, so this would be a good estimate of the stock of invested capital. Those investments tend to be leveraged at least 1 to 1, meaning the portfolio company values would exceed $2.4 trillion. This represents almost 10% of the value of the US stock market during that period.

Table 1.3 illustrates the diversity of fund types and variation in fundraising by tabulating total amount of capital committed to various sub-sectors of private equity from 2006 to 2019. Buyout fundraising decreased

Table 1.2 Private Equity Funds Raised by Geography

	2006	2007	2008	2009	2010	2011	2012	2013	2014	2015	2016	2017	2018	2019
Rest of world	$1.02	$3.45	$3.57	$0.91	$3.97	$9.99	$1.54	$1.87	$3.29	$1.62	$1.87	$1.75	$0.96	$2.01
Africa	$1.15	$4.19	$2.76	$1.74	$1.81	$1.52	$0.95	$3.48	$0.89	$4.16	$2.66	$0.67	$1.34	$0.61
Middle East	$5.00	$4.39	$9.54	$1.21	$1.68	$0.99	$5.05	$1.74	$1.50	$1.42	$2.09	$1.66	$0.21	$0.49
Oceania	$3.65	$1.42	$4.93	$0.55	$2.75	$1.67	$3.61	$0.81	$1.48	$2.03	$2.68	$2.82	$2.96	$0.00
Asia	$16.65	$28.15	$35.89	$14.51	$28.32	$29.81	$38.16	$24.87	$69.59	$37.37	$35.70	$28.76	$169.42	$71.66
Europe	$90.16	$108.40	$78.04	$51.59	$27.61	$54.34	$33.15	$79.81	$61.01	$57.55	$72.62	$98.15	$89.64	$108.33
North America	$162.55	$237.40	$166.98	$99.64	$63.80	$78.46	$101.41	$163.92	$184.99	$154.92	$232.97	$263.21	$211.85	$322.30

Source: Pitchbook

Table 1.3   Capital Raised by Fund Type

	Buyout	Diversified Private Equity	Mezzanine	PE Growth/ Expansion	Restructuring/ Turnaround
2006	$226.01	$0.16	$30.91	$20.97	$2.12
2007	$333.01	$0.55	$27.18	$22.07	$4.60
2008	$245.85	$0.12	$22.52	$29.78	$3.45
2009	$139.95	$0.04	$8.82	$20.54	$0.82
2010	$91.90	$1.25	$9.09	$26.02	$1.71
2011	$128.32	$0.23	$11.78	$35.45	$1.00
2012	$144.04	$0.00	$17.78	$22.06	$0.00
2013	$231.85	$0.19	$15.36	$24.36	$4.75
2014	$257.62	$2.17	$11.16	$49.75	$2.04
2015	$204.51	$0.00	$16.06	$38.50	$0.00
2016	$264.76	$3.10	$37.75	$40.02	$4.95
2017	$336.01	$0.05	$18.97	$41.80	$0.20
2018	$302.90	$0.39	$27.06	$140.00	$6.04
2019	$398.89	$0.33	$6.76	$90.12	$9.29

Source: Pitchbook

substantially after the financial crisis, declining to $91.9 billion in 2010, but then growing to $398.9 billion in 2019. As befits its name, the largest percentage growth has been in growth-stage private equity, which increased by almost seven times from only $21 billion in 2006 to $140 billion in 2018. Mezzanine and turnaround investing, in contrast, have been relatively smaller sub-sectors.

Over the past 30 years, the growth in global private equity fundraising has led to the emergence of global players managing many billions of dollars in capital. Table 1.4 lists the top 20 private equity firms based on capital under management and highlights their investment focus, namely the asset class and strategies in which they invest, as well as their geographies. Most of the global private equity firms invest across multiple geographies and multiple asset classes. Nine of the top 10 global private equity firms are headquartered in the US. Carlyle, KKR and Blackstone are the three largest, with each managing more than $100 billion. CVC is the largest non-US headquartered fund with $108 billion under management and headquartered in the UK. There are a few exceptions. Sino-IC Capital

Table 1.4 Largest Private Equity Firms in 2020

Firm Name	Total Funds Raised (USD mn)	Funds in Market	Estimated Dry Powder (USD mn)	Asset Class	Strategy	Geographic Focus	Headquarters
Carlyle Group	$129 743	19	$31 609	PE, VC	Buyout, growth	Asia, North America, Europe, US, Japan, Brazil, China, Germany, Middle East, Peru, South America, Tanzania, UK, West Europe	US
KKR	$116 579	10	$19 894	PE, VC	Buyout, growth	US, North America, Europe, Asia, Greater China	US
Blackstone Group	$116 564	13	$12 289	PE, VC	Buyout, growth	US, North America, Mexico, Asia, China	US
TPG	$109 073	4	$18 880	PE, VC	Buyout, growth, turnaround	US, Asia, China, North America, South America	US
CVC	$108 762	0	$34 482	PE, VC	Buyout, growth	Asia, Europe, West Europe	UK
Apollo	$79 148	8	$19 073	PE	Buyout	North America, US, Asia	US
Bain Capital	$71 781	5	$12 115	PE	Buyout	US, North America, Europe, Asia, Japan	US
Advent International	$70 520	1	$16 135	PE	Buyout	Americas, North America, Central and East Europe, West Europe, Europe	US
Silver Lake	$62 687	2	$21 178	PE, VC	Buyout, growth	North America, US	US

(Continued)

Table 1.4 (Continued)

Firm Name	Total Funds Raised (USD mn)	Funds in Market	Estimated Dry Powder (USD mn)	Asset Class	Strategy	Geographic Focus	Headquarters
Hellman & Friedman	$53 251	2	$12 494	PE	Buyout	North America, US	US
SINO-IC Capital	$52 315	0	$23 400	PE, VC	Growth	China	China
Permira	$51 900	0	$11 037	PE, VC	Buyout, growth	Europe, France, UK, Germany	UK
The Goldman Sachs	$50 650	4	$4 569	PE, VC	Buyout, growth	North America, Asia, China	US
Apax Partners	$46 439	1	$765	PE, VC	Buyout, growth	Europe, Israel, North America	UK
Vista Equity Partners	$45 276	3	$13 167	PE	Buyout	North America	US
EQT	$44 762	2	$22 466	PE	Buyout, turnaround	Europe, Asia, US	Sweden
Clayton Dubilier & Rice	$43 375	1	$14 654	PE	Buyout	North America, US	US
Cinven	$41 624	0	$9 490	PE	Buyout	Europe	UK
Leonard Green	$39 523	0	$12 030	PE	Buyout	North America, US	US
Providence Equity Partners	$36 937	1	$5 870	PE, VC	Buyout, growth	North America, Europe	US

Source: Preqin

invests solely in China, while Cinven focuses on Europe. Sino-IC focuses on growth equity, while all of the other firms invest in buyouts. This is consistent with the younger maturity of the Chinese market, where there are fewer buyout opportunities.

The prior statistics looked at fundraising by private equity firms. Because many of the deals include leverage, and because funds are invested over a three- to five-year period, it is useful to also examine the amount of actual investments made in a given year. Table 1.5 looks at the geography and value of private equity transactions from 2017 to 2019. The US was the largest market for transactions, with more than $300 billion in transaction value in each year, peaking at $372 billion

Table 1.5 Private Equity Value of Transactions by Country

	2017	2018	2019
United States	$349 943	$338 485	$372 056
China	$97 344	$120 647	$84 071
United Kingdom	$61 294	$44 321	$68 443
Germany	$17 997	$25 649	$36 901
Spain	$24 145	$30 254	$24 279
France	$20 118	$47 322	$22 182
Canada	$12 306	$41 053	$21 320
South Korea	$11 029	$19 064	$21 139
India	$18 958	$17 651	$19 421
Switzerland	$4 134	$3 796	$19 165
Australia	$16 800	$22 098	$16 733
Netherlands	$9 386	$28 417	$14 402
Japan	$32 109	$3 092	$14 150
Brazil	$3 672	$5 885	$13 028
Hong Kong	$2 923	$6 789	$11 266
Sweden	$5 873	$7 857	$9 584
Chile	$480	$113	$8 898
Italy	$12 158	$21 623	$8 416
Israel	$5 057	$4 226	$7 603
Bermuda	$4 568	$8 036	$6 118

Source: Bureau van Dijk (BVP)

Table 1.6   Global Private Equity Transactions 2014–19

	Number of Deals	Total Deal Value (USD mn)
2014	26 470	$845 561
2015	27 123	$905 995
2016	25 742	$811 298
2017	25 565	$609 791
2018	27 703	$767 991
2019	25 923	$564 627

Source: Bureau van Dijk (BVP)

in 2019. China represented the next largest market in terms of transaction values, ranging from $84 billion in 2019 to $120 billion in 2018. The UK, Germany, Spain and France were the four next largest markets. Several emerging economies also appear on the list, including India, Brazil and Chile. Overall, the table clearly shows the global impact of private equity.

Table 1.6 provides a summary of total private equity transaction value from 2014 to 2019. While the data source differs from Table 1.5, Table 1.6 identifies more than 25 000 transactions in each year, with aggregate transaction values between $564 and $905 billion. The largest single category of investments is buyouts whose fundraising from 2000 to 2019 we tabulate in Table 1.7. Aggregate capital raised increased substantially in the early 2000s before declining after the financial crisis. Over the past 10 years, we have seen a consistent increase in both the aggregate capital raised and average fund size. In 2019, a record $387 billion of buyout capital was raised with an average fund size of $1.5 billion.

The investment activity of buyout funds from 2009 through 2019 is tabulated in Table 1.8. Over the period, buyout funds engaged in 54 816 transactions with an aggregate deal value of $3.9 trillion. The average deal size was $306 million. In 2009, the buyout industry engaged in 2565 transactions for a total aggregate transaction value of $118.7 billion. Aggregate transaction value peaked in 2018 when 6673 buyouts had a total transaction value of $435 billion. These data show that the private equity industry has clearly been transformative in the overall economy. Subsequent chapters will explore exactly how private equity firms operate, how they add value and the role that they play in the overall economy.

Table 1.7   Leveraged Buyouts Funds Raised from 2000 to 2019

	Number of Funds	Aggregate Capital Raised (USD bn)	Average Size (USD mn)
2000	146	$89.90	$676.00
2001	118	$55.05	$496.00
2002	114	$62.97	$606.00
2003	107	$43.88	$418.00
2004	146	$67.41	$485.00
2005	215	$143.15	$698.00
2006	262	$225.61	$899.00
2007	278	$250.09	$947.00
2008	251	$233.78	$974.00
2009	151	$113.07	$825.00
2010	148	$79.21	$587.00
2011	153	$94.13	$672.00
2012	185	$103.11	$614.00
2013	226	$191.07	$932.00
2014	252	$187.51	$808.00
2015	291	$179.89	$689.00
2016	314	$243.90	$856.00
2017	358	$309.34	$937.00
2018	273	$238.57	$921.00
2019	286	$387.87	$1 498.00

Source: Prequin

Table 1.9 ranks global private equity firms by the number of transactions in 2019. Some private equity firms are extremely active yet make middle-market or smaller transactions. Audax, a middle-market private equity firm, generated the most deals, closing 96 transactions in 2019. KKR closed the second most with 92 deals. HarbourVest, a fund-of-funds, closed on 91, primarily through co-investments with underlying partnerships in which they had invested. The list shows a mix of types of private equity firms from the largest, globally diversified firms, e.g., KKR, Carlyle and Blackstone, to more focused private equity managers like Genstar and Insight Partners.

Table 1.8   Leveraged Buyout Transactions 2009–19 (USD bn)

Year	Number of Deals	Aggregate Deal Value (USD bn)	Average Deal Size (USD mn)
2009	2 565	$118.7	$151.6
2010	3 755	$246.7	$212.5
2011	4 505	$292.3	$216.2
2012	4 602	$289.3	$218.3
2013	4 354	$328.8	$263.7
2014	5 205	$386.0	$299.0
2015	5 458	$477.2	$403.1
2016	5 780	$367.2	$314.4
2017	6 230	$448.8	$408.0
2018	6 673	$520.5	$439.6
2019	5 689	$435.3	$448.3
Overall	54 816	$3 910.8	$306.4

Source: Prequin

Table 1.9   Top Global PE Firms by Deal Count

Investor	Number of Deals
Audax Group	96
Kohlberg Kravis Roberts	92
HarbourVest Partners	91
The Carlyle Group	82
Genstar Capital	72
Business Growth Fund	71
Bpifrance	71
TA Associates Management	67
The Blackstone Group	66
Ardian	62
Caisse de dépôt et placement du Québec	60
Government of Singapore Investment Corporation (GIC)	56
EQT	56
Hellman & Friedman	55
Insight Partners	53

Source: Pitchbook

Assessing value creation in private equity

Private equity investors seek to generate attractive returns for their investors by executing well-developed strategies. LPs hope to earn returns that exceed the risk of those returns, so-called positive risk-adjusted returns or returns with a positive alpha. Private equity investors can create risk-adjusted value in three ways: by reducing the riskiness of those cash flows, by buying low or by increasing future cash flows from the company.

Decreasing the riskiness of cash flows is hard to do in practice. Risk is generally thought of in terms of "systematic risk," i.e., how the riskiness of a diversified portfolio is affected by adding the investment in question. The simplest model of systematic risk and return, the capital asset pricing model (CAPM), leaves little room for private equity investors to create value. Other multi-factor models, including the Fama–French model, look at size as a factor for systemic risk. In this framework, growing a company (either organically or through acquisition) may increase value because systematic risk is lower.[2]

Historically, PE firms have tried to buy assets at a below market price. In an increasingly competitive deal environment, this is difficult to do. Accordingly, much of what private equity investors do focuses on improving cash flows and increasing the growth rate of those cash flows. Below we will highlight how improving cash flows relates to the way these firms typically assess investments.

In this section, we discuss how private equity firms typically evaluate their investments in terms of value creation and explicitly tie it to an understanding of the sources of real value creation from academic research. In practice, private equity investors examine three levers that could, at least in theory, generate positive risk-adjusted returns for their investors: operational or cash flow improvements, multiple expansion and leverage. Accordingly, many private equity firms use what is often referred to as a "value bridge" to measure the increase in value both prospectively before an investment is made and, retrospectively, after a deal exit is realized. While the concept of a value bridge is helpful, there are some elements that can be misleading.

The price a private equity firm pays for a portfolio company is the total enterprise value of the firm. This represents the value of the equity and debt that are used to finance the transaction. It helps to think of the enterprise value of the portfolio company as the equivalent of the value of a house. And, like a house, the enterprise value is split between equity (the down payment) and debt (the mortgage). Enterprise values are usually referred to as multiples of the portfolio company's earnings before interest, taxes, depreciation and amortization (EBITDA). EBITDA provides a measure of the cash flow a company generates. The enterprise value at the time of investment represents the total consideration paid by the private equity firm to buy the company which determines an entry EBITDA multiple, $Multiple_{in}$, that can be determined by dividing the total purchase price by current EBITDA, $EBITDA_{in}$.

The private equity investor is interested in understanding the sources of the increase in equity value over the life of an investment. Equity value at the time the investment closes, $Equity_{in}$, is determined by estimating the enterprise value at the time of the investment minus the amount of debt outstanding after the transaction closes. $Equity_{in}$ is the amount of equity that is actually invested by the private equity investors into the transaction. A similar exercise is done for the deal at the time of exit. $Equity_{out}$ is what the private equity investor is trying to determine and represents the equity proceeds that they receive at the sale of the company. The enterprise value at exit represents the total consideration received by the private equity firm at the time the portfolio company is sold. The exit enterprise value then determines an exit EBITDA multiple, $Multiple_{out}$, that can be determined by dividing the total exit price by exit year EBITDA, $EBITDA_{out}$. In order for the private equity firm to estimate its proceeds from the sale, it needs to subtract debt outstanding at the time the deal is sold, $Debt_{out}$, from the enterprise value. $Equity_{out}$ is the gross amount of money that the private equity firm receives to pay returns to investors and carried interest. As mentioned earlier, $Equity_{out}$ is projected at the time of investment to estimate what the potential gross return on the investment might be in order to make a decision about whether it makes sense for the PE firm to undertake.

It is fairly easy to derive the math behind a value bridge. $Multiple_{in}$ represents the EBITDA multiple paid when the firm is purchased, and $Multiple_{out}$ is the EBITDA multiple at which the company is sold upon exit. Total enterprise values (TEV) at purchase (in) and exit (out) are given by:

(1) $TEV_{purchase} = EBITDA_{in} \times Multiple_{in}$ and
$\quad TEV_{out} = EBITDA_{out} \times Multiple_{out}$

The TEV, in turn, is split between debt and equity both at purchase (in) and at exit (out):

(2) But, $TEV_{in} = Debt_{in} + Equity_{in}$ and $TEV_{out} = Debt_{out} + Equity_{out}$
(3) $Equity_{out} - Equity_{in} = (EBITDA_{out} \times Multiple_{out} - Debt_{out})$
$\quad\quad\quad\quad\quad\quad\quad - (EBITDA_{in} \times Multiple_{in} - Debt_{in})$

If we rearrange, (6) shows that the increase in equity value consists of three components: (i) multiple expansion – the increase in multiple between the purchase and sale multiplied by the exit EBITDA, (ii) EBITDA growth – the increase in EBITDA between purchase and sale multiplied by the exit multiple, and (iii) debt reduction.

(4) $Equity_{out} - Equity_{in} = (EBITDA_{out} \times Multiple_{out}$
$\quad\quad\quad\quad\quad\quad\quad - EBITDA_{in} \times Multiple_{in}) - Debt_{out} + Debt_{in}$
(5) $Equity_{out} - Equity_{in} = (EBITDA_{out} \times Multiple_{out} - EBITDA_{out} \times Multiple_{in})$
$\quad\quad\quad\quad\quad\quad\quad + (EBITDA_{out} \times Multiple_{in} - EBITDA_{in} \times Multiple_{in})$
$\quad\quad\quad\quad\quad\quad\quad + (Debt_{in} - Debt_{out})$
(6) $Equity_{out} - Equity_{in} = EBITDA_{out} \times (Multiple_{out} - Multiple_{in})$
$\quad\quad\quad\quad\quad\quad\quad$ [Multiple expansion]
$\quad\quad\quad\quad\quad\quad\quad + (EBITDA_{out} - EBITDA_{in}) \times Multiple_{in}$
$\quad\quad\quad\quad\quad\quad\quad$ [EBITDA growth]
$\quad\quad\quad\quad\quad\quad\quad + (Debt_{in} - Debt_{out})$ [Debt reduction]

Private equity firms typically calculate two measures of return to evaluate deals, internal rate of return (IRR) and multiple on invested capital (MOIC). MOIC is simply calculated by taking the ratio of $Equity_{out}$ over $Equity_{in}$. IRR is the rate of return over the holding period of the investment and is calculated by $(Equity_{out}/Equity_{in})^{1/n} - 1$ where n is the number of years that the investment has been held.

At the time of investment, private equity investors typically use hurdle rates for MOIC and IRR that determine whether the investment is attractive. A typical MOIC hurdle is 2.5 to 3.0 times (over five years) and a typical IRR hurdle rate is 20% to 25%. If the prospective investment has a return above these thresholds, it is usually considered attractive.

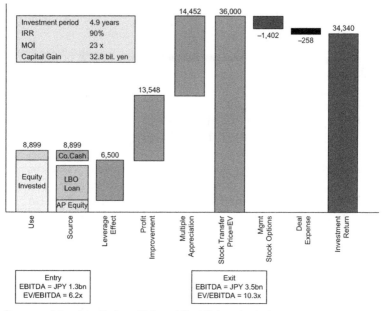

Source: Advantage Partners' Internal Deal Return Analysis

Figure 1.1   Value Bridge from Dia Kanri Investment by Advantage Partners

An example of a real value bridge is helpful in understanding how it is used in practice. Figure 1.1 shows a real value bridge created by Advantage Partners, a Japanese private equity firm, when it evaluated its performance after selling Dia Kanri, a roll-up in the condominium management business.[3]

Dia Kanri was an investment completed in September 2008 that intended to roll up condominium management companies in Japan. The total purchase price (TEV) was 8.0 billion yen (net of cash). The performance of the company improved substantially under Advantage Partners management. Revenue grew from 16.5 billion yen in 2008 to 26.9 billion yen in 2013. EBITDA increased from 1.3 billion yen in 2008 to 3.5 billion yen in 2013. Advantage Partners sold the company in an auction in August 2013 to Tokyu, a publicly traded condominium management company, for 36 billion yen, i.e., the TEV at exit was 36 billion yen. After adjusting for management stock options and deal expenses, Advantage Partners' equity investment of 1.5 billion yen grew by 32.8 billion yen to an exit value of 34.3 billion yen.

Figure 1.1 shows that the debt was completely paid off (labeled "Leverage Effect"), i.e., $Debt_{in} - Debt_{out}$ contributed 6.5 billion yen to the return. The increase in EBITDA ($EBITDA_{out} - EBITDA_{in}$) accounted for a 13.5 billion yen increase in equity value. Similarly, the increase in the EBITDA multiple from the time of acquisition to the time of exit ($Multiple_{out} - Multiple_{in}$) was responsible for 14.5 billion yen of equity value appreciation.

Advantage Partners also calculated its return on the investment using both an IRR and MOIC. Dia Kanir was held within the portfolio for 4.9 years. The IRR on the equity investment was 90% and the MOIC was 23×. These returns are extremely high, but illustrate how most private equity firms seek to attribute value. As mentioned earlier, most private equity firms do a value bridge both prospectively to understand how they may be able to generate returns, as well as retrospectively, in order to understand what actually created value after the fact.

While this general framework is helpful to understand mechanically how value is created, a deeper understanding of the drivers of value is critical to both making better investment decisions, as well as evaluating the contribution of private equity to the overall economy.

Multiple expansion is the process of buying a given dollar of cash flow at a lower valuation than it is ultimately sold for in the future. There are at least three reasons why the exit multiple might be higher than the entry multiple. First, as mentioned earlier, the private equity firm might be able to buy cheaply, i.e., at a cost below a market price, because of some proprietary advantage.

Second, and related to this, some private equity investors believe there are differences between public markets and private markets as to how they value companies, that if they buy an asset in the private markets, they will be able to sell it for a higher multiple in the public market. This belief is often referred to as "public-private arbitrage." This concept is slightly misguided. Private acquisition multiples may be lower because of a lack of competition for a deal. As the private equity industry has grown and more firms target smaller, private companies, acquisition multiples in private markets have increased. The sustainability of executing a private equity program based upon "public-private arbitrage," however, is increasingly questionable.

Third, exit multiples can expand if a strategic acquirer has synergies with the portfolio company, particularly cost overlaps. In this case, the EBITDA available to the acquirer is greater than the EBITDA of the company alone. This does raise the question of why a strategic acquirer did not buy the company in the first place. Some private equity firms claim that one of the ways they add value is to improve a company's processes so that it becomes attractive to a strategic acquirer.

Finally, exit multiples will expand if the private equity investor improves the future or long-term prospects of the portfolio company. Because a multiple can be viewed as a one-step discounted cash flow, a firm's multiple will increase if long-run growth prospects are higher at exit than at acquisition.

It is worth mentioning that multiples do not always expand. If the purchase price is very high or growth does not materialize, the multiple can decline and detract from the equity value created.

In the value bridge calculations, most private equity investors include debt paydown, $Debt_{in} - Debt_{out}$, as value created. While the debt paydown, all else being equal, does increase equity value, the debt paydown does not create firm value. In fact, it is possible that debt paydown reduces overall value. Paying off the debt just reduces the debt claim on the overall enterprise value. As long as the debt is "fairly priced," this is compensation for the debt providers in accordance with the risk they bear. If the cash to pay off the debt had been retained, then the equity holders would own a smaller percentage of a larger enterprise value. This is true because the value of the enterprise is higher by the amount of the cash on the balance sheet. Paying off the debt lowers the enterprise value by the cash payout, so equity holders own a larger piece of a smaller enterprise value. In the absence of taxes or governance effects, the value of the equity is independent of whether you pay off the debt or not.

Financial economists have shown how debt can create value, but it is typically not in the way private equity investors calculate it. First, because interest payments are typically deductible as an expense before taxes, the interest tax shield creates value because it lowers overall taxes paid by the firm. The higher the debt, ignoring any cost of potential financial distress, the higher the tax shield and the higher the enterprise value. In this case, paying off debt actually lowers overall enterprise (and equity) value because the interest tax shield is reduced in subsequent years.[4]

A second potential source of value from increasing debt relates to the governance benefits discussed above. A significant amount of academic research has focused on the disciplining effects of debt on management. Because management has to make fixed payments or risk default, there is an incentive to reduce wasteful spending and to improve operations. Jensen (1986)[5] was among the first to highlight this disciplining role. Jensen (1989)[6] argued that the disciplining role of debt increased the alignment of management incentives and provided a significant advantage to private equity investors. We will highlight the critical role that debt can play in *governance engineering* in Chapter 5.

A second conception among many private equity investors is that taking on more debt increases equity returns because more of the purchase is in the form of debt and this leverage mechanically increases equity returns. Leverage does increase the expected returns on equity, but does so by increasing the underlying cash flow risk of the company. Leverage does not increase the value of the company, i.e., leverage is not a free lunch. Basic finance demonstrates that in the absence of taxes and governance benefits, the increase in expected equity returns is simply a compensation for greater risk.

The ability to generate returns via leverage, however, is also subject to external market conditions and the receptivity of debt providers to leveraged transactions. The market for debt has been highly cyclical with booms in credit over periods such as 2004 to 2007 and 2020 to 2021, as well as severe retrenchment during other periods like the financial crisis in 2008 and 2009. If markets for credit become "overheated" with debt providers willing to provide capital at interest rates below what might reasonably be the riskiness of the investment, then private equity firms may be able to generate value for their investors. Ivashina and Kovner (2008)[7] have shown that relationships with banks often provide private equity investors with access to debt capital at more favorable rates. Kaplan and Stein (1993)[8] examine how the growth in the "junk bond" market in the late 1980s increased the valuation being paid in leveraged buyouts. Other research has highlighted the potential role of investor sentiment in providing credit. If debt markets are subject to these underlying forces, raising favorably priced debt could create value for investors. We will deal with debt and equity financing issues in Chapter 5 on *financial engineering*.

Finally, private equity investors often focus on improvements in the cash flow generating ability of the firms they purchase, i.e., they can make $EBITDA_{out}$ greater than $EBITDA_{in}$. Private equity investors have two levers to grow EBITDA. First, private equity investors can engage in *operational engineering*. By actively helping firms grow sales and become more efficient through consulting and advice, value is increased. Second, private equity investors can improve oversight and incentives of management through *governance engineering*. This provides incentives for the management team to find ways to grow sales and become more efficient. In terms of the ability to sustainably generate value, these two levers are complementary.

Many private equity firms institute detailed operational plans based on their own (or their outside consultants and affiliates') expertise in operations. These efforts typically target growth in EBITDA through increased revenues and efficiencies. These efforts are seen as essential for value creation. It is critical to examine how a particular private equity firm can improve operations. The critical levers by which PE investors can increase operating performance include operational and governance engineering. We will explore the types of activities that PE investors engage in during their ownership of portfolio companies in Chapter 7.

Governance engineering will be discussed in Chapter 6. In that chapter, we look at the ways private equity investors better align the incentives of managers with investors. A common feature of many private equity transactions is a large increase in the equity ownership of management. This equity compensation would better align incentives. In the average Fortune 1000 company, Jensen and Murphy (1990)[9] showed that the typical public company CEO in the 1980s held relatively little of the company's equity, with their total compensation changing by less than $3 for every $1000 change in shareholder value. By comparison, the average CEO of an LBO portfolio company in the 1980s experienced a change of roughly $64 per $1000 – and the entire operating management team, which owned about 20% of the equity, experienced a $200 change. Similarly, equity sponsors of these LBOs typically owned more than 60% of the companies' equity.

As a large outside shareholder, the LBO firms have a strong incentive to monitor their portfolio companies and intervene.

Similarly, private equity firms often bring in knowledgeable board members who take an active role in providing advice and guidance to senior managers of the company. If the portfolio company gets into financial trouble or has operating problems, the board can quickly intervene, potentially appointing a new senior management team if needed. The board members also typically help with the corporate finance function, including negotiations with lenders and the investment banking community. All of these changes are intended to improve operations, i.e., increase EBITDA and growth.

One important caveat to keep in mind is who gets the value of these improvements in the level of EBITDA? There are three possibilities: selling shareholders, LPs and GPs. Arguments for selling shareholders include the fact that with the growth in private equity, competitive bidding has led to higher transaction prices. If private equity firms do not have any comparative advantage in terms of improving operations and no comparative advantage in financing, then selling shareholders may actually get a large fraction of the gains from operating improvements.

Similarly, there are several arguments for why the GPs are the likely beneficiary of the value improvements. If there are proprietary aspects of what specific private equity investors do to improve companies, private equity investors can generate positive risk-adjusted returns at the gross investment level. In this case, better PE investors would charge fees that provide them with the benefit of the value creation, leaving LPs with returns which are just commensurate with the riskiness of the investment.

Finally, LPs may still be able to receive some of the value creation benefits. GPs may need to offer some of the returns to "skill" to induce their investors to allocate capital to their funds. As such, the possibility exists that LPs may get some of this return. The next chapter will discuss the empirical evidence on returns (gross and net) and whether there is any academic evidence on the persistence of performance within private equity investing.

The discussion in this section outlines the issues for assessing value creation in private equity, both prospectively and retrospectively. Much of the way private equity investors evaluate deals makes sense. Some of their approaches, however, are less grounded in a clear relationship to real sources of value. Investors and private equity managers care about earning returns on their investments that are above the risk-adjusted cost of capital.

In the rest of this book, we discuss the evidence for value creation in private equity and provide frameworks for creating value going forward. In Chapter 2, we summarize the evidence for value creation at the portfolio company level. In Chapter 3, we consider the evidence for value creation at the fund level. The next several chapters provide frameworks that private equity investors use to create value. Chapter 4 looks at investment decision making; Chapter 5, financial engineering; Chapter 6, governance engineering; Chapter 7, operational engineering; and Chapter 8, successfully exiting investments. In the remaining two chapters, we consider how private equity firms structure and raise their funds (Chapter 9) and how they manage their firms (Chapter 10).

Notes

1   Carmela Mendoza, 2022, Fundraising Hit a New Full-Year Record in 2021, *Private Equity International*, 18 January 2022.
2   Recent evidence, however, has cast doubt on whether size can be interpreted as a risk factor.
3   Based on Paul A. Gompers and Akiko Kanna, 2013, Advantage Partners: Dia Kanri (A), Harvard Business School Case Number 9-214-016.
4   See Kaplan (1989), who calculates the value of interest tax shields in a set of leveraged buyouts in the 1980s and shows that it was important to those transactions. Steven N. Kaplan, 1989, Management Buyouts: Evidence on Taxes as a Source of Value, *Journal of Finance* 44, 611–32.
5   Michael Jensen, 1986, Agency Costs of Free Cash Flow, Corporate Finance, and Takeovers, *American Economic Review* 76, 323–9.
6   Michael Jensen, 1989, Eclipse of the Public Corporation, *Harvard Business Review* 67, 61–73.
7   Victoria Ivashina and Anna Kovner, 2011, The Private Equity Advantage: Leveraged Buyout Firms and Relationship Banking, *Review of Financial Studies* 24, 2462–98.
8   Steven N. Kaplan and Jeremy Stein, 1993, The Evolution of Buyout Pricing and Financial Structure in the 1980s, *Quarterly Journal of Economics* 108, 313–58.
9   Michael Jensen and Kevin J. Murphy, 1990, Performance Pay and Top-Management Incentives, *Journal of Political Economy* 98, 225–64.

2 Private equity: performance at the portfolio company

Since the first large buyouts in the 1980s, there has been a continued interest in the effect of buyouts and private equity on portfolio companies and, more broadly, on the economy. Private equity investors argue that buyout transactions create value by improving the operations of their portfolio companies in different ways. Critics counter that private equity firms overleverage their companies, underinvest in them and create systemic risk. According to the critics, PE investors generate returns by buying undervalued assets, selling overvalued assets and by firing workers without creating real value. In the critics' view, the large payoffs to and wealth of private equity investors are not deserved. These issues received a great deal of attention from a wide audience when Mitt Romney, one of the founders of Bain Capital, became the Republican nominee for president in 2012.

In the first part of this chapter, we summarize what is known from the academic literature about the effects of private equity on portfolio company financial performance and productivity, as well as on broader non-financial measures. The results on operating performance and productivity are overwhelmingly positive. A wide number of research papers find that private equity portfolio companies have higher operating margins and/or higher productivity. The results are largely positive on non-financial measures, although not uniformly so.

In the second part of this chapter, we consider the reasons for portfolio company outperformance. We show how private equity firms make use of financial engineering, governance engineering and operational engineering. We explore each of these mechanisms for improving portfolio company performance in Chapters 5 through 7.

How have private equity-funded companies performed?

Operating margins and productivity

The first major study of the performance of LBO companies was conducted by one of us. The public-to-private buyouts of the 1980s were studied by Kaplan (1989),[1] who found that buyouts are followed by significant increases in operation margins and cash flows, both in absolute terms, as well as relative to the public companies' operation in the same. Such increases were sustained at least over the three-year period covered by the study. For the deals in Kaplan's sample that could be tracked after the buyouts, the operating gains resulted in increases of roughly 100% in enterprise values. Those gains were divided fairly evenly between the selling shareholders and the private equity investors. We explore how the gains of company improvements are split and why it matters for the investment returns in Chapter 3.

Since that early study, almost every large sample study of private equity portfolio companies has found similar results – outperformance relative to firms in similar industries. In Europe, several papers by Michael Wright, including Harris et al. (2005),[2] find outperformance by buyouts in the UK in the 1990s and 2000s. Boucly et al. (2011)[3] find that buyouts in France are more profitable and grow more quickly than other companies. Acharya et al. (2013)[4] study 395 private equity transactions in Western Europe undertaken by large private equity firms from 1991 to 2007 and find that the unleveraged deal returns outperform unleveraged public company returns over the holding period of the investment. Despite the public rhetoric that returns are driven by slashing employment and expenses, the excess returns are related to greater sales growth as well as greater improvement in operating margins. Biesinger et al. (2020)[5] study a large sample of small European buyouts and find that "company operations and profitability improve."

In the US, using more recent data – corporate tax return data for the years 1995 to 2009 – Cohn, Hotchkiss and Towery (2020)[6] find both significant post-buyout improvements in operating performance and rapid growth. And, in two prominent, recent studies, Davis et al. (2014 and 2019)[7,8] look at a large fraction of all US buyouts from the 1980s to 2011 and find the net effect of a leveraged buyout is a significant increase in productivity. Private equity portfolio companies tend to exit low productivity plants while they enter or build high productivity plants. This only measures what happens in US operations; private equity portfolios are unable to measure what happens outside the US. If private equity portfolio companies were quicker or more likely to move overseas, the productivity increases would be larger.

There are two caveats to these results, one negative and one positive. On the negative side, the results are less consistent for public-to-private firms. Guo et al. (2011)[9] find evidence of significant value creation in public-to-private buyouts, yet only modest (and insignificant) operating gains. Cohn and Towery (2014)[10] also find modest operating gains for public-to-private transactions using tax data. And while Davis et al. (2019)[11] find that public-to-private firms increase productivity as much as other buyouts, the increase is not statistically significant.

On the positive side, most of the large sample evidence uses deals completed before 2012. Operational engineering has increased in importance and, likely, effectiveness since then. Early public-to-private transactions focused largely on creating value through the use of improved incentives and leverage (financial engineering). As the industry has grown and become more competitive, successful buyout firms have had to increasingly focus on other levers of value creation, including operational improvements. If this is the case, the record of operating improvement will also improve as more recent data become available.

The bottom line from all of these studies is clear. On average, private equity ownership leads to value creation as companies become more productive, earn higher margins and grow faster. Of course, this is not true in every deal. Some private equity investments perform poorly. But, the results from the large sample studies show that deals that perform well outweigh the poor performers.

This was true of the US deals in the 1980s; it proved to be true of the second great wave of buyouts in the UK and continental Europe; and it has been true for US buyouts in the 1990s and 2000s. Because it takes from five to seven years for private equity funds to realize their returns, it is still too soon to know how the many deals transacted during the boom of the mid-2010s will materialize. Yet the key finding from these more recent studies is consistent with Kaplan's main finding for US buyouts in the 1980s – namely, the significant and sustainable improvements in the productivity and operating performance of private equity-funded companies.

Employment and workers

Private equity-funded companies have been frequently and repeatedly charged with making their money largely by firing employees, seen and popularized in books such as *Barbarians at the Gate*, or movies such as *Wall Street*. Although the patterns are more complicated, this does not seem to be the general case. In their study of US private equity-owned establishments that we mentioned earlier, Davis et al. (2019) distinguish between employment at buyout firms' existing plants and operations, and employment in the new operations they start or acquire.[12] In the existing operations, employment declines by 4% relative to that of other companies in the same industry. Yet in these same portfolio companies, employment increases by 2.3% relative to competitors in the new operations. The net effect on employment is a decline of 1.7%. The authors also find modestly lower compensation per employee (1.7%) relative to competitors. The results differ for private-to-private deals relative to public-to-privates. In private-to-private deals, employment increases more in those companies than in other companies in the same industry; in public-to-private deals, the opposite is true. And, again, the data do not include non-US operations.

Amess and Wright (2007)[13] study buyouts in the UK from 1999 to 2004 and find that firms which experienced leveraged buyouts have employment growth similar to other firms, but increase wages more slowly. Boucly et al. (2011)[14] find that leveraged buyout companies experience greater job and wage growth than other similar companies. Antoni et al. (2019)[15] find similar or consistent results in a study of post-buyout employment of companies in the Netherlands. The buyout companies became more efficient and profitable; healthier-than-average workers experienced gains in wages and ascending career paths; less healthy workers were more likely to be fired while experiencing reduced wages and further declines in health.

Overall, then, the empirical evidence on employment is largely consistent with the view that private equity portfolio companies create economic value by operating more efficiently. Private equity firms grow less mature companies (and companies in France) and consolidate more mature companies. These findings do not support the concerns over substantial job destruction, but neither do they support the diametrically opposite position that all firms owned by private equity experience especially strong employment growth.

Other non-financial measures

Apart from the questions of jobs and taxes, there are now many studies of the non-financial performance-related effects of private equity. These studies help provide a more complete picture of how companies are transformed by their private equity investors.

On the positive side, Bloom, Sadun and van Reenen (2015)[16] find that private equity-backed firms have better management practices than almost all other ownership groups, based on thousands of firms across 34 countries. Fracassi, Previtero and Sheen (2017)[17] find that private equity firms have been more likely to achieve growth with new products and in new geographic markets instead of raising prices for consumers. Lerner et al. (2011)[18] find that buyout-owned firms that patent become more innovative. Cohn, Nestoriak and Wardlaw (2021)[19] find that private equity-operated companies have fewer workplace injuries relative to their public competitors. Bernstein and Sheen (2016)[20] find that private equity-funded restaurants have fewer health violations. Agrawal and Tambe (2016)[21] find that private equity-backed companies increase human capital by improving technical job skills that are more valued by subsequent employers. And Bellon (2020)[22] finds that private equity ownership for firms in the oil and gas industry leads to a 70% reduction in the use of toxic chemicals and a 50% reduction in CO_2 emissions. This reduction is identified by comparing projects from private equity-backed firms to their close geographical neighbors using novel satellite imaging and administrative datasets from the oil and gas industry. Collectively, these studies demonstrate that along other dimensions, private equity managers appear to improve the firms in which they invest.

On the negative side of the ledger, however, several papers find that private equity companies profit by taking advantage of government regulations in ways that turn out to have social costs. Eaton et al. (2018)[23] find that buyouts in the for-profit college education industry are associated with worse outcomes for students, including higher tuition, higher per-student debt, lower education inputs and lower graduation rates and per-graduate earnings. One thing that these private equity-backed for-profit educators were especially good at – securing funding through a generous, and what now appears to have been a poorly designed, government-subsidized student loan program – has proved to be a mixed blessing.

Pradhan et al. (2014)[24] find that private equity-owned nursing homes had fewer and, on average, less-skilled Registered Nurses and worse health outcomes than their non-private equity counterparts. Consistent with this finding, Gupta et al. (2020)[25] find a negative impact of private equity buyouts on patient health and compliance with care standards, a finding the authors attribute to fewer frontline nursing staff and higher bed utilization. In these cases, the authors point to a kind of "arbitraging" of nursing home regulations and Registered Nurse classifications that effectively encourages excessive reliance on highest-skilled (Level I) and minimally skilled (Level III) caregivers, with too little use of higher-paid, mid-tier (Level II) caregivers. (Again, on the flip side, two recent papers find that private equity-owned nursing homes had better COVID-19 outcomes, so the jury is still out.)

In both positive and negative cases, the private equity-backed companies appear to operate in a profit-maximizing way that, although compliant with laws and regulation, is not always viewed as socially optimal. One might interpret these results as consistent with a view of private equity as "capitalism in high gear." That is to say, private equity is a high-powered way to optimize operations, financing, governance and, ultimately, returns. But this view also carries an important message for policymakers: make sure policies do not create incentives for profit maximizers to take advantage in ways that are not advantageous to society.

Why do private equity firms make their portfolio companies more efficient?

The empirical evidence at the portfolio company level overwhelmingly indicates that private equity investors make companies more efficient and increase the value of their portfolio companies. And, as we will explain below, we expect the evidence to improve over time. The private value at the portfolio company level often comes with positive non-financial externalities, but not always, particularly when government regulations are poorly designed. This is important to remember any time you read something that describes a failed private equity deal or disparages private equity.

The critical question is where does that value come from? Kaplan and Stromberg (2009)[26] lay out an explanation and framework that we copy and rely on throughout the book. Private equity firms apply three sets of changes to the firms in which they invest, which we categorize as financial engineering, governance engineering and operational engineering. Financial engineering provides more effective incentives and capital structures. Governance engineering provides more effective management and monitoring. Operational engineering provides various capabilities that help portfolio companies operate more efficiently. We describe each of these in more detail below.

In this section, we will also refer to the results of two surveys of private equity investors that we conducted with Vladimir Mukharlyamov in 2012 and 2020. In Gompers et al. (2016)[27] or GKM (2016), we surveyed 79 private equity investors with roughly $750 billion of assets under management (AUM), representing almost half of buyout capital at the time. In Gompers et al. (2020)[28] or GKM (2020), we surveyed more than 200 private equity investors with almost $2 trillion of AUM.

Financial engineering

Jensen (1989)[29] and Kaplan (1989)[30] describe the financial and governance engineering changes associated with private equity. These changes were pioneered by KKR in the early buyouts of the 1980s. First, private equity firms pay careful attention to management incentives in their portfolio companies, and typically give the management team a large equity upside through stock and options – a provision that was quite unusual among public firms in the early 1980s. Kaplan (1989) finds that management ownership percentages increase by a factor of four in going from public-to-private ownership. Private equity firms also require management to make a meaningful investment in the company, so that management has not only a significant upside, but a significant downside as well. Moreover, because the companies are private, management's equity is illiquid – that is, management cannot sell its equity or exercise its options until the value is proved by an exit transaction. This illiquidity reduces management's incentive to manipulate short-term performance.

It is still the case that management teams obtain significant equity stakes in the portfolio companies. Kaplan and Stromberg (2009)[31] collected information on 43 leveraged buyouts in the US from 1996 to 2004 with a median transaction value of over $300 million. Of these, 23 were public-to-private transactions. They find that the CEO acquires 5.4% of the equity upside (stock and options) while the management team as a whole acquires 16%. Acharya et al. (2013)[32] find similar results in the UK for 59 large buyouts (with a median value of over $500 million) from 1997 to 2004.

In GKM (2020), the private equity investors report that their portfolio company CEOs receive a median of 5% (average of 10%) of the company equity upside while the management team receives a median of 15% (and average of 20%). These results are remarkably consistent over time, with the percentages having increased somewhat since the mid-2000s.

Even though stock- and option-based compensation have become more widely used in public firms since the 1980s, management's ownership percentages (and upside) are still greater in leveraged buyouts than in public companies. Consistent with a very important role for incentives, improved incentives are the second most frequently mentioned pre-deal source of value by the private equity investors in the survey of GKM (2016).

The second key ingredient is leverage, i.e., the borrowing that is done in connection with the transaction. Leverage creates pressure on managers not to waste money because they must make interest and principal payments. This pressure reduces the "free cash flow" problems described in Jensen (1986),[33] in which management teams in mature industries with weak corporate governance had many ways in which they could dissipate these funds rather than returning them to investors. On the flip side, if leverage is too high, the inflexibility of the required payments (as contrasted with the flexibility of payments to equity) raises the chances of costly financial distress. In the US and many other countries, leverage also potentially increases firm value through the tax deductibility of interest. The value of this tax shield, however, is difficult to calculate because it requires assumptions of the tax advantage of debt (net of personal taxes), the expected permanence of the debt and the riskiness of the tax shield.

Governance engineering

Governance engineering refers to the way that private equity investors control the boards of their portfolio companies – they are more actively involved in governance than boards of public companies. Boards of private equity portfolio companies are smaller than comparable public companies and meet more frequently (Acharya et al. (2013), Cornelli and

Karakaş (2008)[34] and GKM (2016, 2020)). In GKM (2016, 2020), private equity investors report that the typical board of their portfolio companies has seven or fewer directors.

In GKM (2020), at the height of the pandemic, 81% of the private equity investors reported that they met with the typical company in their portfolio at least once per week. Fifty-eight percent met multiple times per week. This is undoubtedly much more frequent than the typical public company director.

At the same time, the private equity investors reported that investment professionals spent roughly 40% of their time, 20 plus hours per week, assisting portfolio companies. While this may have been higher than normal because of the COVID pandemic, it indicates an extraordinary amount of time, particularly compared to the typical director of a public company, who might spend on average three to five hours per week.

Private equity investors also take an active role in replacing management when appropriate. Acharya et al. (2013)[35] report that one-third of chief executive officers of their portfolio companies are replaced in the first 100 days and two-thirds are replaced at some point over a four-year period. In the GKM (2016) survey, the private equity investors reported very similar activity. Thirty percent of private equity investors stated they were actively involved in bringing in a new executive team before closing the investment, while 50% said they were actively involved in bringing in a new team after closing the investment. So, overall, 58% reported bringing in their own senior management team.

Consistent with an important role for improved governance, the private equity investors in GKM (2016) affirmed that improving corporate governance, changing the CEO or CFO and changing other senior management are important sources of value in, respectively, 47%, 31% and 33% of private equity deals.

Operational engineering

From the early 1980s through the early 2000s, most private equity firms relied on financial and governance engineering. Some firms, however, innovated and developed an operational engineering capability. Bain Capital was among the first to make systematic use of management consulting resources. Clayton & Dubilier (now CD&R) was among the first to recruit senior operating executives.

In the 2000s, however, driven by growth in the private equity industry and increased competition for deals, the need to add more value in order to achieve high returns increased significantly. Most private equity firms added their own form of "operational engineering." For example, KKR added Capstone, an "in-house consulting firm," whose principals participate in transactions from their inception and due diligence to the final sale of the firm – they are compensated based on deal success. Additionally, Blackstone created a portfolio operations team that is comprised of former senior operating executives. All of these efforts were meant to provide internal resources that could engage with portfolio companies and enhance operating performance.

Most top private equity firms are now organized around industries. In addition to hiring dealmakers with financial engineering skills, private equity firms now often hire professionals with an industry focus and an operating background. The industry specialization allows the firm to better understand operating levers that can enhance the company's performance. Most top private equity firms also make use of internal or external consulting groups.

Private equity firms use their industry and operating knowledge to identify attractive investments, develop a value creation plan at the time of investment and implement the value creation plan. This plan might include elements of cost-cutting opportunities and productivity improvements, strategic changes or repositioning, acquisition opportunities, as well as management changes and upgrades.

GKM (2016 and 2020) have a number of findings consistent with an important role for operational engineering. First, Table 2.1 shows that the majority of firms in 2012 were organized by industry or the equivalent; only 37% of the sample firms were generalists. At the time, roughly one out of six firm professionals were consultants or operating executives. Almost half of the firms had a CEO council, senior advisors or the equivalent. And roughly one-third of the firms regularly hired strategy consultants to help with operating plans. Organizing around industry is consistent with private equity firms looking for ways to add value and improve portfolio company performance.

Table 2.1 How Is the Firm Organized?

	Mean	Low AUM	High AUM	Low IRR	High IRR	Old	Young	Local	Global
Industry	54.4	54.1	54.8	65.5	55.2	64.7	46.7	54.5	54.3
Criteria	11.4	10.8	11.9	13.8	3.4	11.8	11.1	6.8	17.1
Product	16.5	5.4	26.2	17.2	17.2	29.4	6.7	2.3	34.3
Generalist	36.7	40.5	33.3	27.6	34.5	26.5	44.4	43.2	28.6
Other	6.3	2.7	9.5	10.3	6.9	8.8	4.4	2.3	11.4
Number of responses	79	37	42	29	29	34	45	44	35

Source: Gompers, Kaplan and Muhkarlyamov (2016)

Table 2.2   Deal Selection – Ranking of Factors Considered by Private Equity Investors in Choosing Investments (with Higher Numbers More Important)

	Mean	Median	Low AUM	High AUM	Low IRR	High IRR	Old	Young	Local	Global
Ability to add value	3.6	3.0	3.6	3.6	3.9	3.5	3.5	3.7	3.5	3.8
Business model/ competitive position	4.6	5.0	4.5	4.7	4.5	4.5	4.4	4.7	4.6	4.5
Fit with fund	2.3	2.0	2.7	1.9	2.0	2.2	2.2	2.4	2.5	2.0
Industry/ market	3.2	3.0	3.4	3.0	3.3	3.0	3.3	3.1	3.5	2.8
Management team	3.8	4.0	3.7	4.0	3.9	4.0	4.1	3.6	3.8	3.8
Valuation	3.5	3.0	3.2	3.8	3.4	3.8	3.5	3.5	3.0	4.1
Number of responses	65	65	32	33	24	23	31	34	37	28

Source: Gompers, Kaplan and Muhkarlyamov (2016)

Second, Table 2.2 reports the relative importance of various factors when selecting deals to invest in. The ability to add value is ranked third in importance by private equity investors. Only the firm's business model or competitive position and the management team are more important considerations.

Third, Table 2.3 reports that the private equity firms rank growing revenues and reducing costs as the two most important sources of value. Growth in revenue is rated substantially higher than reducing costs. Leverage and increases in multiples are substantially less important. The importance of growing revenue was greater in the GKM (2020) survey than it had been in the 2012 survey of GKM (2016), suggesting that the private equity firms are increasingly focused on helping their companies grow faster.

Table 2.4 from GKM (2016) reports more detailed results that examine expected sources of value. Private equity investors reported that growing revenues was by far the most important expected source of value (70% of

Table 2.3   Sources of Value Creation

Source of Value	Mean	Median	AUM		Age	
			Low	High	Young	Old
Growth in revenue of the underlying business	8.1	8.0	7.9	8.3	8.0	8.1
Reducing costs	5.4	5.0	5.5	5.4	5.5	5.3
Industry-level multiple arbitrage	4.6	4.5	4.4	4.8	4.6	4.7
Leverage	3.9	4.0	3.9	4.0	4.0	3.8
Refinancing	3.2	3.0	3.2	3.1	3.2	3.2
Other	1.7	1.0	1.5	1.9	1.9	1.6
Observations	145	145	73	72	77	68

Source: Gompers, Kaplan and Muhkarlyamov (2020)

the time). Reducing costs in general (36%), redefining the current business model or strategy (34%), improving IT systems (26%) and introducing shared services (16%) were important.

Summary

To summarize this section, the empirical evidence is exceptionally strong that private equity investors, on average, make their portfolio companies more productive and more valuable. This conclusion mirrors the conclusion more than 10 years ago in Kaplan and Stromberg (2009) that "the empirical evidence is strong that private equity activity creates economic value on average." Furthermore, many of the non-financial results are also positive, although not uniformly so, particularly in the presence of ill-designed government incentives.

The increased value at the portfolio companies comes from three sources or competencies: financial, governance and operational engineering. Private equity firms continue to invest in and improve these capabilities, particularly in governance and operational engineering. Chapters 5 through 7 explore in greater detail how private equity firms exploit each of these capabilities.

Table 2.4   Pre-Investment (Expected) Sources of Value Creation – The Percentage of Deals That Private Equity Investors Identify Having the Following Pre-Deal Sources of Value

	Mean	Median	Low AUM	High AUM	Low IRR	High IRR	Old	Young	Local	Global
Reduce costs in general	35.6	27.5	35.8	35.5	37.1	37.3	39.9	32.0	31.0	41.8
Improve IT/information systems	26.1	20.0	30.8	21.6	22.0	23.3	23.9	28.0	26.7	25.3
Introduce shared services	15.6	2.5	16.4	14.9	11.6	18.3	16.9	14.6	14.9	16.6
Increase revenue/improve demand factors	70.3	80.0	77.5	63.5	75.0	63.5	67.0	73.2	70.6	70.0
Redefine the current business model or strategy	33.8	29.5	27.8	39.5	43.0	29.8	32.1	35.3	32.8	35.2
Change CEO or CFO	30.6	27.5	33.4	28.0	29.2	32.9	30.9	30.4	29.3	32.4
Change senior management team other than CEO and CFO	33.4	30.0	37.3	29.7	32.5	33.1	27.9	38.1	35.4	30.8
Improve corporate governance	47.0	37.0	52.4	41.9	40.1	45.5	39.4	53.5	47.3	46.6
Improve incentives	61.1	73.5	60.7	61.5	58.3	67.0	65.5	57.4	59.0	63.9
Follow-on acquisitions	51.1	50.0	53.9	48.4	52.0	46.9	51.0	51.2	53.2	48.3

Strategic investor	15.6	10.0	16.4	14.8	12.3	14.0	14.4	16.5	15.1	16.2
Facilitate a high-value exit	50.0	43.5	61.0	39.6	45.6	42.0	40.4	58.1	53.5	45.4
Purchase at an attractive price (buy low)	44.3	43.0	49.2	39.6	38.2	43.3	40.9	47.1	44.9	43.5
Purchase at an attractive price relative to the industry	46.6	50.0	54.5	39.2	38.7	47.3	42.9	49.8	50.1	42.0
Other	9.8	0.0	9.4	10.2	0.0	14.3	9.4	10.1	12.4	6.4
Number of responses	74	74	36	38	27	27	34	40	42	32

Source: Gompers, Kaplan and Muhkarlyamov (2016)

Notes

1   Steven N. Kaplan, 1989, Management Buyouts: Evidence on Taxes as a Source of Value, *Journal of Finance* 44, 611–32.

2   Richard Harris, Donald Siegel and Mike Wright, 2005, Assessing the Impact of Management Buyouts on Economic Efficiency: Plant-Level Evidence from the United Kingdom, *Review of Economics and Statistics* 87, 148–53.

3   Quentin Boucly, David Sraer and David Thesmar, 2011, Growth LBOs, *Journal of Financial Economics* 102, 432–53.

4   Viral Acharya, Oliver Gottschalg, Moritz Hahn and Conor Kehoe, 2013, Corporate Governance and Value Creation: Evidence from Private Equity, *Review of Financial Studies* 26, 368–402.

5   Markus Biesinger, Çağatay Bircan and Alexander Ljungqvist, 2020, Value Creation in Private Equity, EBRD Working Paper No. 242, Swedish House of Finance Research Paper No. 20-17.

6   Jonathan B. Cohn, Edith Hotchkiss and Erin Towery, 2020, The Motives for Private Equity Buyouts of Private Firms: Evidence from U.S. Corporate Tax Returns, Working Paper.

7   Steven J. Davis, John C. Haltiwanger, Kyle Handley, Ron S. Jarmin, Josh Lerner and Javier Miranda, 2014, Private Equity, Jobs, and Productivity, *American Economic Review* 104, 3956–90.

8   Steven J. Davis, John Haltiwanger, Kyle Handley, Ben Lipsius, Josh Lerner and Javier Miranda, 2019, The Economic Effects of Private Equity Buyouts (No. w26371). National Bureau of Economic Research.

9   Shourun Guo, Edith S. Hotchkiss and Weihong Song, 2011, Do Buyouts (Still) Create Value? *Journal of Finance* 66, 479–517.

10 Jonathan B. Cohn, Lillian Mills and Erin M. Towery, 2014, The Evolution of Capital Structure and Operating Performance after Leveraged Buyouts: Evidence from US Corporate Tax Returns, *Journal of Financial Economics* 111, 469–94.

11 Steven J. Davis, John Haltiwanger, Kyle Handley, Ben Lipsius, Josh Lerner and Javier Miranda, 2019, The Economic Effects of Private Equity Buyouts (No. w26371). National Bureau of Economic Research.

12 Steven J. Davis, John Haltiwanger, Kyle Handley, Ben Lipsius, Josh Lerner and Javier Miranda, 2019, The Economic Effects of Private Equity Buyouts (No. w26371). National Bureau of Economic Research.

13 Kevin Amess and Mike Wright, 2007, Barbarians at the Gate? Leveraged Buyouts, Private Equity and Jobs, Working Paper.

14 Quentin Boucly, David Sraer and David Thesmar, 2011, Growth LBOs, *Journal of Financial Economics* 102, 432–53.

15 Manfred Antoni, Ernst Maug and Stefan Obernberger, 2019, Private Equity and Human Capital Risk, *Journal of Financial Economics* 133, 634–57.

16 Nicolas Bloom, Raffaella Sadun and John van Reen, 2015, *American Economic Review* 105, 442–6.

17 Cesare Fracassi, Alessandro Previtero and Albert Sheen, 2021, Barbarians at the Store? Private Equity, Products, and Consumers, *Journal of Finance* 77, 1439–88.

18   Josh Lerner, Morten Sorensen and Per Stromberg, 2008, Private Equity and Long Run Investment: The Case of Innovation, Working Paper, Harvard Business School.

19   Jonathan Cohn, Nicole Nestoriak and Malcolm Wardlaw, 2021, Private Equity Buyouts and Workplace Safety, *Review of Financial Studies* 34, 4876–925.

20   Shai Bernstein and Albert Sheen, 2016, The Operational Consequences of Private Equity Buyouts: Evidence from the Restaurant Industry, *Review of Financial Studies* 29, 2387–418.

21   Ashwini Agrawal and Prasanna Tambe, 2016, Private Equity and Workers' Career Paths: The Role of Technological Change, *Review of Financial Studies* 29, 2455–89.

22   A. Bellon, 2020, Does Private Equity Ownership Make Firms Cleaner? The Role of Environmental Liability Risks. Available at SSRN 3604360.

23   C. Eaton, S. Howell and C. Yannelis, 2018, When Investor Incentives and Consumer Interests Diverge: Private Equity in Higher Education (No. w24976). National Bureau of Economic Research.

24   R. Pradhan, R. Weech-Maldonado, J. S. Harman and K. Hyer, 2014, Private Equity Ownership of Nursing Homes: Implications for Quality, *Journal of Health Care Finance* 42(2), 1–12.

25   A. Gupta, S. Howell C. Yannelis and A. Gupta, 2020, Does Private Equity Investment in Healthcare Benefit Patients? Evidence from Nursing Homes. NYU Stern School of Business. Available at SSRN 3537612.

26   Steven N. Kaplan and Per Stromberg, 2009, Leveraged Buyouts and Private Equity, *Journal of Economic Perspectives* Winter, 121–46.

27   Paul A. Gompers, Steven N. Kaplan and Vladimir Mukharlyamov, 2016, What Do Private Equity Firms (Say They) Do? *Journal of Financial Economics* 121, 449–76.

28   Paul A. Gompers, Steven N. Kaplan and Vladimir Mukharlyamov, 2020, Private Equity and Covid-19, NBER Working Paper.

29   Michael Jensen, 1989, Eclipse of the Public Corporation, *Harvard Business Review* 67, 61–73.

30   S. N. Kaplan, 1989, The Effects of Management Buyouts on Operating Performance and Value, *Journal of Financial Economics* 24, 217–54.

31   Steven N. Kaplan and Per Stromberg, 2009, Leveraged Buyouts and Private Equity, *Journal of Economic Perspectives* Winter, 121–46.

32   Viral Acharya, Oliver Gottschalg, Moritz Hahn and Conor Kehoe, 2013, Corporate Governance and Value Creation: Evidence from Private Equity, *Review of Financial Studies* 26, 368–402.

33   Michael Jensen, 1986, Agency Costs of Free Cash Flow, Corporate Finance, and Takeovers, *American Economic Review* 76, 323–9.

34   Francesca Cornelli and Oğuzhan Karakaş, 2008, Private Equity and Corporate Governance: Do LBOs Have More Effective Boards, Working Paper.

35   Viral Acharya, Oliver Gottschalg, Moritz Hahn and Conor Kehoe, 2013, Corporate Governance and Value Creation: Evidence from Private Equity, *Review of Financial Studies* 26, 368–402.

3

Private equity performance at the fund level*

We have seen in Chapter 2 that private equity investors create value at the portfolio company level. The next question to ask is what happens at the fund level. There are two primary frictions that affect whether performance at the company level translates into performance at the fund level. First, the private equity firm must buy the company. If the purchase takes place in a competitive situation, some (or even all) of the gains can end up going to the seller, leaving the buyer with less. Second, private equity firms charge fees to their limited partner investors. It is possible that the fees more than offset the private equity value creation. Phalippou (2020)[1] claims that fees offset private equity value creation to leave private equity returns equal to those of public markets.

The evidence we present in this chapter, however, makes clear that the performance improvements at the portfolio company level have translated into outperformance relative to reasonable public benchmarks at the fund level. In other words, private equity funds have consistently outperformed the equivalent public equity markets over all relevant time periods over the last 30 years. That is undoubtedly a large part of the reason why investors in private equity funds (referred to throughout this chapter as limited partners or LPs) have increased their investments in private equity over that period.

In this chapter, we begin with an overview of the structure of private equity funds. We then discuss the different ways performance is measured at the fund level. That leads us to the most important section that describes the evidence on the average performance of private equity funds. Next, we consider whether superior (or inferior) performance persists from one fund of a private equity partnership to the next. Finally, we will look at whether there is a cyclical component to private equity returns, i.e., what is the performance of private equity across business cycles?

The organization of private equity funds

Private equity funds are financial intermediaries that pool their investors' capital and make investments in portfolio companies. A defining characteristic of the private equity industry is that these portfolio companies are generally either private or become private as part of the private equity transaction, so that there is no organized exchange for the company's equity. The goal of private equity investing is to exit the portfolio company after increasing its equity value. Private equity funds are active investors who attempt to increase value through financing and other contractual structures, value-added monitoring, advice and management staffing. These features distinguish private equity funds from mutual funds and hedge funds, which are primarily passive investors. Successful exit mechanisms include acquisitions by operating companies, IPOs and, in buyout, acquisitions by other buyout firms (known as secondary buyouts).

Although venture capital and private equity funds have a similar organizational form and compensation structure, they are distinguished by the types of investments they make and the way they finance them. Private equity funds, and in particular leveraged buyout (LBO) funds, generally acquire a majority ownership position in the target firm and use leverage. Venture capitalists take minority positions in private businesses and do not use debt financing. Growth equity funds are somewhere in between.

Legally, private equity funds are usually organized as limited liability partnerships (LLPs). The fund is managed by a private equity "firm," such as Blackstone or KKR, which takes the role of the general partner (GP) of the partnership. The fund investors are the limited partners (LPs). These investors are typically large institutions such as endowments, pension plans and banks. LPs retain limited liability for the actions of the partnership in exchange for delegating all management decisions to the GP.

The contracted life of the partnership is typically 10 years. The year the fund makes its first investment, or its first call for LP capital, is known as its "vintage year." At the inception of the fund, LPs commit to a total investment amount ("committed capital"). These committed amounts are not transferred to the GP immediately, but rather are kept by the LPs until called by the GP to fund investments and management fees ("capital calls" or "takedowns"). Investments are made during the first few years of the fund's life, with the subsequent years devoted to efforts to add value and exit investments. New investments are typically sourced and selected in the first three to five years of a fund. Generally, investments are held for three to eight years before exit. The fund's life can be and often is extended for an additional period if portfolio companies have not achieved the desired improvements or if exit markets are relatively weak. Usually the LP agreement allows for automatic extensions of one to three years. If more time is needed, and it usually is, the GPs and LPs must come to a mutual agreement. The median life of private equity funds turns out to be roughly 15 years.

Unlike investors in mutual funds and hedge funds, investors in private equity funds typically cannot redeem their stakes even after a redemption period, because the nature of the private equity investing cycle makes unplanned liquidations of portfolio companies extremely costly. In recent years, a more active secondary market has developed for LP stakes in private equity funds for those investors who require liquidity prior to the winding down of the particular private equity fund. Many of the secondary market players are themselves organized as private equity funds.

The GP is compensated with an annual management fee and a share of the profits generated by the fund, known as the carried interest or carry. The modal management fee is 2% of committed capital per year over the investment period and, then, 2% of invested capital thereafter. There is substantial variation in both the percentage fee and the basis on which it is calculated. Carried interest is almost always 20%, with variation in the value of carry driven primarily by differences in the basis and timing rules for its calculation. A very few funds charge a premium carry of 25% or 30%. Other funds charge a premium carry, but only after investors have received an agreed-upon return using a 20% carry.

In addition, the GP itself invests its own capital in the fund, in order to impose some downside risk on the GP. This is referred to as the GP commitment. Historically, the GP commitment was initially 1% of total capital. As some GPs have succeeded and accumulated wealth, LPs have strongly encouraged the GPs to commit a meaningful amount of liquid wealth to their funds. Accordingly, today, the GP commitment is more commonly 2% or 3% of committed capital, but with a great deal of variance depending on the past successes of the GP and the size of the fund being raised.

Fund-level performance measures

Absolute performance measures – IRR and MOIC

The fact that most of the investments in the typical private equity fund are in illiquid portfolio companies means that there is no completely objective way to mark a private equity fund's investments to market except when an investment is made or exited. The GPs generally report their performance every quarter to LPs. The assessments of the fund's net asset value (NAV) that GPs report – before the GP has exited all of its investments – are necessarily subjective. And the fund NAVs do not necessarily adjust for any transaction costs the fund would bear if it actually tried to sell the underlying investments.

Consequently, industry practice, as well as most academic work, has shied away from the very technical performance evaluation based on factor pricing models that is used for mutual funds and hedge funds. These methods require more frequent and accurate performance reporting that just does not exist in private equity. Any use of relatively frequent returns would lean heavily on the self-reported NAVs. Instead, the practice has been to measure performance using, to the extent possible, the objective cash flows between GPs and LPs.[2]

An LP's cash outflows consist of management fees and capital called for investments. Inflows to the LP result from cash distributions as the GPs exit investments (net of the applicable carried interest the GP withholds from these distributions). Traditionally, industry practice expresses fund performance in two ways: the internal rate of return (IRR) of this cash flow stream; and the ratio of the cumulative returns to the LPs (distributions) to cumulative capital contributions by the LPs (capital calls), known as the multiple of invested capital (MOIC) or total value to paid in capital (TVPI). In both cases, the return measure is net of all fees.

While useful, the IRR and MOIC both have several drawbacks. Most importantly, both the IRR and MOIC are absolute, not relative, measures of performance. They do not control for movements in the overall market or any other source of risk. This makes it difficult to compare funds. Table 3.1 provides a good example of this. Fund A has a high IRR, but a low MOIC. Fund C is the opposite. Fund B is in between. It is hard to know which fund has the better performance.

The IRR is particularly problematic because it is highly affected by timing. A way to see this is to compare fund A and A'. Fund A has two investments. The first is $12 million that returns $23 million in one year. The second is $8 million that turns out to be worthless. Fund A has a 50% IRR largely because the first investment was very good. Fund A' has exactly the same two investments, but fund A' made the bad one first and the good one second. Note that the IRR drops to 8%. But, in a real sense, A and A' have the exact same performance, which the identical MOICs of 1.17 do reflect.

There are two lessons here. First, from an LP perspective, you want to understand if the GP is investing consistently well. Do not be fooled by a very strong first investment. Second, and acknowledging that LPs are not always completely rational, there is a huge incentive for a GP to make sure the first investment or two in a fund perform very well. A strong first investment or two will ensure a strong IRR for the fund.

Survey evidence of private equity firms in Table 3.2 demonstrates the importance of IRR and MOIC. Gompers, Kaplan and Muhkarlamov (2016) found that, on average, 25.4% of private equity firms said that Net IRR was the most important benchmark for their LPs. An additional 27.0% said that Net IRR relative to the fund's vintage year was most

Table 3.1   Calculating Fund Returns

	Year	Fund A	Fund B	Fund C	Fund D
	0	-12	-20	-20	-8
	1	23	21	0	0
	2	-8	0	0	-12
	3	0	5	0	23
	4	0	0	33	0
	5	0	0	0	0
IRR		50%	22%	14%	8%
MOIC		1.17	1.30	1.67	1.17

Table 3.2 The Most Important Benchmark for the Limited Partners (LPs) Investing in the Private Equity Investors

	Mean	Low AUM	High AUM	Low IRR	High IRR	Old	Young	Local	Global
Net IRR	25.4	29.0	21.9	27.3	21.7	26.7	24.2	22.2	29.6
Net IRR vs S&P	7.9	6.5	9.4	9.1	4.3	10.0	6.1	8.3	7.4
Net IRR with respect to fund vintage year	27.0	19.4	34.4	27.3	43.5	40.0	15.2	33.3	18.5
Net multiple/cash-on-cash	38.1	45.2	31.3	31.8	30.4	20.0	54.5	33.3	44.4
IRR of other GPs	1.6	0.0	3.1	4.5	0.0	3.3	0.0	2.8	0.0
Number of responses	63	31	32	22	23	30	33	36	27

Source: Gompers, Kaplan and Muhkarlyamov (2016)

important to LPs. Finally, 38.1% said Net MOIC was the benchmark that was most important.

Market-adjusted performance measures – LN-PME, KS-PME, direct alpha

While IRR and MOIC are useful, they are absolute measures. They do not tell an investor how the private equity fund performed relative to other alternatives, particularly relative to public equities.

The first attempt to deal with this came from Long and Nickels (1996).[3] They propose a method to market-adjust the IRR, in what has become known as the Long-Nickels public market equivalent (LN-PME). Essentially, the LN-PME calculates the IRR an investor would have received from investing in the relevant public equity benchmark and compares that IRR to the IRR from the private equity fund. The LN-PME has the advantage that many investors think in terms of IRRs. At the same time, the LN-PME has two disadvantages. First, it shares with the IRR the unattractive attribute of being unusually sensitive to investment sequencing, particularly the success of a fund's early investments. Second, the LN-PME "blows up" or cannot be calculated for some funds, particularly those that are very successful and return capital quickly. Because of these unattractive properties, the LN-PME is rarely used anymore.

Kaplan and Schoar (2005)[4] proposed a new method to market-adjust performance. Instead of market-adjusting the IRR, they market-adjusted the MOIC. The Kaplan-Schoar (KS) PME is calculated as the ratio of the sum of discounted distributions to the sum of discounted capital calls, where the discount rate is the total return on the relevant public equity benchmark from an arbitrary reference date to the date of the cash flow in question. Following Kaplan and Schoar (2005), the S&P 500 is usually used as the public benchmark. A fund with a KS-PME (hereafter, simply PME) greater than one outperformed the benchmark (net of all fees); a fund with a PME less than one underperformed. For instance, a PME of 1.20 (0.80) means that the investor ended up with 20% more (fewer) dollars by investing in the private equity fund instead of the public benchmark. The PME has the advantages that it can always be calculated and has an intuitive interpretation. One practical disadvantage for practitioners is that it provides a cumulative measure rather than an annualized return measure.

Gredil, Griffiths and Stucke (2014)[5] propose an alternative method to market-adjust the IRR. They calculate the differential alpha to the relevant benchmark that discounts the private equity fund cash flows to a net present value of zero. Accordingly, it is the analog to the KS-PME. While it is an improvement over the LN-PME, it still has some of the disadvantages of IRR and the LN-PME.

Table 3.3 shows the KS-PME and direct alphas for the investments in Table 3.1 under the assumptions that the stock market return over the fund life is 0% and that it is 10% per year. Under the assumption of 0% returns to the stock market, the absolute and relative measures are the same!

Alternatively, if the stock market increases by 10% per year, funds A, B and C all have the same KS-PME of 1.14. This is because the early returns to fund A can be reinvested in the stock market at a 10% return, while fund C returns 14% annually versus the stock market at 10%. Over four years, this works out to a cumulative 14% advantage. Fund A' remains a laggard despite the fact that it has the same investments as fund A because the later successful investment is not reinvested in the growing public market.

Table 3.3 Calculation of Fund Returns, PMEs, and Direct Alpha

	Year	Fund A	Fund B	Fund C	Fund D
	0	-12	-20	-20	-8
	1	23	21	0	0
	2	-8	0	0	-12
	3	0	5	0	23
	4	0	0	33	0
	5	0	0	0	0
IRR		50%	22%	14%	8%
MOIC		1.17	1.30	1.67	1.17
PME (at 0%)		1.17	1.30	1.67	1.17
PME (at 10%)		1.14	1.14	1.14	0.96
Direct alpha (at 0%)		50%	22%	14%	8%
Direct alpha (at 10%)		36%	11%	3%	-2%

The bottom line here is that different performance measures can give different results. Fund A is desirable if you can reinvest in another fund A. If, on the other hand, fund A could be A', then funds B and C look more desirable.

At the end of the day, LPs (and GPs) should look for private equity funds that outperform the public markets (net of fees). If private equity does not outperform public markets (net of fees), then it is harder, although not impossible, to make the case for investing.

Other risk adjustments

Since Kaplan and Schoar (2005) introduced the PME, it has been the standard performance measure in the academic literature measuring private equity returns using fund-level cash flows. Practitioners also increasingly use the KS-PME and direct alpha.

A natural question is to what extent the market-adjustment embedded in the PME suffices to risk-adjust fund returns. Theoretical works by Sorensen and Jagannathan (2013)[6] and Korteweg and Nagel (2013)[7] have tried to link private equity performance measurement to asset pricing theory. These papers establish that the PME suffices to adjust for risks spanned by the benchmark return, regardless of the beta of private equity with respect to the benchmark, under the assumption that investors have log utility.[8] On the other hand, as the authors acknowledge, investors may not have log utility[9] and there are likely relevant risks not spanned by a single benchmark return.

Average performance[10]

Who measures performance?

Currently, the four primary providers of private equity performance or benchmarks are (in alphabetical order) Burgiss Private I, Cambridge Associates, Pitchbook and Preqin.[11]

Burgiss has the advantage that it is sourced exclusively from LPs. LPs use Burgiss's software to manage their private equity investments – record keeping and fund investment monitoring. Burgiss uses those data to measure performance. LPs comprise a wide array of institutions. The data come from "institutional allocators including endowments, foundations, OCIOs, pension funds, and family offices . . . representing over $1.7 trillion in assets" and include data from "more than 1,000 firms in 32 countries, delivering data that represents nearly $9 trillion in private assets." Burgiss believes the private equity funds in the sample represent greater than 70% of funds ever raised.

The advantage of the Burgiss database is that if the fund is in the LP portfolio, the GPs have to report. So, there is no reporting bias. The only possible bias is if the Burgiss LPs do not invest in a representative sample of private equity funds. Given the number of LPs and funds in the database, this seems unlikely. As a result, we view the Burgiss database as likely to be the most reliable for measuring private equity performance.

Cambridge Associates (CA) provides an array of investment management services to LP clients. For many LP clients, this means providing private investment performance reporting and recommending GPs. CA receives roughly two-thirds of its fund-level data from GPs that are in LP client portfolios. They also receive data from other GPs who are not in client portfolios (but, presumably, would like to be). This may create a slight positive selection bias.

The advantage of CA, and particularly Burgiss, is that their data are likely to have relatively little selection and reporting bias. The disadvantage is that they do not report the performance of individual funds or fund names. This makes it difficult for GPs and LPs to perform more detailed benchmarking comparisons.

Pitchbook and Preqin are primarily data providers. These data providers obtain fund-level data by gathering information from (1) public sources, which include using Freedom of Information Act (FOIA) requests (or their parallel outside the US) requiring some LPs to reveal the performance of the funds in which they invest; and (2) from requests to LPs and GPs to voluntarily provide the information. Roughly half of Preqin's data comes from GPs. Some funds report only IRRs, some report cash flows as well.

Pitchbook and Preqin have the advantage of reporting the performance of individual funds and reporting GP names. The disadvantage is that they potentially have a selection bias and a reporting bias in the funds they include.

Harris et al. (2014)[12] compare the performance reported for US buy-out funds by the four data providers. They find that the reported performance is reasonably similar for funds with post-2000 vintages. This is not so true for VC funds. Burgiss and Cambridge Associates tended to show higher performance for VC funds than Pitchbook and Preqin, likely because a number of the best VC funds do not allow their numbers to be publicly reported or used.

What is performance?

Table 3.4 shows the pooled average and median IRR, MOIC and KS-PME for North American buyout and growth funds by vintage year from Burgiss's Private IQ database as of 30 September 2021. Figures 3.1 to 3.4 show the data graphically for vintages from 1991 to 2017. The pooled average puts all the fund cash flows of a vintage year together and is closer to a value-weighted average. These vintages have a reasonable number of data points and are old enough to have meaningful performance information. More recent funds are still investing and performance is continuing to emerge.

Figure 3.1 shows that the average vintage year IRR has varied quite a bit, with some vintages over 20% and some under 10%. Figure 3.2 shows that the average vintage year MOICs are generally between 1.5 and 2 with strong vintage years exceeding 2 and poor years less than 1.5. The interesting result here is that every vintage since 1995 has returned at least 1.3 times the capital invested. For investors concerned with absolute returns and capital preservation, this is a very attractive (and impressive) result.

As discussed earlier, it is difficult to know if this IRR and MOIC vintage year performance is particularly good or bad without being able to compare it to an alternative. The KS-PMEs (relative to the S&P 500) in Figure 3.3 show the stunning result that the pooled average performance of every vintage from 1994 to 2017 – 24 in a row – has outperformed the S&P 500. This is net of fees for private equity funds, but assuming no fees for investing in the S&P 500. The median fund has outperformed the S&P 500 in 22 of 24 vintages, never going below a KS-PME of 0.92. Figure 3.4 annualizes the KS-PMEs and presents direct alphas by vintage year. As with the KS-PME, the direct alphas show that the pooled average of buyouts outperforms the S&P 500 in every vintage since 1994. For post-financial crisis vintages (2009 to 2017), direct alphas are almost 5% on average. The strong relative performance is one of the reasons that

Table 3.4 Historical Private Equity Fund Returns by Vintage Year

Vintage	Capitalization (M)	Number of Funds	IRR Average	IRR Median	MOIC Average	MOIC Median	KS-PME Average	KS-PME Median
1980		2	28.25	23.20	9.34	7.67	2.24	1.91
1982		2	28.17	24.95	2.86	2.77	1.37	1.21
1983		3	20.52	8.51	3.04	1.81	1.21	0.71
1984		2	27.18	23.19	4.40	4.09	1.53	1.38
1985		4	131.67	35.87	7.11	2.43	5.03	1.30
1986	1 453	5	24.42	16.79	5.77	2.36	1.52	1.11
1987	8 371	8	10.81	12.85	2.24	2.19	0.87	0.97
1988	6 060	8	15.17	11.21	2.01	1.60	0.98	0.84
1989	3 129	11	26.74	25.67	2.93	3.05	1.48	1.45
1990	2 306	8	14.56	13.09	2.23	1.96	0.92	0.93
1991		4	26.25	29.02	2.77	2.86	1.22	1.35
1992	4 087	9	32.07	19.95	2.12	1.95	1.20	1.09
1993	4 574	9	18.76	17.43	1.90	1.72	0.97	0.90
1994	6 855	19	16.82	8.75	1.83	1.42	1.12	0.94
1995	16 991	27	11.67	10.49	1.60	1.56	1.12	1.03
1996	4 888	19	15.44	9.05	1.75	1.70	1.30	1.14
1997	26 240	30	8.26	3.81	1.51	1.23	1.24	1.04
1998	39 578	43	5.34	8.46	1.32	1.44	1.21	1.44

(Continued)

Table 3.4 (Continued)

Vintage	Capitalization (M)	Number of Funds	IRR Average	IRR Median	MOIC Average	MOIC Median	KS-PME Average	KS-PME Median
1999	29 891	34	7.79	8.94	1.44	1.53	1.26	1.37
2000	54 914	51	15.12	12.93	1.84	1.66	1.39	1.32
2001	23 338	33	23.11	20.67	1.97	1.92	1.47	1.47
2002	20 639	22	16.89	15.13	1.92	1.74	1.41	1.29
2003	22 018	24	20.46	14.20	2.05	1.90	1.55	1.34
2004	35 760	46	13.40	11.93	1.79	1.67	1.35	1.26
2005	53 678	63	9.14	8.35	1.63	1.60	1.16	1.07
2006	142 122	71	7.76	10.16	1.56	1.61	1.01	1.07
2007	125 896	73	10.90	12.64	1.71	1.73	1.02	1.07
2008	95 164	75	13.97	11.61	1.71	1.66	1.01	0.92
2009	20 653	26	20.18	22.12	2.14	2.17	1.19	1.24
2010	21 470	34	14.10	15.11	1.87	1.82	1.01	1.03
2011	65 082	55	18.40	18.46	2.18	2.06	1.16	1.16
2012	55 791	56	19.43	16.70	2.02	1.88	1.17	1.09
2013	72 623	53	18.99	18.68	1.99	1.91	1.15	1.13
2014	87 733	80	22.22	16.84	2.11	1.82	1.25	1.08
2015	73 299	60	22.02	18.61	1.94	1.65	1.18	1.07
2016	113 295	78	21.86	22.69	1.83	1.77	1.11	1.09

2017	91 169	61	30.60	30.26	1.89	1.72	1.26	1.21
2018	123 938	72	22.88	25.25	1.45	1.42	1.04	1.02
2019	224 975	98	32.13	23.98	1.36	1.26	1.09	1.01
2020	135 003	73	40.47	20.68	1.27	1.17	1.08	1.00
2021	120 793	53	23.99	-3.27	1.08	0.97	1.06	0.97
(All)	1 937 632	1 504	15.86	15.35	1.75	1.62	1.18	1.09

Source: Burgiss

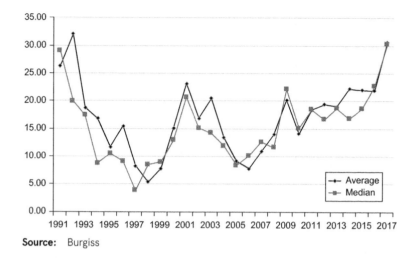

Source: Burgiss

Figure 3.1 US Buyout IRRs by Vintage Year, 1991–2017 Pooled Ave. and Median as of 2021 Q3

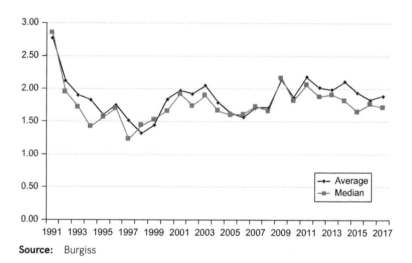

Source: Burgiss

Figure 3.2 US Buyout MOICs by Vintage Year, 1991–2017 Pooled Ave. and Median as of 2021 Q3

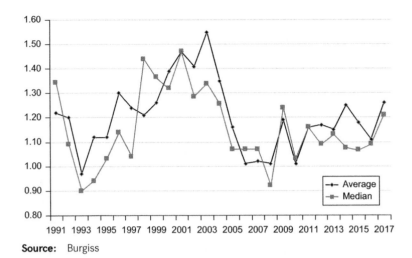

Source: Burgiss

Figure 3.3   US Buyout PMEs by Vintage Year, 1991–2017 Pooled Ave. and Median as of 2021 Q3

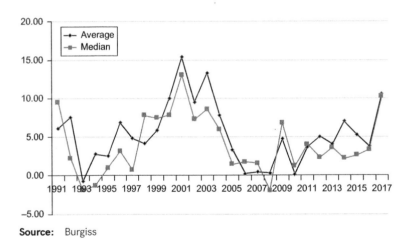

Source: Burgiss

Figure 3.4   US Buyout Direct Alphas by Vintage Year, 1991–2017 Pooled Ave. and Median as of 2021 Q3

institutional investors have increased their allocations/investments to private equity over time. It is worth adding that the results are qualitatively similar for European private equity funds relative to the MSCI World Index or the MSCI Europe Index.

Sensitivities

There are various questions one might have about the basic results.[13] First, the S&P 500 may not be the best benchmark. Buyout funds tend to invest in companies that would be considered mid-cap or small-cap. The most frequently used and most liquid small-cap index is the Russell 2000. Figure 3.5 presents KS-PMEs relative to the Russell 2000. Every vintage from 1999 to 2016 has outperformed the Russell 2000. The KS-PMEs relative to the Russell 2000 tend to be a bit lower than those relative to the S&P 500 pre-financial crises, but much greater post-financial crisis. In fact, for vintages from 2009 to 2017, the average KS-PME relative to the Russell exceeds 1.25. This reflects the fact that the Russell 2000 has greatly underperformed the S&P 500 since the financial crisis.

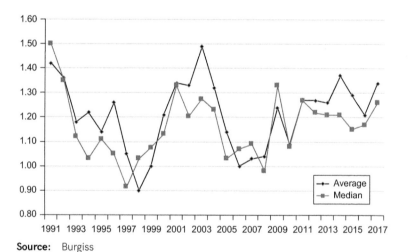

Source: Burgiss

Figure 3.5   US Buyout PMEs by Vintage Year, 1991–2017 Pooled Ave. and Median as Pooled Ave. as of 2021 Q3 Russell 2000

Second, some have argued that buyout investing should be compared to value investing in mid-cap or small-cap public stocks because of the type of companies in which private equity funds invest. According to this argument, buyout performance should be compared to returns to a value index like the Russell 2000 value index. Brown and Kaplan (2019)[14] make this comparison. They find that buyout funds consistently have the Russell 2000 value index except for a few vintages in the late 1990s. The outperformance has been particularly strong post-financial crisis as small-cap value and mid-cap value have markedly underperformed the overall small-cap and mid-cap markets as well as the S&P 500.

A third alternative is to try to adjust for leverage and the level of market risk (i.e., the CAPM beta). Ilmanen et al. (2019)[15] assume that the market risk inherent in a portfolio of US buyout funds is equivalent to having a beta of 1.2 and adjust accordingly. Because buyout funds are illiquid, it is difficult to estimate betas directly. The academic literature on this is inconclusive with betas typically ranging from 1.0 to 1.3. In general, using a beta above 1.0 has the effect of lowering the PMEs and direct alphas of buyout funds because the stock market, on average, has gone up.

We note that, empirically, beta does not do a good job of explaining realized returns, i.e., a portfolio of higher beta public stocks does not perform much differently from a portfolio of low beta stocks. Evidence for this comes from Frazzini and Pedersen (2014).[16] It is further not clear to what extent risk measures based on volatility and covariance are particularly meaningful for illiquid investments, where cash flows are somewhat at the discretion of the fund manager. Nevertheless, Brown and Kaplan (2019) compare the performance of buyout funds to a leveraged investment (with a beta of 1.2) in the S&P 500 and Russell 2000. Buyout funds still outperform, albeit by less than when using a beta of 1.0.

The bottom line to take from this section is that buyout funds of vintages from 1995 to 2017 have performed very well, both in an absolute sense and relative to various public market benchmarks. This consistent outperformance is an important reason why investors have markedly increased their allocations to buyout and growth equity funds over recent time periods. While impressive, it is important to note that there is no guarantee that outperformance will continue in the future.

Performance persistence

The next logical question is whether particular GPs can consistently outperform. Figure 3.6 shows quartile performance cutoffs by vintage year for all buyout and growth equity funds in the Burgiss database as of the third quarter of 2021. For most vintage years, top-quartile funds have PMEs above 1.2 while bottom quartile funds have PMEs below 1.0. It would be very valuable if one could know in advance to invest in funds that were going to be in the top quartile while avoiding funds that were going to be in the bottom quartile. For post-2000 buyout funds, Harris et al. (2020) report that funds in the top quartile have an average PME of 1.70 while funds in the bottom quartile average only 0.71.

A common strategy employed by investors in private equity is to invest in GPs whose previous funds have done well. This is a good strategy if there is persistence in performance. Kaplan and Schoar (2005) were the first to study performance persistence in private equity. They found that the performance (PME or IRR) of a given fund was positively related to the performance of the previous fund raised by the same private equity firm. This was an unusual result given the fact that there is little

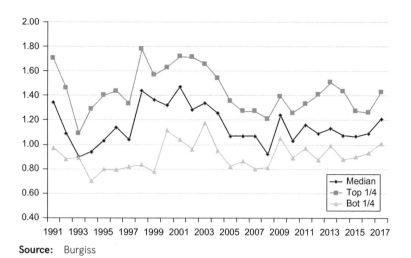

Source: Burgiss

Figure 3.6   US LBO PMEs by Vintage Year, 1991–2017 Top 1/4, Median and Bottom 1/4 as of 2021 Q3

evidence of persistence in mutual fund performance (Carhart (1997),[17] Fama and French (2010)[18]), and, at best, modest evidence of persistence in hedge fund performance (Ammann et al. (2013)[19] and Jagannathan et al. (2010)[20]).

More recently, however, using the Burgiss database (through June 2019), Harris et al. (2020)[21] revisit the question of persistence, focusing on funds raised since 2001 – after the period studied by Kaplan and Schoar. Using ex post or most recent fund performance as of June 2019, they find there is modest persistence from fund to fund for post-2000 funds – the final performance of a GP's fund predicts the latest performance of the next fund. For example, if fund 2 of a particular GP is in the top quartile, there is a 33% chance that its next fund, fund 3, will be in the top quartile. If it were random, the likelihood would be 25%. Subsequent funds of funds that were in the top quartile had PMEs of 1.27 while funds previously in the second, third and bottom quartiles had PMEs of 1.18, 1.15 and 1.02. This is modestly good news for GPs. Good risk-adjusted performance persists somewhat.

The news for LPs is more complicated. When Harris et al. (2020) look at the information an LP would actually have – previous fund performance at the time of fundraising rather than final performance – they find little or no evidence of persistence for buyouts, both overall and post-2000. This occurs because GPs can choose when to raise their funds. They tend to try to raise funds when performance of their current fund is strong. GPs with poorly performing funds often decide to wait. If performance improves, they raise another fund; if performance is sufficiently poor, they are unable to raise another fund. This means LPs should be wary of relying on the conventional wisdom to invest in top-performing private equity funds.[22] The results and advice are different for venture capital funds where persistence appears to have persisted.

Blackstone Capital Partners (BCP) provides a nice example of a lack of persistence. Table 3.5 shows the MOIC and IRR for BCP IV to VII according to Pitchbook as of 30 September 2021. For each fund, the table also reports the vintage year quartile both for MOIC and IRR where the BCP fund sits based on the Burgiss Private IQ performance data. BCP IV performed very well and is in the top quartile of funds raised in 2002 for both MOIC and IRR. In fact, the performance is in the top 10%. Contrast that with BCP V which is in the second quartile for MOIC for funds

Table 3.5 Blackstone Capital Partners IV–VII Fund Returns

	Vintage Year	Fund Size (bn)	MOIC	Burgiss Quartile	IRR	Burgiss Quartile
Blackstone Capital Partners VII	2016	$18.90	1.52×	3	21.0%	2
Blackstone Capital Partners VI	2011	$17.50	1.73×	3	13.0%	3
Blackstone Capital Partners V	2006	$21.70	1.64×	2	8.0%	3
Blackstone Capital Partners IV	2002	$6.77	2.46×	1	36.0%	1

Source: Pitchbook and Burgiss

raised in 2006. BCP VI and BCP VII are both in the third quartile for MOIC for funds raised, respectively, in 2011 and 2016. The IRR quartiles also move around. Thus for BCP, since 2002, there is essentially no consistency.

The discussion in this chapter demonstrates that, as an asset class, private equity has performed quite well and has outperformed public equity benchmarks across any reasonable time horizon. Efforts to risk-adjust private equity returns leave that outperformance intact. As such, the dramatic growth in the private equity industry can be understood as institutional investors understanding that performance and increasing their allocation accordingly. We do want to end with the caution that successful past performance is no guarantee that that performance will continue.

Notes

[*]   This chapter borrows from and updates Kaplan and Sensoy (2015).

[1]   Ludovic Phalippou, 2020, An Inconvenient Fact: Private Equity Returns & The Billionaire Factory, https://papers.ssrn.com/sol3/papers.cfm?abstract_id=3623820.

[2]   For active funds, it is usually assumed that the last observed NAV is a fair measure of the true value of the fund, so the last observed NAV is treated as a liquidating distribution for the purposes of calculating performance.

[3]   A. M. Long and C. J. Nickels, 1996, A Private Investment Benchmark, AIMR Conference on Venture Capital Investing.

[4]   S. N. Kaplan and A. Schoar, 2005, Private Equity Returns: Persistence and Capital Flows, *Journal of Finance* 60, 1791–823.

5   O. Gredil, B. Griffiths and R. Stucke, 2014, Benchmarking Private Equity: The Direct Alpha Method, University of North Carolina Working Paper.

6   Morten Sorensen and Ravi Jagannathan, 2015, The Public Market Equivalent and Private Equity Performance, *Financial Analysts Journal* 71, 43–50.

7   Arthur Korteweg and Stefan Nagel, 2016, Risk-Adjusting the Returns to Venture Capital, *Journal of Finance* 71, 1437–70.

8   Technically, it is the difference between the sum of discounted distributions and the sum of discounted capital calls that provides the appropriate risk adjustment, rather than their ratio.

9   Log utility implies that risk aversion and the intertemporal elasticity of substitution are both equal to one. The asset pricing literature has found these implications hard to reconcile with the equity premium and risk-free rate in the data.

10   This section relies on data and analysis in Robert S. Harris, Tim Jenkinson and Steven N. Kaplan, 2014, Private Equity Performance: What Do We Know? *Journal of Finance* October, 1851–82; Robert S. Harris, Tim Jenkinson and S. N. Kaplan, 2016, How Do Private Equity Investments Perform Compared to Public Equity? *Journal of Investment Management* 14, 1–24; Robert S. Harris, Tim Jenkinson, S. N. Kaplan and R. Stucke, 2018, Financial Intermediation in Private Equity: How Well Do Funds of Funds Perform? *Journal of Financial Economics* 129, 287–305; Robert S. Harris, Tim Jenkinson, S. N. Kaplan and R. Stucke, 2020, Has Persistence Persisted in Private Equity? Evidence from Buyout and Venture Capital Funds, https://papers.ssrn.com/sol3/papers.cfm?abstract_id=2304808; and G. Brown and S. N. Kaplan, 2019, Have Private Equity Returns Really Declined? *Journal of Private Equity* 22(4), 11–18.

11   Kaplan serves on the board of directors of Morningstar, the owner of Pitchbook.

12   Robert S. Harris, Tim Jenkinson and Steven N. Kaplan, 2014, Private Equity Performance: What Do We Know? *Journal of Finance* October, 1851–82.

13   See Ludovic Phalippou, 2020, An Inconvenient Fact: Private Equity Returns & The Billionaire Factory, https://papers.ssrn.com/sol3/papers.cfm?abstract_id=3623820, who raises several of these questions (albeit in a misleading way).

14   G. Brown and S. N. Kaplan, 2019, Have Private Equity Returns Really Declined? *Journal of Private Equity* 22(4), 11–18.

15   Anti Ilmanen, Swati Chandra and Nicholas McQuinn, 2019, Demystifying Illiquid Assets: Expected Returns for Private Equity, AQR Working Paper.

16   A. Frazzini and L. H. Pedersen, 2014, Betting Against Beta, *Journal of Financial Economics* 111, 1–25.

17   M. Carhart, 1997, On Persistence of Mutual Fund Performance, *Journal of Finance* 52, 57–82.

18   E. F. Fama and K. R. French, 2010, Luck versus Skill in the Cross-Section of Mutual Fund Returns, *Journal for Finance* 65, 1915–47.

19   M. Ammann, O. Huber and M. Schmid, 2013, Hedge Fund Characteristics and Performance Persistence, *European Finance Management* 19, 209–50.

20   R. Jagannathan, A. Malakhov and D. Novikov, 2010, Do Hot Hands Exist among Hedge Fund Managers? An Empirical Evaluation, *Journal of Finance* 65, 217–55.

21   Robert S. Harris, Tim Jenkinson, S. N. Kaplan and R. Stucke, 2020, Has Persistence Persisted in Private Equity? Evidence from Buyout and Venture Capital Funds, https://papers.ssrn.com/sol3/papers.cfm?abstract_id =2304808.
22   Performance persistence has also been documented at finer levels of detail than the private equity fund. R. Braun et al. (2019) study individual buy-out managers. They find deal-level gross PME performance persistence; the individual is around four times more important than the GP organi-zation. R. Braun, N. Dorau, T. Jenkinson and D. Urban, 2019, Whom to Follow: Individual Manager Performance and Persistence in Private Equity Investments, University of Oxford Working Paper.

4   Investment decision making

Access to attractive investment opportunities is a critical factor that influences the ultimate returns generated by private equity investors. Industry professionals typically refer to the deal "funnel" to describe the process of sourcing potential investments and then winnowing them down to those that justify an investment.

In this chapter, we explore how private equity investors bring investment opportunities into the firm, evaluate the attractiveness of the deal and decide which opportunities to invest in. We start by understanding deal sourcing and deal selection. How do private equity managers gain access to their deals, and what factors are most important for their selection? We then move on to discuss the analytical tools private equity investors use to evaluate deals. We review the theory and practice of the finance tools taught in most business schools and then evaluate which tools are utilized while exploring how they are employed by decision makers. Finally, we present an investment framework that can assist in determining which deals are attractive.

Deal sourcing

Private equity investors emphasize the importance of deal sourcing in the value creation process. There are numerous channels that private equity managers utilize to gain access to attractive deals. The GKM (2016)[1] survey of a large group of PE investment managers examined this issue. Many outsiders are under the illusion that private equity managers just bring great companies in the door and quickly close a transaction. Table 4.1 shows that this is not the case. For every 100 opportunities that come in the door, the typical investor does deep due diligence on fewer than 24, signs an agreement with fewer than 14 and ultimately invests

Table 4.1 Private Equity Deal Funnel

	AUM				IRR		Age		Offices	
	Mean	Median	Low	High	Low	High	Old	Young	Local	Global
All considered opportunities	100.0	100.0	100.0	100.0	100.0	100.0	100.0	100.0	100.0	100.0
Review with partner group/investment committee	61.8	50.0	56.9	66.6	65.8	61.3	63.0	60.8	56.5	69.2
Meet management	52.8	40.0	38.1	67.0	58.5	53.2	62.2	44.5	42.0	67.5
Limited due diligence	49.1	40.0	35.2	62.6	56.7	46.5	59.1	40.4	42.5	58.1
Deep due diligence	23.7	20.0	16.3	30.9	29.0	21.2	29.5	18.7	19.1	30.0
Offer term sheet/negotiate detailed terms	22.5	19.0	14.4	30.3	25.7	22.9	27.1	18.5	16.2	31.1
Sign LOI	13.6	8.0	9.1	17.9	15.2	11.0	14.5	12.8	8.0	21.2
Close	6.1	4.0	4.0	8.1	7.0	5.4	7.3	5.0	4.1	8.8
Number of responses	71	71	35	36	26	26	33	38	41	30

in only six. This indicates that private equity investors devote considerable resources to evaluating transactions, despite the fact that they will ultimately invest in only a very few. The winnowing process is a critical part of what private equity managers do. A key element of this process is quickly deciding which deals make sense to examine intensively and which merit a quick pass.

When we compare the deal funnel at different types of private equity firms, larger private equity firms have an investment rate nearly twice as high as smaller private equity firms (8.1 deals per 100 opportunities considered versus 4.0 deals per 100 opportunities considered). There are several potential explanations. First, larger private equity firms may have higher quality initial deal sourcing and hence do not need to weed out as many deals at all stages. Alternatively, the larger fund sizes may reduce the investment hurdle rate relative to the investment hurdle rate of small funds given their abundance of capital. In other words, larger funds may be doing more marginal deals compared to smaller funds. Finally, there may simply be fewer large deals to evaluate.

It is also important to understand exactly how quality deals are introduced to the private equity firms. Table 4.2 looks at the source for closed deals within each private equity firm, i.e., where do the deals they do come from. Not surprisingly, a large fraction of deals that are done are considered "proprietary," 35.6%. Proprietary deals are potentially important to the ability to achieve high returns. Academic research tells us the greater the competition for the deal, the higher the acquisition price paid is likely to be. Private equity firms would be willing to pay a price which reflects a portion of the operating improvements that they can create in their portfolio companies. In fact, auction theory states that the winning bidder in an auction pays a price that is equal to the value that can be created by the second-best bidder. As such, multiple bidders give more of the total value created to the seller as opposed to the buyer. Proprietary deals are one way to keep from paying a higher price (that translates directly into lower returns).

On a more granular level, private equity managers indicate that 7.4% of deals come from solicitations by management and 8.6% come from their executive network. These have the potential to be proprietary as well. Another third come from investment banks that shop deals on behalf of sellers, 8.6% are from deal brokers and 4.3% from other private equity funds. These deals are unlikely to be proprietary. In total, private

Table 4.2 Source of Private Equity Closed Deals

	AUM				IRR		Age		Offices	
	Mean	Median	Low	High	Low	High	Old	Young	Local	Global
Proactively self-generated	35.6	30.0	37.7	33.5	39.3	35.5	35.8	35.4	35.3	35.9
Investment bank generated	33.3	25.0	30.5	36.0	33.0	37.0	38.2	29.1	33.0	33.7
Inbound from management	7.4	5.0	5.8	8.9	6.1	9.0	7.4	7.3	7.2	7.6
Other PE firm	4.3	0.0	5.4	3.3	4.1	2.2	4.1	4.5	5.0	3.5
Deal brokers	8.6	0.0	9.5	7.7	6.8	7.1	8.4	8.7	8.7	8.5
Executive network	8.6	5.0	8.3	9.0	8.8	8.5	4.6	12.1	9.1	8.0
LPs/investors	1.7	0.0	2.5	0.9	0.6	0.7	0.4	2.7	1.2	2.3
Conferences	0.6	0.0	0.3	0.9	1.0	0.3	1.1	0.3	0.5	0.8
Other	0.0	0.0	0.1	0.0	0.1	0.0	0.0	0.1	0.1	0.0
% of deals considered proprietary	47.9	50.0	54.0	41.9	48.0	43.9	41.5	53.4	47.6	48.3
Number of responses	71	71	35	36	26	26	33	38	41	30

equity managers viewed nearly half (48%) of their deals to be proprietary. Clearly, a significant amount of time and effort are put into bringing in deals that are not "over-shopped."

There are many examples of deal sourcing employed in the PE industry. A number of firms like Summit Partners and TA Associates proactively "cold call" numerous private companies in order to assess the owner's willingness to potentially take private equity. Often referred to as "smiling and dialing for deals," this often occurs many years before any contemplated transaction is made, and is meant to introduce the firm and the concept of private equity to companies. Even in new markets, this strategy could work well. In 2012, TA partners Michael Berk and Ed Sippel led TA's first investment out of its Hong Kong office by proactively contacting P.J. Beylier, CEO of satellite communication company SpeedCast. Beylier hoped to buy SpeedCast – a wholly owned subsidiary of AsiaSat, a Hong Kong-based publicly traded company. The wrinkle was that not only would TA have to convince Beylier that the deal made sense, they would have to convince AsiaSat, the parent, to sell. Their persistence led to the opportunity for the buyout and consolidation of several other regional players in the industry in what was ultimately a highly successful transaction.[2]

Other private equity firms attempt to gain proprietary access by meeting with management of public companies and getting them to agree to a "take private." In order to avoid an auction, some private equity firms attempt to convince senior management that a negotiated transaction makes sense for both shareholders and management. These transactions typically require an independent special committee of the board of directors to negotiate with the private equity firms prior to agreeing to the transaction. They also generally require the selling company to "check the market" by considering other bids for some fixed amount of time. This process is necessary to ensure that outside shareholders' interests are taken into consideration.

Michael Chu of Catterton Private Equity had been courting Bill Allen, CEO of Outback Steakhouse, for more than six months about the possibility of taking the restaurant chain private. Chu convinced Allen that the deal made sense only after he brought in Andrew Balson and Mark Nunnelly of Bain Capital, a much larger private equity firm that could provide Allen with assurances that the deal would get done. Through a multi-month period of negotiation, Bain and Catterton were able to take Outback private in November 2006 without the company going to a formal auction.[3]

Another strategy to access deals is to use networks to identify a potential investment. These networks can typically come from past employment or business associates, but can also come through social networks. Brazos Private Equity's partner, Randall Fojtasek, used connections through his Southern Methodist University alumni network to identify Cheddar's (a restaurant chain in the Southwest) as a potential investment opportunity. Aubrey Good, the company's founder, had deep ties in Dallas and was an alum of Southern Methodist University. Even though the Cheddar's deal had been previously shopped by an investment bank, Fojtasek was able to utilize his connections and shared alma mater connection to make Cheddar's a proprietary deal.[4]

A critical takeaway from this discussion is that the deal funnel matters immensely for PE investors. Many strategies are employed to generate deal flow, and that process is an integral part of the PE process. Because there is not always the ability to bring unique value-add to a portfolio company, avoiding competition for a transaction is often a necessary step for generating attractive returns.

Deal selection

The winnowing process that private equity managers undertake is critical to picking the best opportunities for the capital they have to deploy. We start by understanding the qualitative factors utilized by PE investors then move to the quantitative tools employed by PE managers. Both are critical drivers of the selection process.

A central debate among economists as well as practitioners has been whether the business model (horse) or the management team (jockey) is more important in deal selection for investors in private companies.[5] Is it more important to have a great set of senior executives in place to implement the plan for improvement or are the industry and business model of the company more important? Clearly, having both is ideal, but when forced to rank which is more important, how do PE managers respond? Good business models likely have the ability to keep and attract customers, have important competitive advantages and have the ability to grow and defend the company's position. Still, the management team has to run the business.

In order to better understand how PE investors select and differentiate among investments, our GKM (2016) survey asked about the qualitative factors that PE investors considered when investing. PE managers ranked the factors they considered when choosing their investments. Table 4.3 shows that the highest ranked factor was the firm's business model/competitive position (i.e., the horse). We obtained the same relative ranking in our more recent GKM (2020) survey. This would indicate that PE investors believe that generating returns with a bad business is difficult to achieve. Most private equity managers are, generally, not interested in turning around dramatically poorly performing companies. These rankings indicate that PE investors are looking for companies that they can grow in a variety of ways.

Somewhat behind the business model were the management team and the ability of the PE firm to add value to that particular investment. Again, the focus on these choices aligns with the desire for growth. The image of private equity firms slashing expenses and headcount seems at odds with these rankings. This was confirmed when the survey asked private equity investors to rate the source of returns. Table 4.4 shows that the dominant source of returns was growth in the value of the underlying business followed closely by operational improvements. Again, the importance of growth is even stronger in our more recent survey.

These results stand in sharp contrast to much of the received wisdom about private equity. The popular press often paints private equity managers as "barbarians at the gate" who take a cleaver to jobs and massively reduce expenses. The advice, services and incentives that private firms provide through operational and governance engineering therefore are critically important to the process of generating returns by growing the business. We explore each of these in subsequent chapters and look at the granular nature of the activities that PE managers employ to achieve that growth.

Interestingly, the results are somewhat different for venture capital investors. Similar survey evidence shows that the management team (i.e., the jockey) is the most important qualitative selection criterion, particularly for early-stage venture capitalists.[6] The difference likely reflects the fact that the business is nascent and, therefore, must rely more on the management team.

Table 4.3   Factors for Selecting Private Equity Deals

	AUM				IRR		Age		Offices	
	Mean	Median	Low	High	Low	High	Old	Young	Local	Global
Ability to add value	3.6	3.0	3.6	3.6	3.9	3.5	3.5	3.7	3.5	3.8
Business model/competitive position	4.6	5.0	4.5	4.7	4.5	4.5	4.4	4.7	4.6	4.5
Fit with fund	2.3	2.0	2.7	1.9	2.0	2.2	2.2	2.4	2.5	2.0
Industry/market	3.2	3.0	3.4	3.0	3.3	3.0	3.3	3.1	3.5	2.8
Management team	3.8	4.0	3.7	4.0	3.9	4.0	4.1	3.6	3.8	3.8
Valuation	3.5	3.0	3.2	3.8	3.4	3.8	3.5	3.5	3.0	4.1
Number of responses	65	65	32	33	24	23	31	34	37	28

Table 4.4 Sources of Private Equity Deal Value before Investment

	Mean	AUM		IRR		Age		Offices	
		Low	High	Low	High	Old	Young	Local	Global
Growth in the value of the underlying business	100.0	100.0	100.0	100.0	100.0	100.0	100.0	100.0	100.0
Industry-level multiple arbitrage	64.8	74.3	55.6	50.0	65.4	66.7	63.2	61.0	70.0
Leverage	76.1	74.3	83.3	65.4	88.5	81.8	71.1	73.2	80.0
Operational improvements	97.2	74.3	100.0	100.0	96.2	100.0	94.7	95.1	100.0
Refinancing	97.2	28.6	44.4	34.6	42.3	45.5	28.9	29.3	46.7
Other	26.8	28.6	25.0	23.1	19.2	21.2	31.6	31.7	20.0
Number of responses	71	35	36	26	26	33	38	41	30

Investment frameworks for private equity and buyout transactions

In every deal they do, private equity investors create an investment memorandum that describes the deal and the reasons they want to do the deal. These investment memos can be over 100 pages. The investment memos generally combine both qualitative and quantitative analyses. In this section, we present an investment framework for the qualitative aspects of deal evaluation. In the next section, we outline the quantitative tools that private equity investors apply when evaluating deals.

Our qualitative framework can be summarized with the pneumonic OUTSX-CUPID. OUTSX stands for Opportunity, Uncertainty, Team, Structure and eXit. CUPID describes the different pieces for evaluating the opportunity and determining whether it is qualitatively attractive. The pieces of CUPID are Competition/industry, Undervalued, Proprietary, Improvements and Debt capacity. It is worth noting in advance that the components of OUTSX-CUPID interact.

The first questions to ask about the opportunity (O) are: how attractive are the industry dynamics and how attractive is the company's competitive position within the industry? Industry dynamics include industry growth prospects, technological change, customer concentration and competitors, among other aspects. Competitive position considers whether the company has existing or potential competitive advantages that will allow the company to compete and do well given the industry dynamics. The analysis of competition and industry (C) generally occupies a large fraction of the typical investment memorandum. In these analyses, investors will consider whether the industry is growing and whether that growth will support the investment thesis.

The next question to ask is whether the deal is undervalued (U) or, equivalently, whether the price is attractive. This reflects the possibility that one can buy an average company at a below average price. Alternatively, one can pay too much for a great company. This analysis generally includes several quantitative analyses that we present in the next section.

Proprietary (P) asks whether there is anything proprietary about the deal. P can also stand for why is the deal positive present value, i.e., a good, valuable deal. Today, because almost every deal is competitive in some way, this is arguably the most important question to answer. At a University of Chicago private equity conference, Bill Conway, the co-founder of Carlyle, paraphrased this thinking by pointing out that PE investors need to ask on every deal what their unique edge is. If you cannot come up with some unique advantage relative to others bidding for the transaction, you are likely overpaying. This is particularly true in deals that are auctioned.

In a recent conversation with one of us, a very senior partner of a megafund reiterated this. His firm will not commit to a deal unless they have conviction in a well-thought-out plan that will increase the value of the company and that they have some advantage over other bidders.

Examples of having an edge or a proprietary advantage would include knowing the particular industry or subsegment better than anyone else, having an idea for a new initiative that no one else has, bringing in a better management team or having a better relationship with the seller or selling management team that no one else has. In some cases, particularly with private company sellers, this can be as simple as having the seller like you more than the other bidders.

Improvement (I) asks if there is room for improvement in the company. Is it possible to reduce costs? Is it possible to reduce taxes? Is it possible to make value-increasing acquisitions? Are there new "bolt-on" investments to make that will increase firm growth? Are there strategic changes that will increase growth, reduce costs or both? The greater opportunity that exists to improve operations, the more likely the deal is undervalued and the more likely the private equity investor has some proprietary angle. In Chapter 7, we discuss operational engineering and the many ways in which private equity firms help their portfolio companies improve.

A good example is Silver Lake Partners' buyout of Instinet.[7] Instinet was an institutional broker with old and high-cost back-end systems. Silver Lake realized that if Instinet could rip out those existing systems and replace them with new ones, Instinet would reduce costs substantially and make themselves more attractive to a strategic buyer. Instinet, with Silver Lake's support, hired top talent who implemented the changes in little more than a year. Shortly thereafter, a strategic investor bought the company for six times what Silver Lake had paid.

The final piece of CUPID is to understand the debt capacity (D) of the company being bought. A deal should use enough leverage to take advantage of interest tax shields and potentially lower cost debt, but should not use too much leverage that it constrains the company from operating efficiently and risks putting the company into financial distress.

In basic corporate finance terms, this means understanding the probability of financial distress/constraints and the costs of financial distress/constraints. Other things equal, firms in industries with lower downside risk, less volatile cash flows and less competitive pressure can take on more debt. Similarly, firms that are less adversely affected by financial distress can take on more debt. Distress and excess leverage are very costly if capital and R&D expenditures are crucial and non-deferrable, or if key employees and customers are likely to leave when the company hits a rough spot. Alternatively, more leverage is feasible if employees will not leave and those investment expenditures are deferrable.

Attractive investments will have favorable CUPID components. In our view, understanding P, the investor's edge or proprietary advantage, is the most important. Deals with P will tend to have favorable industry and competitive dynamics, tangible expected improvements, and, as a result, are more likely to be acquired at a price that generates attractive returns.

Even for investments with favorable CUPID components, there are always aspects that are uncertain (U). This is the U in OUTSX. Or, in other words, all deals have some risk. For some companies, the greatest uncertainty may revolve around the technology or product. For others, competitors and their response to entry may be most critical. For others, the management team and their ability to navigate strategy is the most important. Private equity investors keep close track of the aspects of the deal that are uncertain or risky. To the extent possible, they focus due diligence on resolving those uncertainties. If the uncertainties resolve favorably, the deal becomes more attractive; unfavorably, less attractive. Even after due diligence is done, some uncertainty invariably remains. It is rare for a deal to be a sure thing. Accordingly, investors will continue to keep close track of those uncertainties after the deal closes, to be ready to respond as the uncertainty resolves.

As we mentioned earlier, the team (T) is also important to a successful investment. Is the management team capable of executing the strategy that is implicit in CUPID? If it is the same management team, why will they be able to implement the expected improvements? Why didn't they do so before? If it is a new management team, why will they be better than the existing management team? Will the management team work well together in a more leveraged environment? Private equity investors spend a great deal of due diligence effort evaluating the management team and conducting reference checks. Increasingly, private equity firms have relied on executive assessment firms, like ghSMART, or have hired their own executive assessment and search professionals or both.[8] As we will see in Chapter 6, governance engineering is a critical lever that many private equity firms pull.

The structure of the deal (S) also matters. There are three pieces to deal structure. The first is the deal's capital structure. Investors want to make sure that the capital structure and leverage are consistent with the firm's debt capacity identified in CUPID. Second, investors want to make sure incentives are well-structured. In particular, investors will want the management team to have sufficient upside to motivate them to perform. At the same time, investors will want the management team to have sufficient downside or "skin in the game" to ensure that they are really committed to the deal and will suffer along with the private equity investors if the deal does not succeed. Third, investors should ensure that the deal provides the appropriate board governance and oversight. Chapter 6 looks more closely at incentive and governance structures.

The final piece of OUTSX-CUPID is the exit (X). Successful private equity investors think about a deal's exit before they commit to the deal. At some point, investors need to get their money out. Good deals have clear paths to do so. A deal can be exited through (1) a sale to a strategic acquirer, (2) a sale to another financial buyer(s) or (3) an initial public offering (IPO) or, more recently, a merger with a publicly traded special purpose acquisition corporation (SPAC). Chapter 8 explores where, when and how private equity firms exit their investments.

It is useful to apply the OUTSX-CUPID framework to Bill Conway's "Ten Rules for Private Investing." Conway is a co-founder of Carlyle

Partners, one of the world's largest private equity firms, who is considered among the best individual private equity investors. Conway's 10 rules are: (1) Develop your own idea of what a business is worth. Constantly assess the valuation [Opportunity–Undervalued]. (2) Avoid auctions. "What is our edge?" [Opportunity–Proprietary]. (3) Pick your spots [Opportunity–Proprietary]. (4) Approach each potential transaction with overwhelming force [Uncertainty]. (5) Follow the cash [Opportunity–Debt capacity]. (6) Get help! [Uncertainty]. (7) Keep your emotions in check [Opportunity–Proprietary and Undervalued]. (8) Develop trust with your managers and vice versa [Team and Uncertainty]. (9) Make sure managers concentrate on the few vital objectives [Team and Structure]. (10) When management is not working out, change them sooner rather than later [Team].

OUTSX-CUPID provides a framework that private equity investors can use to help structure their analyses and avoid missing out on a critical piece of the evaluation. All private equity firms cover these issues and use some version of this framework. A huge amount of work and due diligence go into each of the components of the framework. In the next section, we outline the financial tools that private equity managers utilize in their investment decisions. We also highlight the relative importance of those tools in practice.

Financial tools utilized by private equity investors to evaluate investments

Valuation is one of the central concepts in finance. Given the high leverage and substantial sums of investor capital at risk in private equity, getting the valuation right is absolutely critical, perhaps more so than in many other settings. Private equity investors have developed a number of financial tools and analyses that help them get to the right place.

We begin with a brief discussion of various financial tools that are taught in most business schools and utilized by private equity investors. Private equity managers employ many (if not all) of these financial tools during the course of evaluating an investment opportunity. Our goal is not to dive into any one of these methodologies in detail, but to help the reader become familiar with the types of analysis that can be employed. The interested reader can find other sources of information to dive more deeply into each approach in the reference section of this book.

We first discuss discounted cash flow (DCF) analysis, the method that most business schools teach. DCF not only provides one method for valuing an investment, but it also is helpful in understanding other valuation approaches used by private equity investors. We then move on to the methods that private equity professionals employ most in practice, the LBO model and comparable companies' approaches. In the LBO model, the private equity investor models out cash flows and exit values. Based on the amount of equity invested, the private equity investor calculates an expected annualized internal rate of return (IRR) and a concomitant multiple on invested capital (MOIC). The projected IRR or MOIC is then compared to the firm's "hurdle rate," i.e., the rate of return or multiple necessary to justify the investment. In the comparable companies approach, private equity investors use the values of similar companies and transactions to value the investment they are considering.

Discounted cash flow methods

Both DCF methods and LBO investment models start by projecting future financial performance for a potential investment opportunity. Private equity firms will often take the projections prepared by the company as the starting point for their own projections.

From that starting point, private equity investors devote a great deal of effort to drilling down on the forecasts. In many cases, this means going to the granularity of individual customers (particularly in business-to-business deals) and individual plants or operations. It seems natural to assume that the initial management forecasts turn out to be optimistic. In fact, this is usually what happens. In our survey of PE managers in GKM (2016), we asked how they typically ended up adjusting management's forecasts. As a fraction of EBITDA – earnings before interest, taxes, depreciation and amortization – a measure of pre-tax cash flow, the private equity managers told us that, on average, they discounted management's projections by about 20%.

The key economically significant input that DCF and LBO models look to is the operating cash flows of the company. Cash flows pay down the debt and generate value for equity holders. Estimating cash flows requires a detailed understanding of the firm, its industry and the prospects to grow the business. Because of the vital importance of understanding future performance, private equity managers increasingly specialize by industry.

Once the investor has generated projected operating cash flows, usually for a period of five years, the investor typically assumes that the investment will be exited at the end of that five-year period. As a result, the investor will calculate a terminal exit value for both DCF and LBO methods. The terminal value captures the value of the company at the end of the explicit projection period.

There are (at least) three possible ways to estimate the terminal value: (1) using the (discounted) value of a growing perpetuity of the final year cash flow in a CAPM-framework; (2) using the value of comparable or similar public companies; and (3) using the value of acquisitions or transactions involving comparable or similar companies.

In the DCF, once the terminal value is estimated, the stream of cash flows and terminal value are valued as of today or the present using an appropriate "discount rate" in the DCF. Most DCF approaches use some form of the capital asset pricing model (CAPM) to estimate a discount rate. The discount rate in the CAPM depends on three elements: the current risk-free rate (usually taken to be the current interest rate on the long-term government bond), the equity market risk premium and the firm's beta. Beta captures how the company's value moves up and down with the overall market returns.

When you calculate a beta and discount rate for a firm, you should not regard this as *the* discount rate. Considerable controversy exists about the validity of the CAPM that underlies the calculation of costs of capital in this way. Without going into the academic debate, we just warn that betas can be very difficult to estimate, so they should be used with caution. However, it is not clear if there is a better alternative. Consistent with this, in acquisition cases, the Delaware Courts look favorably on this approach. A detailed discussion of these issues is beyond the scope of this book, but basic finance textbooks deal with how to approach each of these elements. The key point is that the discount rate for cash flows depends upon the systematic risk of the company, i.e., how much its returns correlate with the market, not the firm-specific riskiness.

DCF methods also factor in the value created by the deductibility of interest payments. There are two ways to do this. The difference between the two methods is where the tax advantages of debt come into the calculation. The weighted average cost of capital (WACC) method includes the value of the interest tax shield in the discount rate by lowering the cost of capital. Alternatively, adjusted present value (APV) DCF method uses a higher discount rate, but adds the value of the interest tax shield as a separate (discounted) stream of cash flows. In both methods, the net present value of the firm is calculated by discounting the appropriate cash flows by the appropriate discount rate.

The advantage of the APV method is that it models a company's actual capital structure which varies over time. The disadvantage is that it requires two sets of cash flows. The advantage of WACC is that it only requires one set of cash flows. The disadvantage of WACC is that it requires the incorrect assumption for most buyouts that the debt-to-total-capital ratio is constant.

LBO investment models

Many, if not most, private equity investors eschew DCF models, and instead utilize an LBO model for making decisions. The method starts with a similar approach to a DCF analysis by projecting a company's revenues, income and cash flows over some period of time. In our survey, we asked the PE investors to tell us the time horizon of the investment cash flows they evaluate. The great majority of PE investors – almost 96% of our sample – use a five-year forecast horizon. At the end of the five years, they typically calculate a terminal or exit value. When asked why they always use five years, they responded that it makes it easier to compare investments against each other.

If the firm has taken on debt, the cash flow in each projection year – after paying interest, and funding capital expenditures and net working capital – is assumed to "pay down" existing debt, so the amount of outstanding debt each year changes. As noted above, the PE investors then calculate an "exit value" in the final year of the projections. This exit value captures what PE managers believe they can sell the company for (or receive if they take it public) at that future time.

The exit value is usually determined by applying an exit multiple to the portfolio company's projected EBTIDA or revenues at the time of the exit. Clearly, the exit multiple chosen has a large effect on the perceived attractiveness of a deal. Accordingly, selecting the right exit multiple requires judgment. If the investor selects an exit multiple that is too high, the investor is more likely to win that deal, but also more likely to regret it later if the investor turned out to have overpaid. Alternatively, if the investor chooses a multiple that is too low, the investor is more likely to lose the deal – and regret it later if the winning bidder makes a lot of money.

Many private equity investors begin by assuming that the exit multiple will equal the multiple they plan to pay for the deal. This is known as multiple in/multiple out (MI/MO). They then adjust around that depending on judgment. And that judgment will consider a number of factors. For example, investors also will look at current industry multiples. While those are informative, if the industry is growing more quickly today (because it is a young industry or is in an expansion phase) than it will be at exit, then exit multiples are likely to be lower in the future than they are today. Alternatively, if values are currently depressed, perhaps at the bottom of a recession, it is more likely that exit multiples will be greater in the future.

Private equity investors also will look subjectively at the deal dynamics. If the private equity firm believes that it "got a good deal" because the deal was proprietary or they bought the firm cheaply, then they might assume the exit multiple in year 5 will be higher than the multiple they purchased the firm for today.

Given this uncertainty and judgment, while investors will have a mean/ point estimate of exit value, they also will typically use a range of multiples and report a range of possible deal outcomes.

Based on the cash flows and the assumed exit value, the private equity investor calculates the amount of exit value going to equity by subtracting the debt projected to be outstanding at exit (akin to paying off a mortgage) and adding back any firm assets (including cash) whose value is not reflected in the cash flows or exit value. The investor then uses the equity at exit and the amount of equity invested up front to calculate an (annualized) IRR and a (cumulative) MOIC.

The investor then compares the IRR or MOIC on their equity investment to their required IRR or MOIC. These are sometimes referred to as investment hurdle rates. If the expected return is above the required return or hurdle rate, the investment is attractive. Investments that have a projected return below the hurdle rate would not likely receive a bid for investment by the PE firm.

Where do these required returns or hurdle rates come from? Many are derived from industry rules of thumb. If a firm is doing an LBO with substantial leverage, it may look for a higher return. Similarly, deals with riskier business models or in riskier industries may require higher returns to compensate for the underlying risks of the investment.

It is important to understand how the IRR and MOIC in an LBO model are driven. The discussion in Chapter 1 presented an overview of sources of value. Because it is so important, we refresh that concept here. First, the value created by the interim paydown of debt is captured by subtracting a lower debt number at exit than the total debt outstanding when the deal is consummated. As mentioned in Chapter 1, this is not value creation in the true sense because the paydown of debt only represents a fair return on the capital provided by lenders. Value of the equity increases as debt is paid off in intervening years, but this just represents a return on equity. Value is created only in situations in which this return on equity is above the firm's cost of capital. Second, improvements in operating performance, e.g., growth revenue and EBITDA, will also result in growth in enterprise value. Finally, differences in the entry and exit multiples, especially if a private equity firm can "buy right," can lead to increases in value creation for the private equity firm. This is often referred to as "selling right."

Multiples valuation methodology

As we mentioned, the common methods for valuation that are often utilized by investment bankers, private equity investors and investment analysts in addition to or rather than discounted cash flow are comparable company valuation methods. These methods entail finding a comparable company or set of companies that are either trading publicly or have been recently acquired. In this method, the value of a company or set of companies is used to estimate the value of another company or project. The comparable companies are chosen to be as similar as possible to the company that is to be valued. Typical dimensions that are utilized to gauge comparability include industry, past performance, size, growth rates and business model.

The comparable company valuation calculates "multiples" for the benchmark company, or companies, and then applies the average or median multiple to the company that is to be valued. A multiple is generally the ratio of company value (measured in different ways) to a performance measure. The calculated multiple is adjusted (if appropriate) and then multiplied by the utilized performance measure for the company of interest in order to derive a valuation of that company. This performance measure can be revenues, EBITDA, earnings, etc.

If a person valuing a particular firm only has one comparable company, then it is imperative to adjust the multiple of the comparison company for any differences in factors that may affect the multiple of the firm. Close scrutiny of the growth rates, riskiness and cash flow generation of the firms must be undertaken.

Implicit in every multiple is the relationship between the chosen metric (EBITDA, net income, EPS, revenues, etc.) and cash flows. An EBITDA or revenue multiple implicitly assumes that companies with the same EBITDA or revenue generate similar cash flows. To the extent this is not true, the multiple can be misleading.

For example, if two firms have the exact same revenues, but one firm has twice the cash flow margin as the other, the firm with the higher cash flow margin will have a higher value. If one uses the revenue multiple from the firm that is more profitable to value the less profitable firm, the revenue multiple would overvalue the less profitable firm. Similarly, if two firms have the same EBITDA, but one has higher capital expenditures and working capital needs, an EBITDA multiple will overvalue that firm. A simple rule to follow when valuing a company using a multiples method is to use a multiple that is derived from a performance measure that is as close to cash flow as possible.

It is also important to benchmark the expected long-run growth and the discount rates of the comparable firms to those of the firm that is being valued. The higher the growth rate of the firm, the higher the value of the multiple, all else being equal. Therefore, if the comparable firm that is chosen to value a particular firm is actually expected to grow faster than the firm to be valued, the comparable company method will overvalue the firm of interest. In essence, the multiple implies a future growth rate for the firm that is too high.

Similarly, the (systematic) riskiness of the comparable firms and the firm to be valued need to be compared. As the systematic risk and discount rate of a particular firm go up, the multiple that applies to that firm will be lower.

What do private equity managers do in practice?

The description above provides a context for understanding what PE investors do, in practice, when quantitatively evaluating investment opportunities. Most MBA programs teach that DCF is the most appropriate way to evaluate such opportunities. One of the core principles of finance is that the value of any asset is just the present value of expected future cash flows. In terms of what actually happens in practice, however, our PE survey provides a much different picture.

Table 4.5 shows that gross IRR and MOIC are almost universally utilized by PE managers, with more than 90% of firms saying that they utilize those methods when evaluating investment opportunities. PE investors are far more likely to use comparable methods than discounted cash flow methods as well. Nearly 72% of PE managers use comparable company EBITDA multiples while only 9.3% use APV DCF methods and 10.9% use WACC DCF methods. PE investors appear to be skeptical of CAPM-based methods for valuing companies relative to the use of multiples-based approaches and LBO investment models.

A similar approach is taken to terminal/exit value calculations. Most finance courses and books teach that terminal values should be calculated using a growing perpetuity. Table 4.6 shows that only about 27% of PE managers utilize that approach. Instead, 70% to 80% use a comparable companies (public or transaction) approach to estimating terminal/exit value with industry comparables being by far the most commonly used metric. Firm riskiness ranks seventh among the different criteria. Again, PE investors appear to be skeptical of using measures of risk that have strong foundations in academic finance. In fact, more than 20% simply use the entry or purchase multiple as the exit multiple.

Given the predominance of IRR and MOIC, two natural questions arise: what do these hurdle rates look like in practice, and how do private

Table 4.5   Quantitative Investment Metric Used to Select Investments

| | AUM | | | | IRR | | | | Age | | Offices | |
	Mean	Median	Low	High	Low	High	Old	Young	Local	Global
Gross IRR	92.7	100.0	88.5	97.0	99.9	96.9	100.0	86.4	94.2	90.5
Multiple of invested capital	94.8	100.0	92.1	97.7	99.1	93.3	96.1	93.7	95.5	93.8
APV DCF	9.3	0.0	7.1	11.5	9.3	7.3	3.9	13.9	10.5	7.6
WACC-based DCF	10.9	0.0	9.3	12.5	5.5	15.2	8.9	12.5	9.4	12.9
Comparable company EBITDA multiples	71.7	100.0	71.4	72.1	63.0	90.7	75.9	68.1	76.7	64.8
Free cash flow return to equity	43.8	33.0	29.7	58.3	45.2	43.7	44.4	43.2	40.7	48.1
Other	13.8	0.0	10.3	17.4	7.0	21.7	12.1	15.3	8.3	21.4
Number of responses	67	67	34	33	25	23	31	36	39	28

Table 4.6 Method for Calculating Terminal Value

| | AUM | | | | IRR | | Age | | Offices | |
	Mean	Median	Low	High	Low	High	Old	Young	Local	Global
Comparable companies	81.4	100.0	75.3	87.7	81.3	88.6	87.3	76.3	78.2	85.8
Comparable transactions	71.4	99.0	67.8	75.0	73.2	80.3	79.5	64.4	76.1	64.8
DCF-based growing perpetuity	27.3	10.0	20.5	34.3	28.1	16.4	26.6	27.9	21.0	36.0
Other	25.6	0.0	33.5	17.4	20.7	31.1	22.8	27.9	28.7	21.3
Number of responses	67	67	34	33	25	23	31	36	39	28

equity firms adjust those hurdle rates? Hurdle rates vary from firm to firm and also depend upon the size, stage and industry of the investment. These hurdle rates are based upon gross return, i.e., before fees and carried interest are taken out by the PE manager. Our survey, GKM (2016), showed that the average (median) IRR hurdle rate was 27.0% (25.0%). Table 4.7 shows that smaller private equity firms and those with global investment operations tend to target higher IRRs. A rough calculation suggests that this target exceeds a CAPM-based rate by a wide margin. In 2012, long-term Treasury bond rates did not exceed 4%. One research paper estimated an average portfolio company equity beta of 2.3,[9] which would imply a CAPM-based discount rate of less than 18%. This beta estimate is higher than most beta estimates for private equity funds.

MOIC hurdle rates are 2.85× on average (2.50× at the median) in our sample. At a five-year time horizon, this implies a gross IRR of approximately 20%. The mean MOIC of 2.85 times implies a gross IRR of 23%. Once again, smaller and younger private equity firms have MOIC hurdle rates that are about 0.6× higher than larger and older PE firms.

In our more recent survey from the summer of 2020, GKM (2021), both IRR and MOIC hurdle rates had declined from our 2012 survey. IRR hurdle rates in the summer of 2020 were 22.6% on average and MOIC hurdle rates were 2.69× on average. This reduction in hurdle rates is likely driven by the tremendous growth in PE which likely increased competition for deals and lowered industry-wide hurdle rates. The declines, however, are modest.

It is relatively easy to understand the high target rates of return, especially relative to CAPM-based returns. PE investors take management fees and receive their carry or share of the profits from gross returns. (We describe this in greater detail in Chapter 9.) PE limited partners (LPs) receive their returns net of those fees. Therefore, in order to generate a rate of return that is above the public market return net of fees, target hurdle rates must be above the CAPM or public market discount rates. As we saw in Chapter 3, PE investors have been successful historically in generating net returns in excess of the public market.

Finally, most PE firms do adjust their hurdle rates depending on a variety of factors. Table 4.7 tabulates factors that affect hurdle rates. These risks can be divided into macroeconomic risks (unexpected inflation, interest rate, term structure, business cycle and foreign exchange) and

Table 4.7 Private Equity Required Return Targets and Their Determinants

	AUM				IRR		Age		Offices	
	Mean	Median	Low	High	Low	High	Old	Young	Local	Global
Panel A: IRR										
Gross IRR target	27.0	25.0	30.0	24.1	24.5	24.9	24.8	29.3	25.7	28.9
Number of responses	62	62	31	31	24	22	31	31	36	26
Panel B: IRR determinants										
Firm's riskiness	86.2		84.4	87.9	91.7	91.3	90.3	82.4	91.9	78.6
Leverage	47.7		40.6	54.5	58.3	52.2	51.6	44.1	54.1	39.3
Historical return expectations of LPs	30.8		40.6	21.2	20.8	30.4	22.6	38.2	37.8	21.4
Other	9.2		6.3	12.1	8.3	17.4	16.1	2.9	10.8	7.1
Not applicable	4.6		6.3	3.0	0.0	0.0	0.0	8.8	2.7	7.1
Number of responses	65		32	33	24	23	31	34	37	28
Panel C: adjustments to the cash flows or the IRR										
Risk of unexpected inflation	17.7	0.0	8.2	26.9	26.0	13.9	21.2	14.5	12.2	25.0
Interest rate risk	25.5	2.0	22.6	28.3	33.5	26.5	26.3	24.8	26.3	24.5
Term structure risk	18.5	0.0	16.6	20.3	14.9	26.9	22.9	14.4	13.5	25.0

(Continued)

Table 4.7 (Continued)

	AUM				IRR		Age		Offices	
	Mean	Median	Low	High	Low	High	Old	Young	Local	Global
GDP or business cycle risk	55.0	50.0	47.8	61.9	63.6	55.7	59.4	51.0	54.2	56.0
Commodity price risk	28.8	21.0	22.8	34.7	35.5	27.1	30.6	27.2	28.0	29.9
Foreign exchange risk	20.2	10.0	15.7	24.5	25.6	16.6	23.5	17.1	12.9	29.8
Distress risk	13.0	0.0	8.7	17.2	13.8	11.9	17.2	9.1	9.0	18.2
Size	28.6	10.0	31.8	25.5	25.1	25.5	22.9	33.8	31.1	25.3
Market-to-book ratio	7.5	0.0	5.3	9.6	9.3	5.6	7.4	7.6	6.6	8.6
Momentum	11.8	0.0	9.6	13.9	17.0	10.3	18.9	5.4	12.9	10.4
Illiquidity	20.3	0.0	22.2	18.5	19.8	6.8	15.2	25.0	15.8	26.3
Other	1.4	0.0	2.8	0.0	0.0	0.0	0.0	2.6	2.4	0.0
Number of responses	65	65	32	33	24	23	31	34	37	28

firm-specific risks (distress, size, market-to-book, momentum and illiquidity). The results indicate that PE investors are somewhat sensitive
to macroeconomic risks, particularly GDP or business cycle risk, where
PE investors make some adjustment in roughly half of their deals. This
is consistent with PE investors taking market or equity risk into account.

Firm-specific adjustments appear less important, although there are a
variety of firm-specific factors that at least some of the PE firms use to
adjust their target hurdle rates. The most common firm-specific factor is
an adjustment for firm size. Larger deals create a less diversified portfolio
for the PE firm and, as such, would require a higher gross IRR to justify
the investment from the perspective of the PE firm. These adjustments
appear to suggest that PE managers use ad hoc factor models to assess the
attractiveness of prospective returns.

These results along with the terminal value results indicate that PE investors do not use (CAPM-based) DCF techniques very often. This contrasts
markedly with the results in Graham and Harvey (2001) for CFOs. In
that paper, they find that CFOs rely on net present value techniques
almost as frequently as IRR. This also is in sharp contrast to methods
taught in MBA finance courses at all top business schools as well as typical valuation analyses seen in investment banker fairness opinions for
mergers and acquisitions. CAPM-based discounted cash flow analyses
are the primary method taught and used in those settings.

Conclusion

In this chapter, we have seen that the sourcing and evaluating of deals
(both qualitatively and quantitatively) are critical elements of generating
attractive returns.

A critical strategic choice that PE firms make is their approach to deal
sourcing and deal selection. Focus both on proprietary deals and deals
that match a private equity firm's ability to add value is important; significant amounts of time and money are spent in this process. Getting
the "funnel" right is a necessary beginning to the PE process.

We also presented an investment framework, OUTSX-CUPID, that can
help private equity managers frame the decision-making process. The

qualitative framework combined with the quantitative tools we outline are critical elements of evaluating and selecting those opportunities that have the greatest potential to provide strong returns. In the subsequent chapters, we explore various levers of value that can increase returns, namely financial, governance and operational engineering. Finally, we sketched the LBO model that private equity investors use to evaluate their deals quantitatively.

Notes

1   Paul A. Gompers, Steven N. Kaplan and Vladimir Mukharlyamov, 2016, What Do Private Equity Firms (Say They) Do? *Journal of Financial Economics* 121, 449–76.
2   Paul Gompers and Monica Baraldi, 2015, TA Associates and Speedcast, Harvard Business School Case Study.
3   Paul Gompers, Kristin Mugford and J. Daniel Kim, 2012, Bain Capital: Outback Steakhouse. Harvard Business School Case Study.
4   G. Felda Hardymon, Josh Lerner and Ann Leamon, 2006, Brazos Partners and Cheddar's Inc., Harvard Business School Case Study.
5   Steven Kaplan, Berk Sensoy and Per Stromberg, 2009, Should You Bet on the Jockey or the Horse? Evidence from the Evolution of Firms from Early Business Plans to Public Companies, *Journal of Finance* 64(1), 75–115.
6   Paul Gompers, Will Gornall, Steven Kaplan and Ilya Strebulaev, 2020, How Do Venture Capitalists Make Decisions? *Journal of Financial Economics* 135, 169–90.
7   Steven Kaplan and Rich Jones, 2005, Silver Lake, Nasdaq and Instinet.
8   Steven Kaplan and Morten Sorensen, 2021, Are CEOs Different? Characteristics of Top Managers, *Journal of Finance* 76, 1773–1811; and Steven Kaplan, Mark Klebanov and Morten Sorensen, 2012, Which CEO Characteristics and Abilities Matter? *Journal of Finance* 67, 973–1007.
9   Ulf Axelson, Morten Sorensen and Per Stromberg, 2013, The Alpha and Beta of Buyout Deals, Unpublished Working Paper.

5 Financial engineering

Most buyout investments are leveraged buyouts, or LBOs, i.e., they are executed with a combination of debt and equity. For many of them, the amount of debt is greater than the amount of equity raised. The factors that affect the financial choices of private equity are critical to value creation. Financing or the financial engineering of the deal is often the difference between winning a deal and generating attractive rates of return or not deploying capital. In this chapter, we explore the empirical patterns of financing patterns in private equity. We begin by examining typical capital structures in private equity transactions. We then explore the ways in which financial engineering has been shown to enhance value. The ability to structure a deal has increasingly become commoditized and, hence, financial engineering as a competitive advantage among private equity firms has declined in importance. At the same time, financial engineering was one of the first sources of value identified by research and continues to be important for private equity firms.

Types of debt

While many people consider debt and equity as monolithic financial instruments, there is a broad spectrum of types of both debt and equity. The structure of a "typical" private equity transaction varies with industry, geography and deal size.

Table 5.1 provides an overview of deals from 2006 to 2019. Buyouts of non-public companies represent the single largest category of debt deals during the time period with 6385 deals raising over $1 trillion of debt. Growth capital deals were the next most frequent transaction type with 3245 transactions, but they raised relatively little debt overall. From 2006 to 2019, there were 429 public-to-private transactions that raised more than $950 billion of debt.

Table 5.1   Private Debt Deals Breakdown (2006–19)

Number of Deals by Type		Aggregate Deal Value (USD bn) by Type	
Investment Type	Number of Deals	Investment Type	Aggregate Deal Value (USD bn)
Buyout	6 385	Buyout	1 022.3
Growth capital	3 245	Growth capital	43.8
Recapitalization	1 972	Recapitalization	47.8
Add-on	1 912	Add-on	258
Public to private	429	Public to private	950.8
Merger	266	Merger	84.7
Restructuring	136	Restructuring	15.4
PIPE	56	PIPE	24.1
Turnaround	1	Turnaround	-

Number of Transactions by Capital Structure		Aggregate Deal Value (USD bn) by Capital Structure	
Capital Structure	Number of Deals	Capital Structure	Aggregate Deal Value (USD bn)
Unknown	6 343	Unknown	1 832.9
Senior debt	4 584	Senior debt	434.7
Mezzanine	3 390	Mezzanine	256.7
Unitranche	976	Unitranche	116.7
Junior/subordinated	858	Junior/subordinated	64.4

Number of Deals by Region		Aggregate Deal Value (USD bn) by Region	
Continent	Number of Deals	Continent	Aggregate Deal Value (USD bn)
North America	9 463	North America	1 645.9
Europe	4 385	Europe	649.2
Asia	233	Asia	96.5
Africa	109	Africa	11.7
Australasia	106	Australasia	28
Latin America and the Caribbean	64	Latin America and the Caribbean	8.1
Middle East	41	Middle East	7.5

Source: Preqin

These leveraged transactions require crafting a capital structure that at the same time gets the deal done, imposes discipline on management, provides value creating tax shields, but is also at a level at which the company can service the debt.

Financing sources vary by deal type and location. For example, smaller private equity investments typically have simple capital structures and are primarily financed by banks and, increasingly, direct lenders. Larger deals often have both greater amounts of debt and different sources of debt that fund different "layers." While a complete exploration of these underlying patterns is beyond the scope of this chapter, we describe broad types of debt below to provide some general understanding of the choices. This chapter largely focuses on the debt structure of private equity investments at deal closing. Every private equity investment, however, includes common equity and other equity-like instruments such as preferred equity. As a source of value, the equity structure of the deal is less important. Academic research has focused on the disciplining nature of debt, and most research points to the importance of debt as the critical lever.

Debt raised by private equity investors can typically be divided into two broad layers: senior (secured) debt and junior (subordinated) debt. Senior secured debt has a first lien, i.e., the right to seize the assets of the company in the case of default. Junior debt stands next in line. After junior debt is paid, preferred equity (if it exists) gets paid before common equity, which stands last in line. Tables 5.2 to 5.4 provide data on the typical capital structure of private equity investments.

As we explained in Chapter 4, transaction values and debt levels in most deals are typically expressed as multiples of earnings before interest, taxes, depreciation and amortization (EBITDA). EBITDA provides a measure of the cash flow generated by the company that can be used to pay interest and principal to the debt holders.

Table 5.2 looks at how LBOs were financed from 2004 through the first half of 2020. Average purchase price multiples have risen substantially, increasing from 7.3 times EBITDA to 11.5 times EBITDA in 2019. These increased purchase multiples have been driven, in part, by low nominal and real interest rates as well as the growth in private equity fundraising and concomitant competition among PE firms. Equity's share of the transaction has grown as purchase price multiples have increased

Table 5.2   Purchase Price Multiples for All LBOs

	Senior Debt/ EBITDA	Sub Debt/EBITDA	Equity/EBITDA	Others	Total
2004	3.37	1.27	2.58	0.1	7.32
2005	4.42	0.97	2.95	0.1	8.44
2006	4.48	0.77	3.05	0.08	8.38
2007	5.5	0.57	3.47	0.14	9.68
2008	4.12	0.84	4.03	0.13	9.11
2009	3.01	0.8	3.76	0.11	7.68
2010	4.04	0.55	3.8	0.1	8.49
2011	4.6	0.32	3.68	0.17	8.78
2012	4.85	0.27	3.49	0.07	8.68
2013	5.18	0.09	3.39	0.13	8.79
2014	5.7	0.03	3.89	0.05	9.67
2015	5.51	0.09	4.49	0.17	10.26
2016	5.31	0.1	4.49	0.12	10.02
2017	5.72	0.01	4.85	0.03	10.61
2018	5.78	0	4.77	0.04	10.6
2019	5.81	0.02	5.59	0.08	11.51
1H20	5.1	0	5.38	0.16	10.64
2Q20	4.93	0	4.32	0	9.24

Source: LCD, S&P Global Market Intelligence

commensurately with the increase in purchase multiples. Equity to EBITDA ratios have increased from a low of 2.6× in 2004 to 5.6× in 2019.

For the typical deal, senior debt is the largest and most important source of debt financing. Table 5.2 shows that senior debt-to-EBITDA levels range from 3.4× to 5.8×. Senior debt to EBITDA has been substantially higher over the past five years than during the prior decade. Junior debt is relatively modest for deals on average, ranging between 0.0× and 1.3× for middle- and large-market LBO investments. It is more important for the largest deals. The availability of debt financing is often tied to financial market cycles. At various times, interest rates are low and credit is readily available. At other times, credit may become expensive and harder to acquire.

Table 5.3   Average Debt Multiples of Large Corporate LBO Loans

	FLD/EBITDA	SLD/EBITDA	Other Senior Debt/EBITDA	Sub Debt/ EBITDA	Total
2004	2.90	0.10	0.30	1.60	4.80
2005	3.27	0.46	0.23	1.30	5.25
2006	3.73	0.67	0.30	0.73	5.43
2007	4.07	0.70	0.64	0.81	6.23
2008	3.37	0.17	0.55	0.82	4.90
2009	3.22	0.24	0.26	0.31	4.02
2010	3.51	0.10	0.76	0.35	4.71
2011	3.89	0.24	0.94	0.17	5.24
2012	3.75	0.69	0.70	0.13	5.26
2013	3.99	0.87	0.46	0.09	5.41
2014	4.25	1.18	0.39	0.00	5.83
2015	4.24	0.96	0.44	0.05	5.69
2016	4.29	0.90	0.29	0.03	5.50
2017	4.50	0.97	0.32	0.00	5.79
2018	4.72	0.93	0.21	0.00	5.86
2019	4.74	0.92	0.30	0.02	5.98
1H20	4.18	0.34	0.50	0.09	5.12
2Q20	3.94	0.00	0.71	0.28	4.93

Source: LCD, S&P Global Market Intelligence

Senior secured debt

Senior secured debt is typically provided by banks or bank syndicates. The most senior debt instruments in a PE investment are asset-backed loans (ABLs) and leveraged loans.

ABLs

ABLs and leveraged loans stand first in line in the case of default and are secured by collateral. ABLs are secured by physical assets, either property, plant and equipment or working capital. These loans are limited by the liquidation value of the underlying asset. For example, a working capital line of credit will typically look through to the value of the inventory and accounts receivable. The "quality" of those assets will determine

Table 5.4   Average Debt Multiples of Middle-Market Corporate LBO Loans

	FLD/EBITDA	SLD/EBITDA	Other Senior Debt/EBITDA	Sub Debt/ EBITDA	Total
2004	3.00	0.40	0.10	0.80	4.20
2005	3.39	0.71	0.17	0.43	4.69
2006	3.65	0.51	0.00	0.56	4.72
2007	4.01	1.13	0.08	0.38	5.61
2008	3.24	0.48	0.01	0.80	4.53
2009	2.52	0.00	0.00	0.73	3.25
2010	3.24	0.16	0.00	0.85	4.25
2011	3.64	0.14	0.00	0.52	4.30
2012	3.48	0.29	0.00	0.76	4.53
2013	3.95	0.68	0.00	0.19	4.82
2014	4.16	0.82	0.16	0.14	5.28
2015	4.25	0.82	0.02	0.24	5.33
2016	4.17	0.66	0.00	0.43	5.26
2017	4.60	0.81	0.00	0.04	5.46
2018	4.53	0.96	0.01	0.00	5.50
2019	4.74	0.48	0.00	0.16	5.37

Source: LCD, S&P Global Market Intelligence

the size of the loan relative to the value of those assets. Private equity deals that involve considerable real estate, equipment or high levels of quality inventory and receivables are able to raise a larger fraction of the deal in the form of ABLs.

Because potential losses on an ABL are tied to the value of the underlying assets, ABL lenders invest heavily in people and technology that can both value and track assets that are pledged as collateral. When the collateral backing the loan is working capital, lenders must assess the ability to sell inventory and collect on receivables. Assessing credit worthiness of the borrowers' customers is also therefore a part of the loan process. Banks are the primary provider of ABLs and the loans are typically structured as private, floating-rate instruments. Given the focus on collateral value, ABLs generally have fewer covenants than other types of corporate debt.

Leveraged loans

A second type of senior secured debt is a leveraged loan. Leveraged loans are generally underwritten on the basis of cash flow that is available to pay interest and principal payments. Leveraged loans typically have a general first lien on the assets of the company. However, given that valuing all of the collateral of the company is difficult and that the secondary market for the underlying assets is illiquid, the principal amount of the leveraged loan is not typically tied to the collateral value securing the loan. Instead, it is tied to the company's ability to generate cash flow.[1]

Leveraged loans are typically private, unlike many types of junior debt that may be publicly traded. While leveraged loans can be bought and sold, the market is typically relatively illiquid and settling trades typically takes considerable time. Leveraged loans are typically arranged by a single bank and can be syndicated to a number of other lenders. The close relationship between the lender and the lead bank is necessary as the lead bank monitors compliance with the financing agreement. Private relationships allow for the frequent exchange of confidential information. Leveraged loans typically have a significant number of covenants, and covenant violations are often used to renegotiate the terms of the debt. In the absence of a renegotiation mechanism, a tight covenant structure would lead to frequent defaults; whereas, a breach of a covenant is just a technical default which rarely leads to an actual default and a seizing of collateral. Covenants can be both positive and negative, i.e., they can require certain actions or prohibit others. Typical positive covenants focus on financial ratios that ensure the financial health of the company and the company's ability to pay interest and principal.

Like ABLs, leveraged loans typically have floating interest rates that are tied to a fixed spread over some base rate. The most frequently used base rate in the US has been the London Interbank Offered Rate (LIBOR). European transactions typically have leveraged loans that are spread over euro-based EURIBOR. The historical time series for these rates is shown in Table 5.5. More recently, the Secured Overnight Financing Rate (SOFR) has replaced LIBOR. Additionally, borrowers usually have the ability to pre-pay leveraged loans (i.e., they are callable) at any time with no pre-payment penalty.

Table 5.5 Sources of Proceeds for LBO Transactions

	2000	2001	2002	2003	2004	2005	2006	2007	2008	2009	2010
Bank debt	47.9%	44.1%	43.7%	37.3%	43.7%	49.4%	51.2%	53.3%	39.1%	33.1%	41.6%
Secured debt	0.5%	1.0%	0.0%	0.0%	1.0%	2.1%	3.2%	1.7%	2.4%	0.0%	1.3%
Senior unsec'd debt	0.5%	0.0%	0.0%	0.0%	2.5%	4.2%	3.1%	5.1%	6.1%	4.7%	5.8%
Public/144a high yield	1.8%	3.8%	6.3%	11.9%	9.9%	6.2%	3.3%	3.5%	1.8%	2.0%	0.7%
Bridge loan	1.4%	2.7%	2.5%	0.3%	0.6%	1.3%	0.5%	0.3%	0.4%	4.7%	0.3%
Mezzanine	8.2%	5.8%	3.7%	5.0%	4.1%	3.2%	4.1%	1.8%	6.3%	7.1%	5.1%
HoldCo debt/seller note	2.0%	4.4%	3.2%	1.6%	1.2%	0.8%	0.4%	0.3%	0.4%	0.0%	0.5%
Preferred equity	8.8%	6.8%	6.8%	4.9%	2.6%	0.9%	0.2%	0.1%	0.0%	0.0%	0.9%
Common equity	23.2%	23.8%	27.4%	28.3%	28.8%	28.1%	30.4%	30.4%	38.4%	45.5%	40.0%
Rollover equity	3.9%	5.5%	2.7%	4.7%	2.7%	2.3%	2.5%	2.0%	3.8%	5.1%	2.4%
Other	2.0%	2.2%	3.8%	6.1%	3.4%	1.4%	1.0%	1.3%	1.3%	2.2%	1.4%
Total senior debt	48.9%	45.1%	43.7%	37.3%	47.2%	55.8%	57.5%	60.1%	47.6%	37.8%	48.7%
Total sub debt	11.4%	12.3%	12.6%	17.1%	14.7%	10.7%	8.0%	5.7%	8.5%	13.7%	6.1%
Total equity	37.8%	40.6%	40.0%	39.4%	35.3%	32.1%	33.6%	32.9%	42.6%	50.6%	43.8%
Average loan size	$200M	$195M	$262M	$300M	$354M	$418M	$459M	$540M	$454M	$251M	$414M
Average sources	$351M	$389M	$540M	$716M	$706M	$972M	$1309M	$2095M	$1732M	$640M	$1014M
Observations	116	51	40	66	133	134	178	207	69	23	78

	2011	2012	2013	2014	2015	2016	2017	2018	2019	1H20	2Q20
Bank debt	45.4%	48.8%	54.1%	55.8%	52.1%	51.2%	52.5%	55.6%	46.7%	41.0%	38.9%
Secured debt	0.3%	0.6%	2.0%	0.8%	0.3%	0.6%	0.2%	0.4%	2.1%	1.6%	1.8%
Senior unsec'd debt	7.0%	6.9%	4.3%	3.2%	2.9%	2.4%	2.7%	1.7%	2.5%	4.0%	5.5%
Public/144a high yield	0.9%	0.4%	0.6%	0.0%	0.0%	0.1%	0.0%	0.0%	0.0%	0.0%	0.0%
Bridge loan	0.0%	0.0%	0.0%	0.0%	0.3%	0.0%	0.0%	0.0%	0.0%	0.0%	0.0%
Mezzanine	2.7%	2.9%	0.4%	0.4%	0.6%	0.7%	0.2%	0.0%	0.0%	0.0%	0.0%
HoldCo debt/seller note	0.5%	0.3%	0.0%	0.1%	0.0%	0.1%	0.2%	0.1%	0.0%	0.5%	0.0%
Preferred equity	0.3%	0.3%	0.6%	0.0%	0.2%	0.7%	0.1%	0.1%	0.1%	0.0%	0.0%
Common equity	37.5%	37.4%	35.1%	36.9%	40.3%	40.3%	41.8%	40.2%	45.4%	49.2%	53.0%
Rollover equity	3.6%	1.6%	1.4%	1.5%	1.9%	2.4%	1.6%	1.6%	1.9%	2.8%	0.8%
Other	1.8%	0.6%	1.5%	1.2%	1.3%	1.5%	0.5%	0.3%	1.0%	0.8%	0.0%
Total senior debt	52.8%	56.3%	60.5%	59.9%	55.4%	54.2%	55.4%	57.6%	51.3%	46.6%	46.3%
Total sub debt	3.6%	3.3%	1.0%	0.4%	0.9%	0.8%	0.2%	0.0%	0.0%	0.0%	0.0%
Total equity	41.8%	39.7%	37.1%	38.5%	42.4%	43.5%	43.7%	42.1%	47.5%	52.5%	53.7%
Average loan size	$454M	$537M	$913M	$676M	$669M	$878M	$808M	$1031M	$1138M	$1445M	$1692M
Average sources	$1139M	$1010M	$1484M	$1099M	$1178M	$1776M	$1365M	$1749M	$2301M	$3260M	$4386M
Observations	87	97	95	136	114	105	152	157	109	31	10

Source: LCD, S&P Global Market Intelligence

A leveraged loan package can contain several facilities. As with capital structure more broadly, the structure of the loan package depends on the deal size and market conditions. Small and medium-sized leveraged loans, like the ones backing middle-market transactions, tend to be funded by one or a few banks. More recently, these have been funded increasingly by direct lenders such as private debt funds and BDCs. Senior secured loan packages financing a large LBO typically include a revolving line of credit and an amortizing term loan (together these are called the "pro-rata" tranche), as well as term facilities syndicated to institutional investors (including collateralized loan obligations (CLOs), hedge funds, mutual funds and insurance companies).

The "pro-rata" tranche is comprised of facilities syndicated primarily to banks. This typically includes a revolving credit facility (revolver) and an amortizing term loan (TLa). A term loan is an installment loan which is typically fully funded at the outset and repaid over the life of the loan. A revolver functions like a corporate credit card. As funds are needed, the company draws down the revolver and can repay any or all of the amounts due until the maturity date of the loan. Borrowers pay a commitment fee for amounts not drawn down while they pay a rate which is typically pegged to the rate on the term loan. Term loans are typically designed to finance the purchase of the company while revolvers are generally meant to fund working capital needs or periodic investment in capital expenditures.

For large LBOs, the largest portion of the leveraged loan financing is the institutional tranche. A typical LBO has approximately 80% in the institutional tranche, although that percentage does move over time. (Figure 5.1 shows the composition of different portions of a leveraged loan facility.) The institutional tranche is typically comprised of a term loan (TLb) that has a first-lien and a second-lien facility. The second-lien facility is a term loan that has a claim on the firm's collateral that stands behind the senior secured loans. Because the investors in the institutional tranche are typically worried about reinvestment risk, the loans have bullet repayment schedules as opposed to the amortization schedule of the term loans in the pro-rata tranche.

Second-lien loans are part of the senior secured loans, however they have a junior claim to the collateral ("lien") backing the transaction. Being a riskier position, second-lien loans are priced at a premium to first-lien

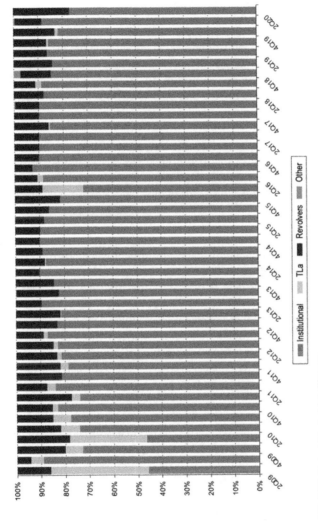

Source: LCD, S&P Global Market Intelligence

Figure 5.1 Loan Structures for US LBOs

loans. The spread differential ranges from 200 bps at a minimum to over 1000 bps in select cases. Second-lien loans tend to appear in buoyant capital markets when there is higher tolerance for risk among investors and then disappear again in a downturn. For example, in the period post-2008, few second-lien loans have been issued.

The institutional tranche also includes at times a delay-draw special purpose facility, such as acquisition lines. A special purpose facility is a credit which can be drawn down over a certain period for a specific purpose – for example to fund an acquisition. In contrast to RCFs, special purpose facilities are not revolving and once drawn they are equivalent to a traditional term loan.

Given that all first-lien tranches have the same seniority and claim over the collateral, the pricing of the institutional tranche is similar to the pricing of the pro-rata tranche. (See Figure 5.2.) Because the TLb tranche have longer maturities and bullet repayment, their spreads tend to be more volatile than the spread on the pro-rata tranches.

The next layer of the capital structure in most private equity transactions is commonly referred to as junior debt. Junior debt has a claim on the value of the capital that comes after senior secured debt, but its claim is senior to equity. Junior debt is typically unsecured, i.e., their claim is only paid off after the senior lenders have received their interest and principal. There are a number of categories of junior debt, and any one transaction may have multiple junior debt issuances. Unlike the senior secured loans in which all tranches are governed by one credit agreement, each category of junior debt is governed by separate loan contracts and can have substantially different terms.

For most large private equity transactions in the US, junior debt takes the form of high-yield bonds, regularly referred to as junk bonds. High-yield bonds are typically publicly issued and require registration with the Securities and Exchange Commission. Over the past decade, high-yield bonds have been increasingly utilized in Europe as well.

Because high-yield bonds have an unsecured claim that comes after the leveraged loans, they are relatively risky and are typically rated as non-investment grade. These bonds can be issued either publicly or privately. Underwritten public bond issuances are utilized by larger transactions

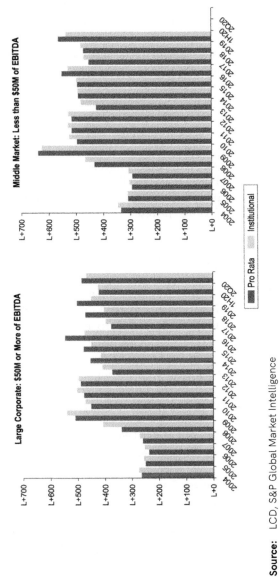

Source: LCD, S&P Global Market Intelligence

Figure 5.2 LBO Pro-Rata and Institutional Spreads by Size

and carry a higher fee structure. Additionally, bonds have a wider investor base which includes retail as well as institutional investors. All high-yield bond issuances in the US are also regulated by the Securities Act of 1933, including updates to the Regulation like Regulation Fair Disclosure ("Reg FD"). As such, the borrowing company cannot convey any private information to investors. Because of the difficulty coordinating renegotiation of bond indentures given the dispersed nature of holders, these indentures typically only contain incurrence covenants. Incurrence covenants are only tested when the borrower takes a particular action. Typical incurrence covenants take effect when firms engage in an acquisition or divestiture, issuance of new debt senior to existing debt, etc.

High-yield bonds have maturities which extend beyond the senior secured loans, typically eight to 10 years. While leveraged loans can be repaid at any time, bonds are typically protected from pre-payment for half of their maturity. Bonds also typically require a premium over par value if they are pre-paid before they mature. Similarly, while leveraged loans typically charge floating interest rates, high-yield bonds typically charge fixed interest rates.

Figures 5.3 and 5.4 graph the volume of high-yield public bond issuances in the US and Europe. There are important differences between the US and Europe in terms of PE debt financing. US private equity capital structures rely more on public markets (or quasi-public markets) as sources of capital. European structures rely more on banks for their financing needs, which has to do with the historical development of the debt markets in each region. This explains several differences between US and European capital structures, including the higher prevalence of high-yield bonds in the US versus a higher share of bank term loans, mezzanine and other private junior debt in Europe.

Differences in the development of the debt markets between the US and Europe are largely due to the legal and regulatory environment as well as the historic importance of regional commercial banks in Europe. In particular, the US and Europe have different bankruptcy and financial regulations. For example, Chapter 11 bankruptcy regulation in the US is focused on restructuring companies through a public, in-court process, whereas most bankruptcies in Europe are still focused on either liquidation or an out-of-court private settlement. Because of these differences, junior debtors typically have a weaker voice in European restructurings.

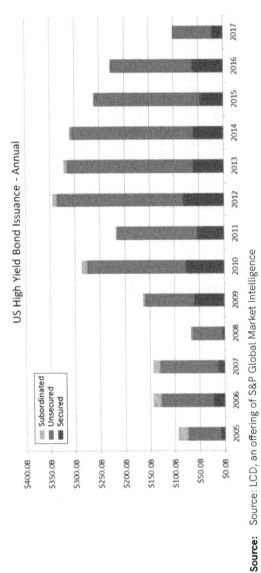

Source: Source: LCD, an offering of S&P Global Market Intelligence

Figure 5.3 High-Yield Public Bond Issuance in the US

Source: AFME Finance Europe, Q3 2020 European High Yield and Leveraged Loan Report

Figure 5.4   High-Yield Public Bond Issuance in Europe

Restructuring deals there are either worked out privately between senior lenders and the debtor, or companies are liquidated according to a strict priority rule, giving the junior public lenders limited control over the process.

The predominance of regional banks in Europe is tied to pre-European Union currencies differences, different languages and national regulations. These differences across countries have made it difficult for pan-European institutional investors to accurately assess risks and directly provide credit to companies across Europe. Instead, this situation has provided regional banks with an advantage over institutional investors, as regional banks focus on dealing with regional differences. While several drivers, including the introduction of the common Euro-currency, provided a boost to eliminating regional differences, many remain. However, the differences between the US and Europe are not static. The convergence between the two regions is facilitated by the globalization of firms and financial sources. Large companies are increasingly able to fund themselves abroad. The increasing presence of global banks is also a reality which drives convergence of financing markets.

European private equity deals and smaller deals in North America often use mezzanine financing in place of high-yield bonds. Mezzanine financing is junior to the leveraged loans, but senior to equity. Mezzanine financing is typically raised in private placements. Dedicated funds, often managed by large private equity firms, often participate in mezzanine finance. Terms can vary considerably given that the contracts are negotiated for each deal and can be adapted to different situations as necessary. While rates charged on the borrowing can vary, mezzanine has typically charged floating interest rate. Some mezzanine facilities include provisions which allow some of the interest to be "paid in kind" (PIK). PIK interest accumulates over time and increases the principal amount of the mezzanine. Regularly, the cash-interest component of mezzanine is supplemented with a PIK component. Mezzanine debt also often includes warrant payment.

Table 5.5 examines 20 years of LBO transaction financing structure data at a granular level. Banks have been the dominant source of capital for LBOs, never accounting for less than 33.1% of capital to more than 55.8% for the average transaction in a given year. Common shares have been the second most important element of financing LBOS, accounting for between 23.2% and 53% of the transaction consideration, although most years equity is approximately 35% of the capital provided. Other sources of debt are, in aggregate, less important and vary from year to year.

What factors influence financial engineering in private equity?

As discussed in Chapter 1, financial engineering increases value by reducing taxes and providing discipline on managers not to waste free cash flows. The tax advantage of debt results from the ability to deduct interest payments from profits before taxes. The governance benefits arise because debt is a fixed obligation that must be paid periodically making it costly to engage in wasteful activities. In this section, we explore how private equity managers think about financial engineering and how it is executed in practice.

Financial economics assesses various theories as to how firms set capital structure policy. In the trade-off theory popularized by Stew Myers,[2] managers are assumed to set the level of debt at a point that balances the value benefits of debt (taxes and disciplining benefits) with the costs of debt (increasing risk of default). The assumption is that at some point, the expected costs of default of additional debt outweigh any additional value benefits. In the pecking order theory, firms issue the maximum amount of safe debt (senior secured) before issuing riskier debt (subordinated debt).[3] Behavioral financial economists propose a different theory, market timing, in which managers attempt to time when interest rates are low and issue more debt in those periods.

Recent research by Axelson, Jenkinson, Stromberg and Weisbach[4] (AJSW) argues that the trade-off theory implies that industry factors play a primary role in leverage decisions because industries vary in cash flow volatility over time. In periods in which the cash flows of an industry are more volatile, the probability of default is higher. Similarly, factors that affect investment decisions, e.g., investment opportunities and tangibility, also affect the costs of distress. The authors predict that firms that are owned by private equity investors in the same industry would have similar levels of debt. On the contrary, the market timing theory would predict that leverage decisions would be influenced by the overall economy and, hence, PE investments consummated at the same time would have similar capital structures. For a large sample of PE investments, AJSW do not find any support for the trade-off theories. Private equity capital structures are not related to capital structures of similar public companies. Rather, debt levels for PE transactions are more similar depending upon the time period in which the deal closed. This empirical fact is more consistent with a market time view of capital structure.

Our two surveys, GKM (2016)[5] and GKM (2020),[6] asked numerous questions about how PE firms set capital structure at the time of investment. The questions tested whether capital structure policy was set via a trade-off view or a market timing view of the world. Table 5.6 compares the target capital structure from both surveys to understand how capital structure targets changed from 2012 to 2020. In our earlier survey, PE investors said they targeted a median debt-to-total capital of 60% and a median debt-to-EBITDA ratio of 4.0 times. Target maturity of senior debt was 5.25 years and target maturity for junior debt was 6.89 years. In the more recent survey during the COVID-19 pandemic, target

Table 5.6 Targeted Capital Structure

a. GKM (2016)

Capital structure measure	AUM				IRR		Age		Offices	
	Mean	Median	Low	High	Low	High	Old	Young	Local	Global
Debt-to-capital (percent)	55.7	60.0	54.3	57.2	56.6	56.9	55.0	56.4	55.0	56.8
Number of responses	62	62	31	31	22	23	23	32	37	25
Debt-to-EBITDA ratio	3.9	4.0	3.6	4.2	4.1	4.2	4.2	3.6	3.8	4.1
Number of responses	60	60	31	29	22	21	29	31	36	24

b. GKM (2020)

	AUM				Age	
	Mean	Median	Low	High	Young	Old
Maturity of bank/senior debt (years)	4.2	4.0	3.9	4.6	4.0	4.5
Observations	145	145	73	72	79	66
Maturity of other long-term debt (years)	5.0	5.0	4.8	5.2	4.8	5.2
Observations	133.0	133.0	67	66	71	62
Total debt-to-capital ratio, D/(D + E) (%)	44.6	50.0	41.8	47.4	43.8	45.5
Observations	142	142	71	71	77	65
Debt-to-EBITDA	3.8	3.6	3.0	4.6	3.4	4.2
Observations	143	143	72	71	78	65

debt-to-capital ratios had fallen to 44.6% while debt-to-EBITDA ratios had remained roughly similar at 3.8 times. Consistent with the reduction in debt-to-total capital, target senior debt maturity in 2020 had fallen to 4.23 years and target junior debt maturity was 5.0 years. This reduction supports a trade-off theory of capital structure in which a reduction in cash flows and potentially greater uncertainty about cash flows lead to a lower target level of debt in order to avoid costly default.

We illustrate the structure of private equity debt by examining two contrasting private equity deals. First, we look at one of the mega-private equity deals from the mid-2000s, Harrah's Entertainment. We then explore how a smaller private equity investment, Hanson Manufacturing, was structured. Both deals demonstrate the value that can be created by careful financial engineering.

In December 2006, Harrah's Entertainment announced that it had entered into an agreement to be purchased by affiliates of Apollo Global Management ("Apollo") and TPG Capital ("TPG").[7] Apollo and TPG had to be approved for gaming licenses in Harrah's markets, which delayed the closing until January 2008. The total purchase price, including fees and expenses, was $30.9 billion or approximately 10.7 × 2007 EBITDA, and included $25.2 billion of debt and $5.7 billion of equity. At the time of the acquisition, Harrah's was the world's largest gaming operator, making the deal the fourth largest LBO of all time.[8]

Apollo and TPG purchased Harrah's with the belief that they were acquiring a leading gaming and lodging company with significant scale, diversification and strong gaming brands (Caesars, Harrah's, Horseshoe and World Series of Poker). Gaming was often categorized as a "defensive" rather than "cyclical" sector, evidenced by the growth in the industry through the 1991 and 2001 recessions. The sheer scale of the transaction drove the need for a tiered capital structure. Given its significant real-estate holdings, Harrah's was a logical candidate to raise commercial mortgage-backed securities ("CMBS"), backed by a portion of its real estate. In total, Harrah's financed the transaction with $25.2 billion of debt, including $4.6 billion of rolled over debt and $20.5 billion of new financing.

Six properties – four in Las Vegas (Harrah's Las Vegas, Paris, Flamingo and Rio), Harrah's Atlantic City and Harrah's Laughlin – were placed into a real-estate holding subsidiary and those properties were pledged as collateral against $6.5 billion of CMBS. CMBS was a form of asset-backed debt. Asset-backed debt was typically structured based upon loan to hard asset value rather than multiples of cash flow. Lenders expected to get their recovery through a liquidation of these hard assets rather than a sale of the future cash flow streams. As such, the asset-backed credit agreement tended to focus on protecting loan to value. Typically, banks, insurance companies and structured vehicles ("CDOs") would own these types of asset-backed facilities.

The CMBS debt was tranched into $4.0 billion of senior mortgage debt (first lien), $1.125 billion of senior mezzanine debt and $1.125 billion of junior mezzanine debt.[9]

To finance the LBO, Harrah's also formed an operating holding company and raised a three-tiered capital structure comprised of $9.3 billion of new senior secured credit facilities, $6.8 billion of new senior notes and $4.6 billion of Existing Senior Notes that were rolled over into the new structure. Leverage at close was approximately 9.1 × EBITDA.

The operating company had three tiers of financing. First came the $9.3 billion of senior secured credit facilities (also known as "bank loans"), which was comprised of a $2.0 billion revolver undrawn at close, and a $7.3 billion term loan. As of December 2008, the bank debt had a first priority lien, or mortgage, on the assets of 22 domestic properties.[10]

Large institutional banks issued a $2.0 billion revolver, which was a line of credit for the borrower to regularly draw from and pay back the lender. This loan was typically used to fund operating expenses depending upon the company's cash flow needs. The $7.3 billion term loan was fully drawn at close and had been broadly syndicated to a variety of investors, which included institutional investors, mutual funds and structured vehicles ("CLOs"). The term loan traded hands regularly and when it traded below par, it attracted hedge funds and other distressed debt players.

Senior secured loans were typically callable at any time at par. They charged a floating interest rate which in this case was LIBOR+300. The loans also had covenants which the company needed to comply with. Some of these covenants were negative covenants that detailed things the borrower could not do including the ability to: (1) incur additional debt, (2) create liens on certain assets, (3) enter into sale and lease-back transactions, (4) make certain investments, (5) sell or acquire assets, (6) pay dividends or make other restricted payments, (7) enter into certain transactions with its affiliates and (8) make restricted subsidiaries unrestricted.[11]

Bank loans also typically had maintenance covenants – minimum performance standards the company had to *maintain* to remain in compliance. Harrah's senior secured credit facilities had only one maintenance test, a leverage test, that required the ratio of senior secured debt to last 12 months ("LTM"). Pro forma EBITDA needed to be below 4.75 to 1 when tested at the end of each quarter.

Next in line in the capital structure was $6.8 billion of new senior notes. These were unsecured notes, which meant that they did not have a lien on any assets. Like the bank loan, these notes were issued by the operating company. The new senior notes came in two forms – $5.275 billion of bonds that matured in 2016 and $1.5 billion of bonds that matured in 2018. The 2018 notes also had a PIK Toggle feature, which meant that the company could choose to pay the interest in cash or "pay-in-kind" (PIK) by giving debt holders their interest payment in the form of new bonds rather than cash.

High-yield bonds were typically non-callable for half their life (four years on an eight-year maturity bond, five years on a 10-year bond, etc.). The new senior notes also had covenants that were typical of high-yield bonds. They had negative covenants, but not maintenance covenants. Similar to the term loan, the negative covenants restricted asset sales and restricted the ability to dividend cash from the borrower. The negative covenant that restricted additional indebtedness and the ability to make future acquisitions was a standard "incurrence test" that limited additional debt.[12]

Third in line in terms of priority stood Harrah's pre-existing notes. Prior to the LBO, Harrah's had issued a series of unsecured senior notes with covenants typical of investment grade bonds. Similar to a high-yield rated bond, investment grade bonds had fixed coupons and were non-callable for some time period. There were, however, major differences between the two types of bonds. Investment grade bonds had very few covenants compared to unsecured senior notes. Similar to the bank loans and the new senior notes, the old senior notes were also issued by Harrah's operating company. They were unsecured, which meant that they did not have a lien on any assets or a pledge of any stock.

The rather lengthy description of Harrah's capital structure illustrates that financial engineering can be complex. The ability to access many different forms of debt and to place it with many different types of investors increases the availability of capital to execute transactions. The Harrah's deal also highlights important market timing elements within the private equity sector. Figure 5.5 shows the average debt-to-EBITDA ratio for large private equity transactions over time; 2006–2007 was clearly at a secular peak in terms of debt availability. The extreme level of debt availability influenced the manner in which private equity firms financed their transactions. Similarly, the perceived counter-cyclical nature of gaming supports the trade-off theory in which strong, stable cash flows support higher debt levels because of the ability to ensure interest and principal repayment.

Table 5.6 reports the typical capital structure that private equity investors reported they target at closing based in GKM (2016). Private equity managers target a median debt-to-total capital of 60% and a median debt-to-EBITDA ratio of 4.0 times. While these ratios may seem low (for example, they are much lower than the ratios that were common in the 1980s), GKM (2016) surveyed private equity managers primarily in 2012, soon after the financial crisis. The results also are somewhat lower than the median ratios of 70% and 5.2 times, respectively, in AJSW.

Table 5.7 from our PE survey also supports a market timing motive. The survey asks what factors the PE investors consider in determining capital structure. The trade-off theories suggest a role for firm industry, tax benefits, default risk and the ability to generate operating improvements/reduce agency costs. The results suggest that the trade-off theory and market timing are equally important. Virtually all PE investors consider both industry factors and current interest rates in determining capital structure. They also rank much higher than any of the other factors. In terms of explicitly trading off tax benefits and risk of default, more than two-thirds of PE managers explicitly consider that factor while 65% say they raise as much debt as the market will bear. These factors rank third and fourth in terms of importance. Finally, just under 40% consider the ability of debt to force operational improvements.[13] Overall, then, the survey indicates that PE investors consider both trade-off theories and market timing.

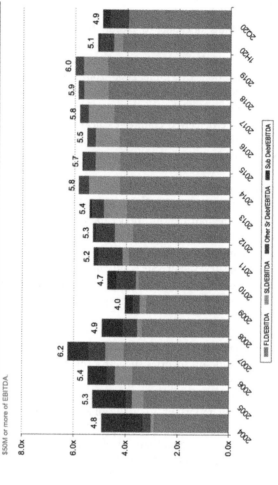

Source: LCD, S&P Global Market Intelligence

Figure 5.5   Debt Levels for Large LBOs over Time

Table 5.7 Capital Structure Factors Considered Important and Ranked

	AUM				IRR		Age		Offices	
	Mean	Median	Low	High	Low	High	Old	Young	Local	Global
Panel A: IRR										
Gross IRR target	27.0	25.0	30.0	24.1	24.5	24.9	24.8	29.3	25.7	28.9
Number of responses	62	62	31	31	24	22	31	31	36	26
Panel B: IRR determinants										
Firm's riskiness	86.2		84.4	87.9	91.7	91.3	90.3	82.4	91.9	78.6
Leverage	47.7		40.6	54.5	58.3	52.2	51.6	44.1	54.1	39.3
Historical return expectations of LPs	30.8		40.6	21.2	20.8	30.4	22.6	38.2	37.8	21.4
Other	9.2		6.3	12.1	8.3	17.4	16.1	2.9	10.8	7.1
Not applicable	4.6		6.3	3.0	0.0	0.0	0.0	8.8	2.7	7.1
Number of responses	65		32	33	24	23	31	34	37	28
Panel C: Adjustments to the cash flows or the IRR										
Risk of unexpected inflation	17.7	0.0	8.2	26.9	26.0	13.9	21.2	14.5	12.2	25.0

(Continued)

Table 5.7 (Continued)

	AUM				IRR		Age		Offices	
	Mean	Median	Low	High	Low	High	Old	Young	Local	Global
Interest rate risk	25.5	2.0	22.6	28.3	33.5	26.5	26.3	24.8	26.3	24.5
Term structure risk	18.5	0.0	16.6	20.3	14.9	26.9	22.9	14.4	13.5	25.0
GDP or business cycle risk	55.0	50.0	47.8	61.9	63.6	55.7	59.4	51.0	54.2	56.0
Commodity price risk	28.8	21.0	22.8	34.7	35.5	27.1	30.6	27.2	28.0	29.9
Foreign exchange risk	20.2	10.0	15.7	24.5	25.6	16.6	23.5	17.1	12.9	29.8
Distress risk	13.0	0.0	8.7	17.2	13.8	11.9	17.2	9.1	9.0	18.2
Size	28.6	10.0	31.8	25.5	25.1	25.5	22.9	33.8	31.1	25.3
Market-to-book ratio	7.5	0.0	5.3	9.6	9.3	5.6	7.4	7.6	6.6	8.6
Momentum	11.8	0.0	9.6	13.9	17.0	10.3	18.9	5.4	12.9	10.4
Illiquidity	20.3	0.0	22.2	18.5	19.8	6.8	15.2	25.0	15.8	26.3
Other	1.4	0.0	2.8	0.0	0.0	0.0	0.0	2.6	2.4	0.0
Number of responses	65	65	32	33	24	23	31	34	37	28

Source: GKM (2016)

These results also fit with the description of the Apollo/TPG purchase of Harrah's. Given the low interest rates at the time and the tremendous availability of debt, as well as the strong staple cash flows of Harrah's, the PE sponsors clearly had an incentive to raise a significant amount of debt. The ultimate outcome of the Harrah's transaction, however, shows that raising debt at market peaks can be problematic. Ultimately, Harrah's ran into significant cash flow issues during the Great Recession of 2008–2009 and needed to be restructured. Financial distress is not just theoretical, it clearly happens in practice.

For a small private equity deal, Hanson Manufacturing's purchase by Rockwood Capital provides a clear illustration of how financial engineering can make a deal possible and create value. It also represents a private equity investment at the opposite end of the spectrum in terms of size and sophistication.[14] In July 2000 Rockwood, a small private equity firm co-founded by Brett Keith and Owen Colligan, had won the bid for the acquisition of Hanson Manufacturing Company at $13 million. The company specialized in the manufacturing and sale of diesel engine accessories, along with air filtration and heater products for military and commercial markets. Keith and Colligan had sought to leverage the deal as much as possible. By September, they had managed to raise $1 million in equity capital, $2.5 million in seller financing and $7.5 million from a local bank. The remaining $3 plus million of the purchase price was paid using the company's existing cash balance of $809 000 together with marketable securities of nearly $2.5 million and the cash surrender value on two life insurance policies held by the company of nearly $450 000.

The seller financing (as in many small deals) represented the junior debt and was structured as a $2.25 million note and $250 000 in earn-out payments. It held a junior claim to the equity investors. For the senior secured debt, Keith and Colligan solicited financing from eight banks, both regional and national, with offices in Cleveland, where Hanson was located. They received $7.5 million in debt financing comprised of a $4 million revolving credit facility collateralized by inventory and accounts receivable, along with a $3.5 million term note with a senior claim to all other assets including the property, plant and equipment.

The bank they chose submitted the term sheet in Table 5.8. The term sheet indicates that the interest rate charged on the loan would be a floating rate with a spread relative to LIBOR. The spread would depend upon

Table 5.8 Model Bank Loan Term Sheet

Exhibit 5	
Guaranty	To the extent that a holding company is formed and remains in place in connection with the contemplated transaction, then the Facilities will be guaranteed by the continuing, unlimited guaranty of such holding company and secured by a pledge of the holding company's ownership interests in the Borrower.
Repayment	A. The Revolver will mature and be payable-in-full on 30 September 2002. B. The Term Loan will amortize in 59 consecutive, monthly payments of $41 667 plus interest followed by a final payment in the amount of $1 041 647 plus interest (seven-year amortization schedule/five-year maturity).
Mandatory Requirements	A. Not Applicable. B. In addition to the repayment schedule outlined above, the Term Loan will incorporate mandatory prepayments in an amount equal to 50% of Excess Cash Flow on an annual basis. Such mandatory prepayments will be applied in the inverse order of maturity and will be payable on 30 September 2002 (for the fiscal year ended 30 June 2002) and each 30 September thereafter.
Voluntary Requirements	A. At the option of the Borrower, the commitment amount of the Revolver may permanently reduce in minimum amounts of $500 000 and even increments of $100 000 upon prior written notice to the Bank. B. At the option of the Borrower, the principal balance of the Term Loan may be prepaid in minimum amounts of $250 000 and even increments of $50 000 without any type of premium (except for breakage fees associated with any applicable LIBOR contracts) upon prior written notice to the Bank. Such voluntary prepayments will be applied in the inverse order of maturity.
Interest rate	The Borrower will have the option of selecting interest rates based on the Bank's Prime Rate or LIBOR (30, 60, 90 and 180 days). In addition, the Bank will provide a "daily" LIBOR option for the Revolver. The applicable spreads over the Bank's Prime Rate and LIBOR will be performance-driven, based on the Borrower's Leverage as follows:

Leverage	Revolver		Term Loan	
	LIBOR Spread	Prime Rate Spread	LIBOR Spread	Prime Rate Spread
x > 3.25	2.50%	0.25%	2.75%	0.50%
2.75 < x ≤ 3.25	2.25%	0.00%	2.50%	0.25%
2.25 < x ≤ 2.75	2.00%	(0.25%)	2.25%	0.00%
x < 2.25	1.75%	(0.50%)	2.00%	(0.25%)

Pricing for the Facilities will be determined quarterly based on (1) audited financial statements for one quarter of each fiscal year and (2) company-prepared financial statements for the remaining quarters and will be adjusted on the first day of the month following each quarter-end.

Notwithstanding the foregoing, the initial interest spreads for the Facilities are highlighted in the above table. These initial interest spreads will remain in effect from closing through 31 December 2000.

Interest on the Facilities will be payable as follows: (1) monthly for Prime Rate and "daily" LIBOR borrowings; (2) at the end of the term for LIBOR contracts of 20, 60 and 90 days and (3) at the end of each three-month period for LIBOR contracts of 180 days.

All LIBOR contracts (excluding "daily" LIBOR borrowings) will carry a prepayment fee and will be written in minimum amounts of $500 000 and even increments of $100 000.

Fees	Closing Fee in amount of 0.50% of the commitment amount of the Facilities.
	Unused commitment fee in the amount of 0.25% of the unused portion of the Revolver, payable quarterly in arrears.
	The Borrower will be responsible for the payment of all of the Bank's legal fees and out-of-pocket expenses in connection with the Facilities.

(Continued)

Table 5.8 (Continued)

Exhibit 5	
Covenants	The documentation for the Facilities will incorporate affirmative, negative and financial covenants customary for this type of transaction including, but not limited to, the following:
	1. Minimum Cash Flow Coverage Ratio of 1.10:1
	2. Maximum Leverage as follows:
	Closing through 9/29/01 3.50:1
	9/30/01 through 6/29/02 3.25:1
	6/30/02 through 6/29/03 3.00:1
	6/30/03 and thereafter 2.50:1
	3. Minimum Net Worth as follows:
	6/30/01 through 6/29/02 $750 000
	6/30/02 through 6/29/03 $1 500 000
	6/30/03 and thereafter $1 500 000 plus 50% of Net Income on an annual basis.
	4. Limitation on Annual Capital Expenditures of $250 000
	5. Limitation on Annual Management Fees to Rockwood of $300 000

Source: Paul Gompers, 2003, Hudson Manufacturing Company, Harvard Business School Case Number 9-203-064

what the debt-to-EBITDA ratio was at the time. At the time the transaction closed, debt-to-EBITDA was 3.32 times. Additionally, the proposed financing had a number of maintenance covenants, i.e., covenants that would have to hold at all times. These covenants can either be positive (i.e., the company must do something) or negative (i.e., the company cannot do something). The covenants are generally meant as "trip wires" so the lender can have the ability to intervene if the company's performance is lagging. Many of the covenants relate to the financial risk of the firm including cash flow coverage, maximum leverage and minimum net worth. There are also covenants that restrict actions like capital expenditure and the ability to take cash outside the company. If the firm violates a covenant, it typically begins the process of renegotiating the terms of the loan typically called an "amend and extend."

The financing package for Rockwood's acquisition of Hanson demonstrates the critical elements of how debt can create value for even small private equity transactions. First, a conservative estimate of the present value of the interest tax shields is $2 million, a substantial portion of the purchase price. Second, Hanson had been historically highly inefficient, and the high debt levels provided financial discipline for the company. The contrast in size between Harrah's and Hanson demonstrates that while the size of the transaction may influence where a private equity manager goes for debt financing, substantial amounts of value can be created through careful deal structuring.

A final component of financial engineering that we discuss is how to split the equity of the transaction. Management incentives are the second important piece of financial engineering. The ability to leverage a transaction and provide meaningful equity ownership to a portfolio company's management can be a critical source of value. In fact, in our surveys, the private equity investors pointed to improved incentives as one of the two or three most important sources of value. Table 5.9 shows the typical equity structure for PE investors in both GKM (2016) and GKM (2020). As we discuss in Chapter 6, management incentives are also an important component of governance engineering.

Equity ownership of senior management in public companies and, particularly, of managers running divisions of public companies can be relatively low, both as a percentage of the firm and in absolute dollars. Increasing equity ownership, particularly as a percentage of the equity

Table 5.9 Typical Equity Ownership

a. GKM (2016)

	AUM				IRR		Age		Offices	
	Mean	Median	Low	High	Low	High	Old	Young	Local	Global
PE investors	79.6	85.0	74.9	84.3	82.7	83.6	82.9	76.6	81.2	77.3
CEO	8.0	5.0	10.0	6.0	7.1	6.1	7.8	8.2	6.9	9.5
Top ten management (excluding CEO)	7.2	7.0	8.1	6.3	7.1	6.9	7.0	7.3	7.6	6.6
Other employees	1.8	0.0	1.1	2.4	3.0	0.9	1.7	1.8	1.3	2.5
Other	3.5	0.0	6.0	1.1	0.1	2.6	0.6	6.1	3.0	4.3
Number of responses	64	64	32	32	23	23	30	34	37	27

b. GKM (2020)

	AUM				Age	
	Mean	Median	Low	High	Old	Young
PE investors	72.9	80.0	65.6	80.2	70.7	75.4
CEO	10.9	5.0	14.8	7.0	12.1	9.5
Top ten management (excluding CEO)	8.9	7.0	11.0	6.8	9.5	8.2
Top ten management (including CEO)	19.8	15.0	25.7	13.8	21.7	17.7
Other employees	2.4	0.0	2.8	2.1	2.7	2.2
Other	4.7	0.0	5.9	3.4	5.0	4.3
Observations	138	138	69	69	73	65

upside, can dramatically enhance the incentives of management to drive value improvements. Table 5.9 is consistent with this. It confirms previous academic work that demonstrates PE investors provide strong incentives to portfolio company management.[15]

In our earlier survey, we found that PE investors allocate 17% of company equity to management and employees. The CEO received an average of 8%. The growth of PE investing over the decade led to dramatic shifts in our more recent survey. The share of the CEO increased to nearly 11% and the share for all senior management was nearly 20%. When all employees are included, the 2020 share increases to 22%. This is significantly higher than equity ownership of senior management in public companies. A comprehensive study of public companies finds that the average CEO of a public company between 1993 and 2007 held 3.58% of the company's equity and the median CEO held only 1.57%.[16]

Conclusion

Private equity has grown, at least in part, because of the ability to craft financing packages that align incentives of various parties as well as increasing value directly through the tax advantage of debt. Market conditions play an important role in how financing in private equity transactions is structured. While the evidence on the value creation of deal structuring is readily supported in both practice and academic research, the tools of financial engineering are readily available to all investors. Any private equity firm can use leverage and provide equity incentives to management. As the private equity industry has grown, the increasing competition for investments means that much of the value created through financial engineering flows to the sellers. In the next two chapters, we explore differential sources of value, governance and operational engineering that allow private equity managers to both create value and retain a portion of the value they create.

Notes

1   Chen Lian and Yueran Ma, 2021, Anatomy of Corporate Borrowing Constraints (with Chen Lian), *Quarterly Journal of Economics* 136, 229–91.
2   S.C. Myers, 1984, The Capital Structure Puzzle. *Journal of Finance* 39, 575–92.

3   S.C. Myers and N.S. Majluf, 1984, Corporate Financing and Investment Decisions When Firms Have Information That Investors Do Not Have. *Journal of Financial Economics* 13, 187–221.
4   U. Axelson, T. Jenkinson, P. Strömberg and M. Weisbach, 2013, Borrow Cheap, Buy High? The Determinants of Leverage and Pricing in Buyouts. *Journal of Finance* 68, 2223–67.
5   Paul A. Gompers, Steven N. Kaplan and Vladimir Mukharlyamov, 2016, What Do Private Equity Firms (Say They) Do? *Journal of Financial Economics* 121, 449–76.
6   Paul A. Gompers, Steven N. Kaplan and Vladimir Mukharlyamov, 2020, Private Equity and Covid-19, NBER Working Paper.
7   See Paul A. Gompers, Kristin Mugford and J. Daniel Kim, 2012, Harrah's Entertainment, Harvard Business School Case Number 9-213-054.
8   Dennis K. Berman, Christina Binkley and Peter Sanders, 2006, Harrah's in Talks to Be Acquired by Buyout Firms – Deal for Casino Operator Would be Among Largest for Private Equity Investors, *Wall Street Journal*, via Factiva, accessed 27 September 2012.
9   As was typical of asset-backed financing, the CMBS covenants restricted the Propco's ability to incur additional debt, buy or sell assets, engage in new businesses or enter into transactions with affiliates. Source: Caesars Entertainment Corporation, 31 December 2010 Form 10-K (filed 4 March 2010), supplemental discussion of financial results, via EDGAR, accessed September 2012.
10 Caesars Entertainment Corporation, 31 December 2010 Form 10-K (filed 4 March 2010), p. 46, via EDGAR, accessed September 2012.
11 Harrah's Entertainment, Inc., 31 December 2008 Form 10-K (filed 17 March 2009), p. 32, via EDGAR, accessed September 2012.
12 Harrah's Entertainment, Inc., 31 December 2008 Form 10-K (filed 16 March 2009), p. 32, via EDGAR, accessed September 2012.
13 M. Jensen, 1989, Eclipse of the Public Corporation, *Harvard Business Review* 67, 61–74.
14 See Paul Gompers, 2003, Hudson Manufacturing Company, Harvard Business School Case Number 9-203-064.
15 S. Kaplan, 1989, The Effects of Management Buyouts on Operating and Value, *Journal of Financial Economics* 24(2), 217–54; S.N. Kaplan and P. Strömberg, 2009, Leveraged Buyouts and Private Equity, *Journal of Economic Perspectives* Winter, 121–46; Viral V. Acharya, O. Gottschalg, M. Hahn and C. Kehoe, 2013, Corporate Governance and Value Creation: Evidence from Private Equity, *Review of Financial Studies* 26(2), 368–402.
16 B. Page, 2011, CEO Ownership and Firm Value: Evidence from a Structural Estimation, University of Rochester Working Paper.

6   Governance engineering

Governance engineering is another key lever that private equity investors use to create value in their portfolio companies. There are three important governance drivers. First, PE firms focus on making sure the right managers are in place at the firms they finance. Both before and after their investment, PE managers actively replace top management and recruit competent CEOs to run their companies. Second, PE managers look to provide the right incentives for top managers by ensuring that their compensation is largely determined by their equity ownership. As we discussed in Chapter 5, by providing company management with a meaningful stake in the portfolio company, PE investors ensure that they are rewarded when performance improves. Finally, boards of directors at PE-backed companies are very active in providing important oversight and guidance. PE investors as well as outside directors with important experience and insight are brought in to sit on boards and are actively engaged in advising and monitoring company management. In this chapter we examine the specific governance engineering levers that PE managers utilize as well as what research has demonstrated about governance effects on firms' performance.

Does governance matter and what do PE investors do?

Management

Private equity investors are very focused on hiring the right top executives to run their portfolio companies. In GKM (2016)[1] and GKM (2020),[2] as noted earlier, we find that the management team is the second most important criterion for making an investment after the business model/competitive situation.

Table 6.1, drawn from GKM (2016), also shows how active PE investors are in recruiting senior management teams in their portfolio companies. A meaningful fraction of PE investors, 31%, recruit their own senior management teams before investing. These PE investors who bring in their own team do not place a great deal of weight on the value of incumbency. In contrast, most (69%) PE managers do not recruit their own senior management team before the investment. This is consistent with the notion that many private equity firms want to be seen as wanting to remain "friendly" when pursuing transactions. This suggests that different PE investors have very different investment strategies.

After the investment, roughly 50% of the PE investors end up recruiting their own senior management team. This is consistent with PE investors becoming more actively involved in the governance of their companies after the investment. When we combine the PE investors who recruit their own teams before, after or both before and after investing, we find that almost 58% of the PE investors recruit their own senior teams. This indicates that the PE investors are actively involved in monitoring and governing their portfolio companies.

This differs markedly from the typical experience in public companies. Cziraki and Jenter (2020) find that for most of the largest US companies, new CEOs come primarily from within the firm and those that come from outside the firm typically have connections with the firm's board of directors. In work in progress, we are finding, in contrast, that private equity firms primarily bring in new CEOs from outside the company. This means that private equity firms rely much more heavily on an external market for talent (Table 6.2).

Although it is not possible to ascribe any causality at this point, the cross-sectional results suggest that the PE investors who recruit their own teams have experienced better past investment performance.

Recruiting senior management is important for many different types of PE investors. For example, Rockwood Equity, a small PE firm founded by Brett Keith and Owen Colligan, purchased their first company, Hanson Manufacturing, for $10.1 million on 27 October 2000.[3] Hanson was a manufacturer of military heaters and air filtration equipment. The company had been undermanaged for many years and, consequently, showed little growth. As part of the effort to improve operations, Keith

Table 6.1 Private Equity (PE) Recruitment of Management Teams

Senior Management Recruitment	Mean	AUM		IRR		Age		Offices	
		Low	High	Low	High	Old	Young	Local	Global
Before investing									
Yes	31.3	31.3	31.3	26.1	39.1	30.0	32.4	29.7	33.3
No	68.8	68.8	68.8	73.9	60.9	70.0	67.6	70.3	66.7
After investing									
Yes	50.0	40.6	59.4	43.5	52.2	50.0	50.0	37.8	66.7**
No	50.0	59.4	40.6	56.5	47.8	50.0	50.0	62.2	33.3**
Before or after investing									
Yes	57.8	53.1	62.5	47.8	63.4	56.7	58.1	48.6	70.4*
No	42.2	46.9	37.5	52.2	36.6	43.3	41.9	51.4	29.6*
Number of responses	64	32	32	23	23	30	34	37	27

Note: This table reports the percentage of the sample PE investors who recruit their own senior management teams before investing, after investing and before or after investing. The sample is divided into subgroups based on the median of assets under management (AUM), the internal rate of return (IRR) of most recent fund, the age of PE investor and whether PE investor has a global presence. Statistical significance of the difference between subgroup means at the 1%, 5% and 10% levels are denoted by ***, ** and *, respectively.

Table 6.2   PE Replacement of Chief Executive Officers (CEOs) after Investing

CEO Swapped Out	Mean	Median	AUM		IRR		Age		Offices	
			Low	High	Low	High	Old	Young	Local	Global
Percent of deals	33.3	30.0	30.3	36.3	27.9	37.3	27.7	38.2	32.0	35.0
Number of responses	64	64	32	32	23	23	30	34	37	27

Note: This table reports the percentage of deals in which the sample PE investors replace the CEO after the investment is made. The sample is divided into subgroups based on the median of AUM, the IRR of most recent fund, the age of PE investor and whether PE investor has a global presence.

and Colligan replaced the entire management team, bringing on board a new CEO, CFO, VP of Operations and a VP of Engineering. Each of these hires was critical to both setting a new direction and growth. In fiscal year 2000, Hanson generated $21 million in revenue. By 2003, the company had increased revenue to $55 million and grown EBITDA from $3.0 million to $8.0 million. While multiple factors contributed to this improvement, bringing on board new senior management was a critical component.

Key senior hires are important outside the US as well as illustrated by AXA Private Equity's purchase of Diana.[4] At the time, Diana was a producer of specialty chemicals in the food space. They had three main lines of business: pet food ingredients; natural extracts for food, beverages and cosmetics; and culinary ingredients for the food and beverage industry. In 2007, AXA approached Cognetas, the owner of Diana, about purchasing the company. As part of the investment thesis, AXA began an immediate search for a new CEO and CFO for Diana. Ultimately, AXA identified Olivier Caix, the President of Rhodia Organics, a company that was focused on chemicals in the consumer goods, automotive, energy and manufacturing spaces. Caix experience made him perhaps overqualified to be CEO, but AXA's philosophy was to hire senior management for the company they hoped to build, not the company that currently existed. When AXA purchased Diana for €710 million, it was generating €254 million in revenue. Caix and his team were able to nearly double revenue to €454 million when AXA sold the company in 2014 to Symrise, a strategic German acquirer, for €1.3 billion. Caix's background running a large, chemical company was critical to this transformation. He brought specific industry expertise as well as credibility with customers when he assumed the CEO role.

Blackstone and Lion Capital's purchase of Orangina from Cadbury in November 2005 provides another example in which key senior hires were a critical lever of transforming a company.[5] Blackstone and Lion paid €1.85 billion to purchase the underperforming division from Cadbury. The two private equity sponsors replaced the entire senior management team. Importantly, Javier Ferran, who had been president and CEO of Bacardi, became the Executive Chairman of Orangina. The new team was able to restructure and streamline operations, push new product innovation and dramatically grow the business. Blackstone and Lion were ultimately able to exit in 2009 by selling to Suntory Holdings in

November 2009 for €2.6 billion after paying off much of the debt. A critical element of the turnaround for the company was bringing in seasoned executives to manage the turnaround.

Alignment of managerial incentives

The second key lever in governance engineering is increasing the amount of senior managers' compensation that comes from equity ownership. Incentive compensation has been a particularly important area of governance research for a long time. Jensen (1986) argued that managers of publicly traded firms typically owned too little equity to make them sensitive to maximizing shareholder value. Private equity managers who are aware of this seek to align incentives through increases in managerial equity ownership.

Kaplan (1989) examined management ownership changes in a sample of leveraged buyouts from the 1980s and found that, on average, ownership substantially increases. Given that equity ownership was the key driver of incentive alignment, Kaplan concluded that one of the critical levers of PE investing that improves performance is increasing managerial incentive alignment. Peck (2004) looked at a more recent sample of 73 LBOs and found that the management's ownership increases to 20% after the transaction. The average CEO owned 2.87% of the equity prior to the LBO, but this percentage increased to 7.81% after the transaction with an additional 3.42% of equity in the form of stock options. This represents more than a tripling in pay sensitivity.

These results are in line with GKM (2016) who ask PE managers about the typical equity ownership structures. Table 6.3 shows that, on average, (median) CEOs own 8.0% (5.0%) after the transaction. Smaller PE firms and global PE players typically target great ownership for CEOs, 10.0% and 9.5%. Excluding the CEO, the top 10 managers own 7.2% of the equity in the deal. Interestingly, below the top 10 managers, equity ownership is relatively modest, 1.8% on average and a median of 0%. Clearly, from the perspective of the PE managers, equity incentives are most critical at the top of the firm. In fact, the CEO generally owns as much equity as the rest of management.

Table 6.3 Typical Equity Ownership

Ownership Group	Mean	Median	AUM		IRR		Age		Offices	
			Low	High	Low	High	Old	Young	Local	Global
PE investors	79.6	85.0	74.9	84.3**	82.7	83.6	82.9	76.6	81.2	77.3
CEO	8.0	5.0	10.0	6.0	7.1	6.1	7.8	8.2	6.9	9.5
Top 10 management (excluding CEO)	7.2	7.0	8.1	6.3**	7.1	6.9	7.0	7.3	7.6	6.6
Other employees	1.8	0.0	1.1	2.4	3.0	0.9	1.7	1.8	1.3	2.5
Other	3.5	0.0	6.0	1.1**	0.1	2.6	0.6	6.1**	3.0	4.3
Number of responses	64	64	32	32	23	23	30	34	37	27

Note: This table reports the typical equity ownership of the sample PE investors, the CEO and top management. The sample is divided into subgroups based on the median of AUM, the IRR of most recent fund, the age of PE investor and whether PE investor has a global presence. Statistical significance of the difference between subgroup means at the 1%, 5% and 10% levels are denoted by ***, ** and *, respectively.

The potential for improvement in incentives is perhaps greatest in buyouts of divisions of public companies, particularly larger conglomerates. Substantial research has shown that many of the conglomerate mergers of the 1960s and 1970s were value destroying. Managers of divisions had little direct incentive to create value. TA Associates' investment in Speedcast represents just such an example.[6] Speedcast was a wholly owned subsidiary of AsiaSat that provided satellite communications based in Hong Kong. Speedcast's primary customers in the maritime, oil and gas, and mining industries operated in geographies that were typically remote. Speedcast did not own their own satellites, but leased bandwidth from companies that owned and operated those satellites.

Speedcast's CEO, P.J. Beylier, saw an opportunity to grow by consolidating players in the VSAT satellite services sector in Asia and Africa. He approached TA Associates about purchasing Speedcast from its parent, AsiaSat. In the process of generating a growth strategy, Beylier identified several acquisition targets that could provide a greater footprint for Speedcast's services. The complex deal required that TA partners Michael Berk and Ed Sippel negotiate with AsiaSat and the targets simultaneously. In March 2012, they reached an agreement to purchase Speedcast from AsiaSat and one of the targets for $50 million. TA and Beylier negotiated a management incentive plan that offered Beylier and his team a pool of "performance shares" that, if targets were met, would total 20% ownership on a fully diluted basis. The equity incentive plan envisioned a base grant of performance shares in which the team would receive 10% of the equity in an eventual sale if the proceeds were above TA's cost. Four additional tranches of 2.5% sharing rights would be granted at returns of 1.5×, 2.0×, 2.5× and 3.0× compared to TA's cost basis. By providing management with an increasing share of the pie as returns improved, TA provided high-powered incentives for Beylier and his team. This type of an incentive plan would have been impossible as a subsidiary of AsiaSat. The compensation program illustrates the importance of governance engineering. After a number of years of exceptional growth, Beylier and TA took Speedcast public on the Australian Stock Exchange in August 2014. The IPO placed a value of $254 million on Speedcast at the end of the first day of trading.

"Take private" transactions can also provide opportunities to enhance incentives of senior management. HgCapital's purchase of Visma Software illustrates the point.[7] In March 2006, Nic Humphries and HgCapital bid to take Visma ASA, a publicly listed Norwegian company, private in a buyout valued in excess of £330 million (roughly $500 million). Visma provided business software to small and medium-sized enterprises in Scandinavia and had grown through the acquisition of smaller players. While the firm was highly successful, senior management owned little of the equity. For example, Oystein Moan, the CEO who had been with Visma for more than eight and a half years, owned only 180 000 shares (0.6% of the equity) and 300 000 options. Tore Bjerkan, the CFO who had been with Visma for more than 10 years, owned 150 000 shares (0.5%) and 100 000 options. Collectively, the top five executives owned only 1.8% of the firm's equity. At a purchase price of NOK 135 per share, management's equity and options were worth less than $10 million in aggregate. In the course of the transaction, Moan's stake alone increased to 6.6% of Visma's equity, a ten-fold increase in his equity ownership. Moan led the company for the next 14 years and grew Visma through multiple acquisitions and additional HgCapital investments. In 2020, Visma had an enterprise value of $12.2 billion.

Structuring effective boards of directors

Finally, even if top executives are motivated to maximize shareholder value through appropriate incentive alignment, informational asymmetries with providers of external capital can make external financing more costly and drive a wedge between the actions of managers and investors. Myers and Majluf (1984)[8] and Greenwald, Stiglitz and Weiss (1984)[9] develop the intuition around how these asymmetries can be detrimental to firm performance. More generally, contracts between managers and outside investors cannot anticipate every potential situation. When outcomes cannot be readily observed, it is impossible to write contracts contingent upon particular events. Models of ownership and potential problems that can arise (Hart and Moore (1990)[10] and Hart and Moore (1998)[11]) have shown the limitations of contracts in alleviating these problems.

While most of these papers develop theory, the implications are real in practice. Management typically knows significantly more than outsiders about customer demand, future orders, product development, core technology, and so on. These insights may not easily be communicated to investors, especially if the company is public and worries about providing sensitive information to competitors.

An active and incentivized board of directors provides a partial solution to these types of information and incomplete contracting issues. Fama and Jensen (1983)[12] and Williamson (1983)[13] hypothesize that the composition of the board should be shaped by the need for oversight, advice and guidance. Having investors on the board is critical to monitoring management and exercising oversight. Private equity investors, as the owners of the firms in which they invest, typically take board seats and serve this monitoring function.

The simple monitoring function points toward an independent board, composed largely of outsiders. Clearly, having senior management on the board is critical to providing information to the directors whose role is to monitor and advise management. The two most common measures of board effectiveness that have been examined in the academic literature are size (e.g., the number of directors) and composition (e.g., the fraction of insiders, investors, independent outsiders, etc.).[14] Large boards are typically found to be suboptimal. The optimal size of the board of directors balances the costs and benefits of additional directors. Yermack (1996)[15] and Eisenberg et al. (1998)[16] find that performance, measured by market valuation and operating ratios, decreases with the size of the board of directors for public companies. The median public board size in the Yermack sample is 12; firms with a board size less than seven have the highest levels of performance measures.

A second common statistic is board composition. A variety of papers have looked at the determinants of board composition. This work tends to find that companies with a larger fraction of outsiders or independent directors perform better or make better decisions (Weisbach (1988),[17] Hermalin and Weisbach (1998),[18] Denis and Sarin (1999),[19] Byrd and Hickman (1992)[20]) and share price reactions to the enactment of poison pills are higher (Brickley, Coles and Terry (1994)[21]). Outsider-dominated boards are more likely to replace CEOs in response to poor performance (Weisbach (1988),[22] Borokhovich et al. (1996)[23] and Perry (2000)[24]).

In addition to their monitoring role, boards of directors are often viewed as an important governance tool to provide strategic advice and guidance. Fama and Jensen (1983)[25] discuss the role of boards and how boards should function. Hermalin and Weisbach (1998)[26] examine the determinants of board structure and argue that boards should be structured to minimize conflicts and maximize value. Coles, Daniels and Naveen

(2008)[27] examine how board size is related to both firm characteristics and then firm performance. In general, this literature also argues that small boards dominated by outsiders perform better.

As we have seen, PE firms take large ownership positions in firms and perform substantial analysis on ways that firms can be improved. PE investors are typically not passive. By scrutinizing firms before providing capital and then monitoring them afterwards, PE investors can both monitor how the firm is doing and provide key strategic advice to managers.

Prior work on private equity has looked at small samples of PE-financed companies as well as their board compositions. In a sample of UK take private transactions, Cornelli and Karakaş (2012)[28] show that boards typically become smaller and heavily dominated by the PE sponsors. They find that average board size decreases after an LBO, falling from around 6.5 members to between 4 and 5 after the transaction. Interestingly, Cornelli and Karakaş find that LBO sponsors do join the board, but they typically replace independent outsiders on the board, not insiders.

GKM (2016) asked a number of questions related to board governance in PE-financed firms. Table 6.4 confirms previous work in showing in Panel A that PE investors prefer smaller boards of directors, with over 90% including between 5 and 7 members. Larger private equity firms tend to have portfolio companies with larger boards while younger and better performing PE firms tend to have smaller boards. Panel B indicates that PE investors target taking roughly three of the board seats while allocating one or two to management, and one or two to outsiders who are not affiliated with the PE firms. Again, the results for board composition are consistent with theory, with previous work and with conventional wisdom in which private equity managers seek to optimize the board both for monitoring and strategic advice. Small boards with significant representation by PE investors and outsiders are important for monitoring and providing strategic advice.

Table 6.5 indicates that PE investors are actively involved in advising their companies in the great majority of their deals. In fact, the median PE investor claims to be actively involved in all of their deals. We also find some differences across PE firm types. Global PE firms and PE firms with higher IRRs are slightly more active in their deals, indicating an

Table 6.4 Board of Directors' Size and Composition

Size and Composition	Mean	Median	AUM		IRR		Age		Offices	
			Low	High	Low	High	Old	Young	Local	Global
Panel A: Board of directors' size										
3 or less	3.1		3.1	3.1	8.7	0.0	3.3	2.9	0.0	7.4
4	1.6		3.1	0.0	0.0	4.3	0.0	2.9	2.7	0.0
5	32.8		40.6	25.0	21.7	30.4	23.3	41.2	37.8	25.9
6	10.9		12.5	9.4	21.7	8.7	20.0	2.9**	10.8	11.1
7	46.9		37.5	56.3	39.1	52.2	46.7	47.1	43.2	51.9
8	3.1		0.0	6.3	8.7	0.0	3.3	2.9	2.7	3.7
9	0.0		0.0	0.0	0.0	0.0	0.0	0.0	0.0	0.0
10	1.6		3.1	0.0	0.0	4.3	3.3	0.0	2.7	0.0
11 or more	0.0		0.0	0.0	0.0	0.0	0.0	0.0	0.0	0.0
Number of responses	64		32	32	23	23	30	34	37	27

Panel B: Board of directors' composition

Inside directors	1.6	1.0	1.6	1.5	1.4	1.5	1.5	1.6	1.5	1.7
PE directors	2.8	3.0	2.7	2.9	2.8	2.9	2.8	2.7	2.7	2.8
Outside directors	1.7	2.0	1.6	1.9	1.9	1.7	1.9	1.6	1.8	1.6
Other	0.1	0.0	0.1	0.1	0.0	0.2	0.1	0.1	0.1	0.1
Number of responses	64	64	32	32	23	23	30	34	37	27

Note: Panel A presents the desired size of a board of directors reported by the sample PE investors. Panel B presents the desired composition of the board of directors by the sample PE investors. The sample is divided into subgroups based on the median of AUM, the IRR of most recent fund, the age of PE investor and whether PE investor has a global presence. Statistical significance of the difference between subgroup means at the 1%, 5% and 10% levels are denoted by ***, ** and *, respectively.

Table 6.5 PE Involvement in Portfolio Companies

Active Involvement	Mean	Median	AUM		IRR		Age		Offices	
			Low	High	Low	High	Old	Young	Local	Global
Percent of deals	87.5	100.0	84.8	90.1	81.3	90.2	85.2	89.5	83.0	93.6
Number of responses	64	64	32	32	23	23	30	34	37	27

Note: This table reports the fraction of deals in which the sample PE investors become involved in the management of portfolio companies, i.e., actively advising the company on strategic choices. The sample is divided into subgroups based on the median of AUM, the IRR of most recent fund, the age of PE investor and whether PE investor has a global presence.

active involvement in more than 90% of their transactions on average. Much of this activity happens through the active role that PE managers play on boards. As we discuss in Chapter 7, private equity managers are also actively engaged in operational engineering through their involvement in portfolio companies.

The Hanson Manufacturing buyout by Rockwood Equity discussed above provides a clear example of structuring an effective board. Prior to the transaction, there was no board of directors as the company was owned exclusively by one person. The previous owner was 72 years old and had been only modestly active in the firm's operations. After the buyout, in addition to Keith and Colligan's presence on the board, they recruited three important outside directors. First, because the Department of Defense was the key customer, they recruited a retired Two-Star Army general to the board. Second, they identified and recruited the former CEO of a $100 million Cleveland-based defense contractor. Both of these directors provided contacts and credibility with the DoD and were instrumental in facilitating new contracts with the military. Finally, the former president of Brush-Wellman, a Cleveland-based producer of beryllium and beryllium compounds, was added to the board to provide important supply chain and manufacturing insights. In the first three years after the buyout, these additions to the board, as well as the recruiting of an entire new senior management team, led to the largest contract in company history (10 years and $106 million) as well as the introduction of a variety of new products. In 2004, Keith and Colligan were able to sell Hanson to Behrman Capital for $93 million. With only $6 million of debt outstanding, the equity value of Hanson increased from $1 million in 2000 to more than $87 million in four years.

Conclusion

This chapter has explored how private equity managers use governance engineering to increase the value of their portfolio companies. The evidence from academic research identifies three important governance levers that have the ability to improve performance: management replacement, improved incentives and effective boards of directors. PE managers use each of these levers.

Notes

1   Paul A. Gompers, Steven N. Kaplan and Vladimir Mukharlyamov, 2016, What Do Private Equity Firms (Say They) Do? *Journal of Financial Economics* 121, 449–76.

2   Paul A. Gompers, Steven N. Kaplan and Vladimir Mukharlyamov, 2020, Private Equity and Covid-19, NBER Working Paper.

3   See Paul A. Gompers, 2002, Hudson Manufacturing, HBS Case 9-203-064.

4   See William Sahlman and Michael Roberts, 2011, AXA Private Equity: The Diana Investment, HBS Case 9-812-042.

5   See G. Felda Hardymon, Josh Lerner and Ann Leamon, 2006, Lion and Blackstone: The Orangina Deal, HBS Case 9-807-005.

6   See Paul Gompers and Monica Baraldi, 2015, TA Associates and SpeedCast, HBS Case 9-216-010.

7   See Paul A. Gompers, Karol Misztal and Joris Van Goode, 2012, HgCapital and the Visma Transaction (A), HBS Case 9-214-018.

8   Stewart C. Myers and Nicholas S. Majluf, 1984, Corporate Financing and Investment Decisions When firms Have Information That Investors Do Not Have, *Journal of Financial Economics* 13, 187–221.

9   Bruce Greenwald, Joseph Stiglitz and Andrew Weiss, 1984, Informational Imperfections in the Capital Market and Macroeconomic Fluctuations, *American Economic Review* 74, 194–9.

10 Oliver Hart and John Moore, 1990, Property Rights and the Nature of the Firm, *Journal of Political Economy* 98, 1119–58.

11 Oliver Hart and John Moore, 1998, Default and Renegotiation: A Dynamic Model of Debt, *Quarterly Journal of Economics* 113, 1–41.

12 Eugene F. Fama and Michael C. Jensen, 1983, Separation of Ownership and Control, *Journal of Law and Economics* 26, 301–25.

13 Oliver E. Williamson, 1983, Organization Form, Residual Claimants, and Corporate Control, *Journal of Law and Economics* 26, 351–66.

14 Benjamin Hermalin and Michael Weisbach, 2003, Boards of Directors as an Endogenously Determined Institution, FRBNY Economic Policy Review, 7–26 provide a more complete survey of the empirical evidence.

15 David Yermack, 1996, Higher Market Valuation of Companies with a Small Board of Directors, *Journal of Financial Economics* 40, 185–211.

16 Theodore Eisenberg, Stefan Sundgren and Martin T. Wells, 1998, Larger Board Size and Decreasing Firm Value in Small Firms, *Cornell Law Faculty Publications* 393.

17 Michael S. Weisbach, 1988, Outside Directors and CEO Turnover, *Journal of Financial Economics* 20, 431–60.

18 Benjamin E. Hermalin and Michael S. Weisbach, 1998, Endogenously Chosen Boards of Directors and Their Monitoring of the CEO, *American Economic Review* 88, 96–118.

19 D.J. Denis and A. Sarin, 1999, Ownership and Board Structures in Publicly-Traded Corporations, *Journal of Financial Economics* 52, 187–223.

20 John W. Byrd and Kent A. Hickman, 1992, Do Outside Directors Monitor Managers: Evidence from Tender Offer Bids, *Journal of Financial Economics* 32, 195–221.

21   James A. Brickley, Jeffrey Coles and Rory L. Terry, 1994, Outside Directors and the Adoption of Poison Pills, *Journal of Financial Economics* 35, 371–90.

22   Michael S. Weisbach, 1988, Outside Directors and CEO Turnover, *Journal of Financial Economics* 20, 431–60.

23   Kenneth A. Borokhovich, Robert Parrino and Teresa Trapani, 1996, Outside Directors and CEO Selection, *Journal of Financial and Quantitative Analysis* 31, 337–55.

24   Tod Perry, 2000, Incentive Compensation for Outside Directors and CEO Turnover, Indiana University Working Paper.

25   Eugene F. Fama and Michael C. Jensen, 1983, Separation of Ownership and Control, *Journal of Law & Economics* 26, 301–25.

26   Benjamin E. Hermalin and Michael S. Weisbach, 1998, Endogenously Chosen Boards of Directors and Their Monitoring of the CEO, *American Economic Review* 88, 96–118.

27   Jeffrey L. Coles, Naveen D. Daniel and Lalitha Naveen, 2008, Boards: Does One Size Fit All? *Journal of Financial Economics* 87, 329–56.

28   Francesca Cornelli and Oğuzhan Karakaş, 2012, Corporate Governance of LBOs: The Role of Boards, London Business School Working Paper.

7   Operationalizing operational engineering

As we discussed in Chapter 2, private equity (PE) firms have increasingly focused on adding operational value to their portfolio companies. This increase in focus has been driven by the rapid increase in capital committed to the private equity industry and the competition for deals. In order to earn a return, PE firms increasingly have to focus on growing revenues and profits of their portfolio companies. We refer to this as "operational engineering." In the 1980s, Clayton Dubilier and Rice (CDR) pioneered the use of operating partners while Bain Capital (and Mitt Romney) pioneered the use of consulting resources and analyses. Today, many top private equity firms have operating partners and make use of both internal and external consulting groups. In Chapter 10, we will look at how various PE firms organize and recruit to focus on these operational improvements. Most private equity firms today incorporate some form of operational engineering in addition to financial and governance engineering. In this chapter, we look in more detail at the different approaches private equity firms take.

As we see in Table 7.1 taken from Gompers et al. (2020)[1] survey of PE firms, the two most important sources of value creation for private equity firms are, first, growing revenues and, second, reducing costs in their portfolio companies. Both of these operating levers go to increase the profits of the portfolio company and thereby increase value. It is interesting that despite the COVID-19 pandemic, PE firms have a primary focus in increasing revenues.

In our 2012 survey, we asked about those sources in more detail. Table 7.2 provides the breakdown. Again, growing revenues was the most important expected source of value (70% of the time). Other forms of operational engineering also were important – follow-on acquisitions (51%), reducing costs in general (36%), redefining the current business model

Table 7.1 Sources of Value Creation

Source of Value	Mean	Median	AUM		Age	
			Low	High	Young	Old
Growth in revenue of the underlying business	8.1	8.0	7.9	8.3	8.0	8.1
Reducing costs	5.4	5.0	5.5	5.4	5.5	5.3
Industry-level multiple arbitrage	4.6	4.5	4.4	4.8	4.6	4.7
Leverage	3.9	4.0	3.9	4.0	4.0	3.8
Refinancing	3.2	3.0	3.2	3.1	3.2	3.2
Other	1.7	1.0	1.5	1.9	1.9	1.6
Observations	145	145	73	72	77	68

Source: Gompers, Kaplan and Muhkarlyamov (2020)

or strategy (34%), improving IT systems (26%) and introducing shared services (16%). When compared to other sources of potential return generation, improving operating performance is clearly the dominant lever.

Most top PE firms are organized around industries. As we will see in Chapter 10, this industry focus is embodied by the people who execute the investment and operating improvements. PE firms use their industry and operating knowledge to identify attractive investments, to develop a value creation plan at the time of investment and to implement the value creation plan.

Operational value creation levers

The plan for operational engineering or value creation begins when the PE firm decides to pursue a transaction. As we saw in Chapter 4, two of the important drivers of the decision to invest in a deal are a proprietary strategy and capability from the private equity firm to improve the company and the room for improvement in the target company's operations. Often, the proprietary strategy involves the development of the operating plan that has the potential to improve operating performance as well as having people who can help implement that operating plan to achieve those improvements. Chapter 2 also presented the academic evidence on how PE investments affect the performance of the companies they control.

Table 7.2   Pre-Investment (Expected) Sources of Value Creation – The Percentage of Deals That Private Equity Investors Identify Having the Following Pre-Deal Sources of Value

	Mean	Median	Low AUM	High AUM	Low IRR	High IRR	Old	Young	Local	Global
Reduce costs in general	35.6	27.5	35.8	35.5	37.1	37.3	39.9	32.0	31.0	41.8
Improve IT/ information systems	26.1	20.0	30.8	21.6	22.0	23.3	23.9	28.0	26.7	25.3
Introduce shared services	15.6	2.5	16.4	14.9	11.6	18.3	16.9	14.6	14.9	16.6
Increase revenue/ improve demand factors	70.3	80.0	77.5	63.5	75.0	63.5	67.0	73.2	70.6	70.0
Redefine the current business model or strategy	33.8	29.5	27.8	39.5	43.0	29.8	32.1	35.3	32.8	35.2
Change CEO or CFO	30.6	27.5	33.4	28.0	29.2	32.9	30.9	30.4	29.3	32.4
Change senior management team other than CEO and CFO	33.4	30.0	37.3	29.7	32.5	33.1	27.9	38.1	35.4	30.8

Improve corporate governance	47.0	37.0	52.4	41.9	40.1	45.5	39.4	53.5	47.3	46.6
Improve incentives	61.1	73.5	60.7	61.5	58.3	67.0	65.5	57.4	59.0	63.9
Follow-on acquisitions	51.1	50.0	53.9	48.4	52.0	46.9	51.0	51.2	53.2	48.3
Strategic investor	15.6	10.0	16.4	14.8	12.3	14.0	14.4	16.5	15.1	16.2
Facilitate a high-value exit	50.0	43.5	61.0	39.6	45.6	42.0	40.4	58.1	53.5	45.4
Purchase at an attractive price (buy low)	44.3	43.0	49.2	39.6	38.2	43.3	40.9	47.1	44.9	43.5
Purchase at an attractive price relative to the industry	46.6	50.0	54.5	39.2	38.7	47.3	42.9	49.8	50.1	42.0
Other	9.8	0.0	9.4	10.2	0.0	14.3	9.4	10.1	12.4	6.4
Number of responses	74	74	36	38	27	27	34	40	42	32

Source: Gompers, Kaplan and Muhkarlyamov (2016)

Overall, the evidence indicated that PE investors dramatically improve company performance, increasing sales, profits, productivity and innovation. Here, we explore a variety of examples and particular areas within portfolio companies in which performance is enhanced.

The importance of operational improvements has not gone unnoticed in the PE industry. The exemplary implementation of these types of strategies is recognized annually in the Private Equity International's (PEI's) annual Operational Excellence Awards. The awards recognize PE firms that "have delivered operational value to their portfolio companies" in a transaction that has been at least partially realized. One of us (Kaplan) has served for a number of years as a judge for these awards. In 2021, PE firms submitted a record number of entries for the Americas awards. Those entries had a number of commonalities. Several of the examples below are taken from winners in the PEI's Operational Excellence Awards.

Team upgrade/new CEO

It is very common for PE firms to upgrade the existing management team. This often involves bringing in new members of the C-suite including new chief executive officers (CEOs), chief operating officers (COOs) and chief financial officers (CFOs). To do this, PE firms make use of in-house talent management teams that are focused on sourcing talent for portfolio companies. Recent work by Cziraki and Jenter (2021)[2] has demonstrated that the market for CEO talent in public companies is primarily limited to candidates from within the firm or candidates who are connected to the board. The labor market for CEOs in PE-backed companies, however, is very different. Gompers, Kaplan and Muhkarlyamov (2022) show that the majority of PE-financed companies replace CEOs and the replacements are most likely to be company outsiders.[3] It is now common for PE firms to have a head of talent management. This head of talent management has extensive networks and the capability to identify senior executive talent. PE firms also make use of executive assessment firms like ghSMART that systematically assess the candidates. Kaplan and Sorensen (2021)[4] and Kaplan, Klebanov and Sorensen (2012)[5] describe the ghSMART assessments and the information about top executives that is in those assessments. Both papers show that CEO candidates could be characterized by general ability versus communication/interpersonal skills. General ability appears to be a better predictor of performance in a sample of buyout and venture capital-financed companies.

An illustration of the importance of new senior management is illustrated by Ardian's purchase of Diana, a European chemical additive company, in 2007.[6] Ardian purchased in an LBO for an enterprise value of €710 million and €415 million of debt. The advent of the financial crisis severely strained Diana's ability to meet its debt obligations. As Diana was struggling, Ardian hired an outsider, Olivier Caix, to turn the company around. Caix had served as President of Rhodia Organics for nearly four years and had over a decade of experience in the chemical additive business. The ability to reach outside of Diana for management talent was critical to the turnaround.

Clayton, Dubilier and Rice utilized management upgrades in its 2016 investment in agilon health.[7] Ravi Sachdev, a partner at Clayton, Dubilier, led the merger of two companies, Primary Provider Management and Cyber-Pro Systems, and was joined on the board by operating partner, Ron Williams, former chairman and CEO of Aetna. A year later, Central Ohio Primary Care was merged into the company as well. The goal was to create a healthcare company focused on senior patients. A critical element of Clayton, Dubilier's strategy was to hire a senior management team that could provide operational excellence. The entire C-suite of the company was hired including Steve Sell as CEO (former President and CEO of Health Net), Tim Bensley as CFO (former CFO of Blue Apron) and Girish Venkatachaliah as CTO. Agilon health was able to go public on the New York Stock Exchange in April 2021 and generated a 43 times gross multiple for Clayton, Dubilier on its investment.

New strategy

One of the ways for a PE firm to increase growth in portfolio companies is by helping to implement a new strategy. This commonly includes introducing new products and services or expanding to new geographies. In order to do this, PE firms often specialize in particular industries and hire experienced operators. Almost half of the PEI award submissions in 2021 reported implementing a new strategy while almost one-third reported initiating a geographic expansion. Arbor Investments' experience with Rise Bakers illustrates the point. Arbor is a PE firm focused on the food and beverage industry. The firm highlights its focus on operational engineering by touting that 60% of professionals are in non-finance roles.[8] These professionals have deep industry domain expertise and focus on issues that are critical for these types of companies. Ten of Arbor's prior investments had been in bakeries, and this deep domain expertise has been particularly important in helping to drive value.[9] In 2013, Arbor helped create Rise Bakeries through the consolidation of five regional bakeries into one large North American company with a suite of products for in-store retailers and food service operators. Arbor invested in R&D so the company could create and offer new products with a primary focus on frozen cookie dough.[10] The company also focused on the large in-store bakery market and quickly dominated the space. Those changes helped Rise add new national customers like WalMart and Costco that would have been hard to approach as a regional bakery. When Arbor eventually exited their investment in Rise through a sale to Olympus Partners, they ended up earning 7.2 times their money on the investment.

Even in complex service industries, PE can bring substantial value by helping portfolio companies implement new strategies. For example, Apollo Global Management bought budget regional passenger airline, Sun Country Airlines, in 2017 and turned it into a "hybrid low-cost air carrier that dynamically deploys shared resources across our synergistic scheduled service, charter and cargo businesses."[11] Apollo undertook the upgrading of the aircraft fleet by purchasing used planes, a strategy that increased during the COVID-19 pandemic. Similarly, Apollo helped Sun Country negotiate a cargo agreement with Amazon in 2019 that lead to dramatic increases in revenues.[12] Apollo also helped Sun Country move to offer charter flights for college sports teams and other leisure travelers.

IK Investment Partners' buyout of Transnorm in 2014 further illustrates how changing strategy and target market can dramatically improve performance.[13] Transnorm is an automation business that provides systems for the transportation and delivery of goods. Prior to the acquisition, airline baggage systems were a heavy emphasis at the company. Major freight carriers like UPS, DHL and FedEx were also customers as were e-commerce companies like Amazon and Alibaba. A key element of IK's investment strategy was to reposition the firm to focus primarily on e-commerce and parcel delivery. This change in strategy necessitated an investment in new product development that helped drive those customers. Similarly, the primary market prior to IK's investment was the European Union. Over the next four years, Transnorm made major expansions in both North America and the Asia/Pacific region. The strategy grew Transnorm's market share by 50% and led to the sale of the company to Honeywell for €425 million. IK generated a gross multiple on its investment of 6.0 times over four years.

Technology upgrade

Another strategy that PE firms employ is to help their portfolio companies upgrade the companies' technology or help with digital transformation. Cloud-based software, AI and new B-2-B SaaS tools have transformed many industries, and PE investors have specialized internal teams that help companies implement these tools. PE firms invested in such technology upgrades in more than 40% of the 2021 PEI award portfolio company nominees. The importance of implementing technology is illustrated by Rockwood Equity Partners' September 2000 buyout of Hanson Manufacturing, a small manufacturer of military heaters and air filtration units based in Cleveland.[14] When Rockwood co-founders, Brett Keith and Owen Colligan, purchased Hanson, the company did not have an inventory management system, instead having nearly a year's worth of work in progress and raw material inventory. Similarly, Hanson had limited use of message and communication tracking, including basic technology like voice mail. Implementing these changes dramatically improved communication and cash flows. Inventory levels shrank by 75%, dramatically reducing the company's working capital needs.

Similarly, New Mountain's investment in Equian, a healthcare payment integrity provider, demonstrates the ability to accelerate company and industry changes. In 2019, New Mountain was awarded *Buyouts* overall deal of the year for its investment in Equian. New Mountain purchased the company in December 2015 and merged it with Trover Solutions.[15] New Mountain helped Equian invest heavily in technology that ensures that health insurers pay the right claims with the appropriate level of reimbursement, thereby avoiding overpaying for covered medical expenses. The company processes more than $500 billion in healthcare claims a year. New Mountain sold Equian to United Healthcare in 2019 for $3.2 billion, which provided New Mountain with a gross multiple on invested capital of 8.3 times and an IRR of 79%.

Sales reorganization/go to market

As we saw earlier, PE firms focus on increasing portfolio company revenues, noting that top-line growth is the most important source of value for PE-backed portfolio companies. One way to do this is to improve the sales function at portfolio companies. This might involve reorganizing the sales force or changing how the company goes to market. Similarly, PE firms may help portfolio companies access new market segments or innovate their products and services. Consistent with this, over 50% of the 2021 PEI award entries mentioned sales reorganization or a change in go to market strategy as an important source of value. For example, in addition to the other changes mentioned earlier, Arbor helped Rise change its sales team structure and sold to retailers resulting in major new contracts with chains like Walmart and Costco.

Similarly, Riverside's 2014 acquisition of Censis Technologies, a provider of SaaS-based surgical instrument tracking and workflow solutions for sterile processing departments (SPDs) of hospitals, demonstrates how PE firms can accelerate the sales function within portfolio companies.[16] Riverside implemented and aided an expansion of the sales and marketing function within Censis. The PE firm also led the add-on acquisition of Applied Logic in 2018 which expanded Censis's offerings.[17] These changes allowed the company to quadruple the number of hospitals it served and led to a successful exit in November of 2019 when the company was sold to Fortive.

Valor Equity Partners worked with Tesla to design Tesla's unusual and innovative direct sales model and process for selling the Tesla Roadster.[18] This included designing a sales system to maximize test drives, identifying the right type of salesperson, designing a training program for those salespersons and reducing the brick-and-mortar dealership footprint.

New products and services

Another way to increase revenues is to introduce new products. Roughly one-half of the PEI award entries highlighted that the companies and PE firms had introduced meaningful new products. For example, in Riverwood's investment in Hanson Manufacturing, Keith and Colligan helped the company hire three Ph.D. engineers who helped the company develop and market new, more advanced units that successfully competed for a variety of military programs.[19]

As mentioned earlier, Arbor and Rise invested heavily in new baking products. Apollo and Sun Country added cargo operations in addition to its passenger airline business. L Catterton and Peloton added "broader content and equipment options for subscribers and commercial customers." Riverside and Censis introduced new modules and new functionality to its software.

Better marketing and branding

Better marketing can go hand in hand with improvements in sales. In retail settings, this can be critical to a turnaround. Bain Capital's investment in Outback Steakhouse shows the importance of this type of activity.[20] Under operating partner Mark Verdi's guidance, Bain's retail team examined how Outback was advertising and determined that there was insufficient "call-to-action" in Outback's promotions. Historically, Outback had crafted an image as a restaurant for special occasions. The Bain marketing team saw an opportunity to grow revenues by building the image of the restaurant as "an everyday" establishment. Along with the pricing and portfolio changes discussed above, Bain was able to drive greater foot traffic to the restaurants and dramatically improve performance.

Operating improvements

Private equity firms also help create value by improving operations or cutting costs. Such improvements/reductions can come from improving manufacturing, supply chain and procurement. Almost 40% of the PEI award entries cited such improvements as important sources of value. In the example of Hanson Manufacturing discussed above, Keith and Colligan implemented reorganized manufacturing around the Japanese kaizen model of continuous improvement, and sales expanded dramatically. These improvements led to a sale of Hanson to Behrman Capital in 2004 for $93 million, a return of nearly 40 times their invested capital. Over the four years that Rockwood owned Hanson, revenues grew from $21 million to $55 million, and EBITDA grew from $1.5 million to over $8 million.[21]

TPG's 2009 investment in Daphne International, one of the world's largest shoe manufacturers and retailers, also highlights PE firms' ability to transform operations.[22] Jin-Goon Kim, a TPG partner who led TPG's operating group in China, was TPG's representative on Daphne's board. TPG had made their investment in Daphne via a private investment in public equity. Daphne's share price had not performed well and, in 2011, Jin-Goon and TPG successfully transformed Daphne into the world's first fast-fashion shoe retailer. Fast fashion had become a major theme within retail during the 2000s, yet it had not been implemented in the shoe space. The transformation of Daphne included substantial changes to the entire supply chain and manufacturing infrastructure of Daphne. Daphne reduced initial store orders by 69% and was able to identify the best sellers within a few weeks. The transformed supply chain then was able to restock the best sellers quickly. Over the next two years, the stock price of Daphne International increased from around ¥6 per share to more than ¥11 per share.

Valor Equity Partners used the manufacturing expertise of its operating group to help Tesla reduce the cost of the Roadster.[23] Valor was instrumental in redesigning the supply chain, in particular, moving Tesla's battery facility to the US. Valor Partner and Head of Operations Timothy Watkins and his team were instrumental in providing direction to Tesla as it sought to expand its battery supply chain. Initially, the battery packs were manufactured in Asia using low-cost labor. The packs were then shipped to Tesla's manufacturing partner in Europe. Cars were then manufactured in the UK and shipped to the US. Watkins and his team realized that scaling this supply chain at volume would be complex and expensive. Hence, Valor advocated moving the entire supply chain, including manufacturing batteries, to the US. These changes led to a substantial supply and cost advantage for Tesla in the race to supply high quality, yet affordable electric vehicles.

Acquisitions

It is very common for private equity firms to invest in one portfolio company, sometimes called a platform, and then make add-on acquisitions, i.e., investments in other companies in the same industry. Sometimes the acquired companies provide additional capabilities to the platform company. Sometimes, the acquired companies provide entries to new geographies. And sometimes, the acquired companies have overlapping operations or employees that the combined company can eliminate.

Roughly 40% of the PEI award entries noted acquisitions as an important source of value creation.

The acquisition of Hanson Manufacturing by Rockwood Capital, discussed above, also illustrates the value that can be created through "bolt-on" acquisitions.[24] Keith and Colligan identified several synergistic acquisitions that could extend Hanson's product line. In August 2001, they acquired a specialized military heater manufacturer that added $12.5 million to annual revenues. They added a second manufacturer of military heaters in September 2002 that added an additional $4 million in annual revenue. Finally, Keith and Colligan purchased a company that had developed advanced technology for specialized nuclear, biological and chemical (NBC) filtration and hired the company's co-founder and Chief Scientist to upgrade the Hanson team. These product line extensions were critical for growing the underlying revenue and profits of the firm and facilitating the exit to Behrman Capital in 2004.

A version of the acquisition strategy that a number of PE investors pursue is a roll-up strategy. In this strategy, a platform company grows a business by purchasing small players in a highly fragmented industry to achieve economies of scale as well as potential increases in liquidity and exit multiples. Housatonic Partners' investment in Archive One illustrates the success of that strategy. Will Thorndike, founder and managing director at Housatonic Partners, identified Archive One, founded by A. J. Wasserstein in 1998, as a potential investment in the records storage space.[25] The records management industry at the time was dominated by two large industry players, but a large number of small players existed. Wasserstein realized there was an opportunity to create a third player by rolling up these smaller mom-and-pop shops. Housatonic invested in 1998, and Archive One proceeded on a path of rapid acquisition. Over the next six years, the company purchased 16 small records storage companies and substantially grew the revenues and profits of the company. Revenues grew from just under $2 million in 1998 to nearly $21 million in 2004. EBITDA grew from $200 000 to $4.8 million. In 2004, ABRY Partners provided follow-on capital that accelerated the growth. In 2007, Archive One was sold to Iron Mountain.

Optimized pricing

Private equity firms increasingly include or enlist the help of pricing experts to determine whether their portfolio companies are pricing their offerings optimally. Eleven percent of the PEI award entries mentioned change in pricing strategy as an important value creation lever. This often means raising prices, but not always. The purchase of Outback Steakhouse by Bain Capital and Catterton in November 2006 illustrates the dramatic improvements that this can engender.[26] Mark Verdi led Bain's operations team to implement a variety of pricing and promotion changes that dramatically improved profitability. First, Outback had historically been unwilling to offer promotional prices, fearing it would reduce profitability. Bain's team determined that promotions on various days of the week could drive increased traffic into the restaurants. Second, by analyzing plates that were cleared from tables after customers left, Bain's team determined that a significant number of customers were leaving food, i.e., Outback's portions were generally too large. Outback reduced portion sizes and increased profitability.

Apollo's acquisition of Sun Country also illustrates the interplay of operating improvements and improved pricing strategy.[27] With Apollo's assistance in raising additional financing, Sun Country switched from leasing aircraft to ownership, reducing overall costs of assets and improving profitability. Unit costs declined by 20% which allowed Sun Country to lower fares by an average of 43% and increase overall revenue by 25% through increased load capacity. Investments in new information technology also allowed Sun Country to initiate a variety of new pricing models including checked baggage charges and upgrade fees. These changes resulted in an increase in ancillary revenue per passenger of 60%.[28]

Conclusion

In this chapter, we have seen that most private equity firms incorporate operational engineering in addition to financial and governance engineering. The PE firms employ a host of different operational engineering strategies to increase value in their portfolio companies. This active involvement in the companies in which they invest facilitates improvements in operating performance. Over time, PE firms have become increasingly focused on implementing operational improvements. We have provided examples of the different ways PE firms can improve the performance of their portfolio companies. Given the dramatic growth in assets under management in the private equity industry, this trend almost certainly will continue.

Notes

1   P.A. Gompers, S. N. Kaplan and V. Muhkarlyamov, 2020, Private Equity and Covid-19, Harvard Business School Working Paper.

2   P. Cziraki and D. Jenter, 2021, The Market for CEOs, London School of Economics Working Paper.

3   P.A. Gompers, S.N. Kaplan and V. Muhkarlyamov, 2022, The Market For CEOs: Evidence From Private Equity, University of Chicago Working Paper.

4   S. Kaplan and M. Sorensen, 2021, Are CEOs Different? Characteristics of Top Managers, *Journal of Finance* 1773–811.

5   S. Kaplan, M. Klebanov and M. Sorensen, 2012, Which CEO Characteristics and Abilities Matter, *Journal of Finance* 973–1007.

6   P.A. Gompers and M. Roberts, 2014, Ardian – The Sale of Diana, Harvard Business School Case Number 9-215-033.

7   www.privateequityinternational.com/opex-awards-21-americas-lower-mid -market-winner-clayton-dubilier-rice/ accessed on 8 February 2022.

8   www.arborpic.com/our-approach/ accessed on 3 February 2022.

9   www.arborpic.com/news/arbor-investments-gobbles-bakery-cos/ accessed on 4 February 2022.

10 www.arborpic.com/news/rise-baking-co-and-cookie-kings/ accessed on 4 February 2022.

11 IPO Prospectus, 16 March 2021.

12 K. Broughton, 2021, Sun Country Looks to Buy Used Planes at Pandemic Discount, *Wall Street Journal*.

13 PEI Operational Excellence Awards 2019, www.peievents.com/en/wp-con-tent/uploads/2019/06/PEI179_OpExOCT19.pdf accessed on 2 February 2022.

14 P.A. Gompers and V. Broussard, 2009, Hudson Manufacturing, Harvard Business School Case Number 9-203-064.

15 www.buyoutsinsider.com/deal-of-the-year-new-mountain-capital/ accessed on 4 February 2022.

16 www.riversidecompany.com/select-growth-stories/censis-technologies/ accessed on 8 February 2022.

17 www.privateequityinternational.com/opex-awards-winner-americas-riv-erside-company-censis-technologies/ accessed on 8 February 2022.

18 See Kaplan et al. (2017).

19 P.A. Gompers and V. Broussard, 2009, Hudson Manufacturing, Harvard Business School Case Number 9-203-064.

20 P.A. Gompers, K. Mugford and J.D. Kim, 2012, Bain Capital and Outback Steakhouse, Harvard Business School Case Number 9-212-087.

21 P.A. Gompers and V. Broussard, 2009, Hudson Manufacturing, Harvard Business School Case Number 9-203-064.

22 V. Ivashina, 2012, TPG China: Daphne International, Harvard Business School Case Number 9-213-055.

23 https://turnaround.org/chicagomidwest/tesla-investor-valor-equity-part-ners-addresses-ctpctas-luncheon accessed on 2 February 2022.

24 P.A. Gompers and V. Broussard, 2009, Hudson Manufacturing, Harvard Business School Case Number 9-203-064.

25 M.J. Roberts and N.N. El-Hage, 2006. Housatonic Partners and ArchiveOne, Inc., HBS Case number 9-806-193.

26 P.A. Gompers, K. Mugford and J.D. Kim, 2012, Bain Capital and Outback Steakhouse, Harvard Business School Case Number 9-212-087.

27 www.privateequityinternational.com/opex-awards-21-americas-upper -mid-market-winner-apollo-global-management/ accessed on 8 February 2022.

28 www.privateequityinternational.com/opex-awards-21-americas-upper -mid-market-winner-apollo-global-management/ accessed on 8 February 2022.

8   Private equity exits

Private equity (PE) investments are typically executed through closed-end funds in which the PE manager serves as the general partner (GP) and investors in their funds, such as pension funds and endowments, serve as limited partners (LPs). As we will discuss in Chapter 9, funds are typically 10 years in length although extensions are typically permissible and common.[1] The funds' limited life means that PE managers need to assess, plan and execute exits for portfolio companies. The most common exits include going public through a traditional underwritten initial public offering (IPO), being acquired by a strategic buyer, being acquired by a financial buyer and, more recently, merging with a special purpose acquisition company (SPAC). This chapter discusses the process and considerations that affect the timing and manner in which private equity firms exit their investments. We also explore trends and factors that affect the types of exits PE managers choose and how it affects the returns that PE funds can generate.

Exit alternatives

Traditional IPOs

One exit path for a PE manager to pursue is an initial public offering (IPO), the process of selling shares to the public for the first time. By going public, companies are able to gain better access to capital, which growth-stage companies need for expansion, and liquidity, which PE managers need to provide returns to their respective LPs.

To be a credible candidate for a traditional underwritten IPO, it is conventional wisdom that a PE portfolio company needs somewhat predictable revenue, historically positive profits, expectations for growth in revenues and profits, a public company-ready management team and robust financial and compliance controls.

The attractiveness of an IPO relative to other forms of exit depends on several considerations. The first is valuation. There are times when IPOs have higher valuations than either strategic or financial sales. The second is the need for liquidity. IPOs are usually a first step to liquidity, but do not generate immediate liquidity. They are typically time consuming, often taking up to a year to complete. Then, PE firms sell only a small portion of their stake in the IPO. They continue to hold the majority of their equity holdings for an extended period of time. As a result, IPOs leave PE firms exposed to the risk of a significant decline in firm value as well as decreasing the ability of PE firms to time exits to coincide with peaks in valuation. Of course, the PE firm will benefit if the value increases. Third is the burden of disclosure requirements. Some firms and management teams are more willing to weather the disclosure requirements of becoming a public company and the other costs associated with being a public company.

When a portfolio company decides to go public, the process begins with selecting an investment bank to serve as a lead underwriter for the offering as well as choosing additional underwriters. The lead underwriter manages the deal. In addition to providing advice and helping with all the necessary filing requirements, the lead underwriter is ultimately responsible for setting the valuation of the company at issuance, making the market for the firm's shares after the offering and ensuring that the company can sell its listed shares, at the offer price.

To do its job, the underwriter uses a "book building" process. First, it works with the company to prepare projections and valuation analyses that help determine an initial price range for the offering. The underwriter relies on both discounted cash flow analyses and comparable companies' analyses to determine the preliminary filing range.

Next, the company's senior officers go on a roadshow with the underwriter to promote the company to institutional investors. At the end of the roadshow, the underwriter receives indications of interest from investors and adjusts the offer price based on investors' stated demand for the offering.

The lead and other underwriters then purchase shares from the listing company and sell them to investors on the day of the stock's debut. To protect themselves against a loss and ensure market liquidity, underwriters at times exercise a "greenshoe provision," which allows them to sell up to 15% additional shares at the offer price. Underwriters usually sell more shares in the offering than the company has allotted in the offering, i.e., they are naked short. If the price of the IPO goes up in the initial aftermarket and stays above the offering price, the underwriter covers their short position by exercising the greenshoe option. The lead underwriter typically has 30 days in which to exercise the greenshoe option. If the IPO trades down in price, the underwriter covers its naked short position by purchasing shares in the open market. These open market purchases have the effect of stabilizing the IPO share price. In return for their work in bringing companies public, underwriters are paid a fee, called an "underwriters' spread," typically 5% to 7% of the offering size.[2]

The risk of subsequent price movements is exacerbated by the fact that PE firms are generally not permitted to divest any of their equity holdings in the first 180 days following the IPO. This period of time is referred to as the IPO lockup. When the issuing firm and the investment bank enter into an agreement to offer securities in an IPO, they sign an underwriter agreement. As Bartlett (1995)[3] explains, these agreements typically include a covenant such as:

> The Selling Securityholders agree that, without your (the investment bank's) prior written consent, the Selling Securityholders will not, directly or indirectly, sell, offer, contract to sell, make any short sale, pledge or otherwise dispose of any shares of Common Stock or any securities convertible into or exercisable for or any rights to purchase or acquire Common Stock for a period of 180 days following the commencement of the public offering of the Stock by the Underwriters.

The lockup is meant to give confidence to IPO investors that pre-public insiders are not going to take advantage of inside information and sell at an inflated price. The lockup also allows the investment bank underwriting the offering to control the public float. The agreement to not sell or sell-short their equity holdings is written into the underwriting agreement and is imposed by the investment bank, not the SEC or state securities laws that regulate insider trading.[4] Typically, when a firm's equity comes off of lockup, the stock price experiences a significant stock price decline, even though the date is fully known and the expiration is fully anticipated.[5]

In addition, insider trading is likely to be regulated by the firm itself, most of which impose trading windows for insiders. A large proportion of IPO companies have a policy in place restricting insider trading by employees as well as pre-specified blackout periods in which the company prohibits trading by insiders. Insiders who are governed by these self-imposed company restrictions are sometimes granted permission to trade during the blackout periods for liquidity or diversification reasons.

Even after the lockup expires, PE managers will often continue to hold the shares in the company for months or even years. Once they decide to liquidate their positions, there are two alternatives. First, the PE managers can sell the shares they hold on the open market or in a secondary stock offering and distribute cash to limited partners. Alternatively, the PE managers distribute shares to each limited partner and (frequently) themselves. There are several factors that influence this decision.[6]

First, SEC rules restrict sales by corporate insiders. The sale of restricted securities, that is, stock purchased in a private placement directly from an issuer before the company is public, is governed by SEC Rule 144. Rule 144 allows for the sale of restricted securities in limited quantities in the aftermarket. Specifically, a person who has beneficially owned shares of common stock for at least six months (one year if the firm is not subject to reporting requirements) is entitled to sell, within any three-month period, a number of shares that does not exceed the greater of 1% of the number of shares of common stock then outstanding or the average weekly trading volume during the four calendar weeks preceding the filing of a notice on Form 144 with respect to the sale.

Because the private equity fund may hold a large fraction of the company's equity, selling the entire stake may take a long period of time. By distributing shares to limited partners who are usually not considered insiders, the private equity fund can dispose of a large block of shares more quickly.

Second, tax motivations may also provide an incentive for the private equity managers to distribute shares. If they sell shares and distribute cash, taxable limited partners (e.g., individuals and corporations) and the private equity managers themselves are subject to immediate capital gains taxes. These investors might prefer to postpone these taxes by receiving distributions in kind and selling the shares at a later date. These considerations will be unimportant to tax-exempt limited partners (e.g., pension funds and endowments). By distributing stock, private equity funds provide limited partners with the flexibility to make their own decisions about selling the stock.

Third, if selling the shares has a negative effect on prices, private equity funds may want to distribute shares. The method of computing returns employed by private equity funds typically uses the closing price of the distributed stock on the day the distribution is declared. The actual price received when the limited partners sell their shares may be lower.[7] Private equity managers care about stated returns on their funds because they use this information when they raise new funds. Thus, the potential price pressure from selling the shares on the open market will typically lower the value that they can quote compared to the value they can claim if they distribute the shares directly.[8]

Finally, the private equity managers' compensation can be affected by distribution policy. Carried interest payments – usually equal to 20% of the profits of the fund – will be higher the higher the stated return to the fund.

Few SEC regulations cover distributions by private equity investors. Rule 16(a) states that individuals who are affiliates of a firm, such as directors, officers and holders of 10% of the company's shares, must disclose any transactions in the firm's stock on a monthly basis. Provision 16(a)-7, however, explicitly exempts distributions of securities that (1) were originally obtained from issuers and (2) are being distributed "in good faith, in the ordinary course of business." An interpretation widely accepted within the industry is that private equity managers distribute investments in the normal course of business, and that they do not convey any information unless the private equity manager makes an explicit recommendation to hold or sell the shares at the time. Private equity lawyers have applied the same principles when considering the applicability of Rule 10(b)-5, the most general prohibition against fraudulent activity in the purchase or sale of any security.

When one examines the price reaction around the distribution date, i.e., the date that the private equity manager distributes shares to their limited partners, the evidence is consistent with the market reacting to the inside information of the private equity fund: there is a systematic 2% to 3% drop around the distribution that is akin to the reaction to public announcements of secondary stock sales even though private equity distributions are not publicly disclosed.[9]

Regulatory and compliance costs associated with traditional IPOs meaningfully increased as a result of the Sarbanes-Oxley Act of 2002. These costs, typically estimated to be several million dollars annually, have increased the minimum threshold in terms of market capitalization. Similarly, the increase in the share of the market owned by institutional investors has also increased the minimum size of IPOs. These changes likely have reduced the number of IPOs compared to the 1990s.

Finally, insiders often objected to the large share price increase on the first day of trading. Studies with data back to 1980 showed that, on average, IPO shares increased by 20% on their first day of trading.[10] This led many commentators to suggest that underwriters underpriced listing shares intentionally and left value on the table for the companies they represented, i.e., firms felt as if they could have raised more capital by selling the same number of shares at a higher price. Taking the first day underpricing into account can markedly increase the total cost of traditional IPOs.

One proposed path of reform is direct listings, which Spotify and Slack undertook in 2018 and 2019, respectively. Direct listings differ from traditional IPOs in that no new stock is issued in an offering. By contrast, existing shareholder stock is auctioned on a public exchange. As a result, there is also no 180-day lockup period for existing investors and underwriters were not needed to engage in the book building process. Instead, companies hired capital advisors to communicate with institutional investors, offer forward-looking guidance in advance of trading and declare a reference price together with the hosting stock exchange. Proponents for direct listings argued they were cheaper, faster, more transparent and captured more value for the listing company.

The IPO of Globant demonstrates the value that PE firms can realize by taking firms public. Globant was founded in 2003 by Martin Migoya, Guibert Englebienne, Néstor Nocetti and Martin Umaran in Argentina to focus on outsourced software development.[11] In 2007, Francisco

Alvarez-Demalde, a co-founder of Riverwood Capital, led an investment in Globant. Riverwood was a growth-stage PE firm that targeted technology investments in North and South America. Riverwood followed on with two additional investments in Globant in 2007 and 2011, raising their ownership stake to 39%, and investing a total of $20.8 million across all three rounds. Over the next six years, revenue grew from $22.8 million in 2007 to nearly $129 million in 2012. While significant growth potential existed, Riverwood's investment in Globant had been made in its first fund which, by 2013, was fully invested. Taking Globant public would provide the opportunity for Riverwood to demonstrate its investment prowess while retaining the public shares of Globant, which it believed could continue to appreciate. Starting in 2013, Alvarez-Demalde and the Globant founders prepared to take the company public and, on 18 July 2014, Globant raised $59 million at $10 per share, in an IPO. The shares increased 10.2% on the first day of trading and the company had a market capitalization of roughly $400 million at the market close. Riverwood held onto its shares after the IPO and could revalue those shares at the public market value, booking nearly an eight times return on its investment. Based upon the success of Globant as well as another Riverwood investment (GoPro), the PE firm was able to successfully raise its second fund at $378 million.

SPACs

In recent years, special purpose acquisition companies, or SPACs for short, rose in popularity as potential mechanisms for private firms to go public.[12] SPACs, which have been around for decades and historically have had bad reputations, are blank check companies formed for the purposes of finding and merging with a private business, thereby bringing it public. Between 2018 and 2020, SPACs exploded as a means of taking private companies public. While in 2018 there were 34 SPACs raising $6.4 billion, in 2020 there were 219 raising $72 billion, outpacing even traditional IPOs by more than $6 billion. SPACs had gained so much traction so quickly in the tech industry that commentators had begun labeling their growth a bubble. (See Table 8.1 for SPAC funding over time.) Consistent with that, their popularity has declined precipitously since 2022.

SPACs have five core steps. In the first, a SPAC is formed by issuing stock (to the public) and raising capital at $10 per share in an IPO. The median

Table 8.1 Number of SPAC and Operating Company IPOs

Year	Number of IPOs		Total Proceeds ($m)		Average Proceeds ($m)	
	SPAC	Operating	SPAC	Operating	SPAC	Operating
2010	2	91	104	29 822	52	328
2011	6	81	451	26 967	75	333
2012	9	93	475	31 112	53	335
2013	10	158	1 325	41 565	132	263
2014	11	206	1 555	42 200	141	205
2015	20	118	3 620	22 000	181	186
2016	13	75	3 224	12 518	248	167
2017	34	106	8 996	22 979	265	217
2018	46	134	9 935	33 467	216	250
2019	59	112	12 115	39 182	205	350
2020	248	165	75 300	61 900	304	375
Total	**458**	**1 339**	**117 099**	**363 711**	**256**	**272**

Source: Minmo Gahng, Jay Ritter and Donghang Zhang, 2021, SPACs, University of Florida Working Paper

IPO proceeds for the 2019–20 SPAC cohort were $220 million. Second, the SPAC then has up to two years to search for and negotiate with an acquisition target. In the third step, a merger target is identified, a transaction is agreed to and IPO shareholders decide whether to exercise their redemption rights (i.e., forcing the SPAC to repurchase their shares at $10) or not. At the same time, in a fourth step, the SPAC lines up additional capital in the form of a "private investment in public equity" (PIPE) to replace the cash that will be used to pay back shareholders who exercise their redemption rights. Finally, a SPAC merges with the target company, bringing it public. (See Figure 8.1 for the SPAC process and timeline.)

A SPAC is created by a sponsor. The majority of sponsors are private equity funds or senior officers of the world's largest publicly listed companies. Sponsors work with underwriters to bring SPACs public. Prior to the IPO, sponsors purchase SPAC shares or warrants as part of a commit. This commit serves primarily to cover the underwriting fees of the IPO and all operating costs that are incurred during its search for an acquisition target. In addition, sponsors are allocated a sponsor's promote, or

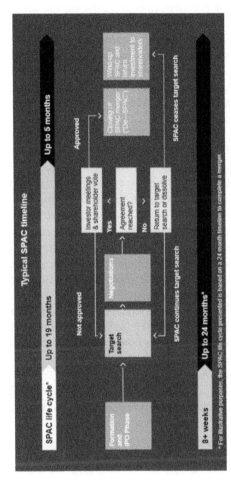

Source: PWC Accounting Advisory, Typical SPAC Timeline, https://www.pwc.com/us/en/services/audit-assurance/accounting-advisory/spac-merger.html, accessed March 2021

Figure 8.1 Typical SPAC Timeline

10% to 20% of post-IPO equity. Sponsors, therefore, end up with 10% to 20% of the SPAC for relatively little money.

Over the next two years, sponsors have to find an appropriate acquisition target, convince existing shareholders to stay on through the merger, bring in required new PIPE investors and close the merger successfully. The promote serves as compensation for their efforts throughout this process. After a successful merger, agreements usually lock up a sponsor's holdings for one year. A recent study examined the performance of SPACs and the return to various stakeholders.[13] In the same research, sponsors experienced a mean return on their investment in the SPAC of 393% and a median return of 202% when performance was measured after three months post-merger.

One apparent benefit of a SPAC for the private company target is that companies seeking to go public view the SPAC process as being less costly than a traditional IPO. To bring a SPAC public, underwriters are paid 2% of proceeds on average from the sponsor's commit. Only upon a successful merger are underwriters paid an additional 3.5%. For underwriters, SPACs have an advantage over IPOs that seems to justify the reduced fee structure. Underwriters are common targets for shareholder lawsuits in traditional IPOs. But because there is little to disclose at the IPO of a SPAC, they are generally protected from Section 11 liability. In fact, there has not been a single lawsuit filed against SPAC underwriters in the past decade. However, while underwriting fees seem more amenable, most SPAC IPO investors exercise their redemption rights when the sponsor proposes a merger candidate. Gahng et al. (2021) evaluate this SPAC mechanism and conclude that the actual median underwriting fee was 16.3% for SPACs, based on the amount of capital that actually remained with the company post-merger. Underwriters can also be paid additional fees to help secure PIPE investors needed to move ahead with a successful merger.

SPACs are sometimes referred to as "poor man's private equity," in which average investors can participate actively in wealth creation. However, by 2020, 70% of SPAC IPO funding came from a group of hedge funds known as the SPAC Mafia – those hedge funds that held at least 100 000 shares in 10 different SPACs that went public between 2010 and 2020. SPAC IPO proceeds are placed in a trust and invested in Treasury notes for two years. As compensation for the illiquidity and as an incentive to make the

IPO investment, SPAC shareholders are given redemption rights. These redemption rights allow SPAC shareholders to redeem their shares at the IPO price ($10 per share) plus accumulated interest when a merger is proposed. As an added incentive to put their money into a SPAC, SPAC IPO shareholders are given warrants and rights. Warrants are call options created by a SPAC company for new stock. The warrants and rights do not expire even after SPAC IPO shareholders exercise their redemption rights, i.e., even if they redeem their IPO shares for $10 plus accrued interest, they continue to hold onto their warrants.

While sponsors offer private deals and discounts to keep existing SPAC IPO shareholders invested through the merger, the majority take advantage of their redemption rights. Klausner and Ohlrogge (2020)[14] find that the median redemption rate, or rate at which SPAC IPO investors opted to exercise their redemption rights, was 73% for the 2019–20 merger cohort. Of those who redeemed, the divestment rate, or the percentage of a position an entity divested, was 98%. Combining the redemptions and the warrants, the mean annualized return for redeeming SPAC IPO shareholders was 11.6% for what was essentially a risk-free investment (Gahng et al. (2021)).

PIPEs are another key piece of the typical SPAC as well as a potential advantage of the SPAC over a traditional IPO. To replenish the cash lost when shareholders redeem before the merger, SPACs often need to raise new capital through the PIPEs. Prospective investors in PIPEs sign nondisclosure agreements and are provided confidential information that allows them to do more thorough due diligence, potentially resulting in more accurate price discovery than what is possible in a traditional IPO roadshow. Because high-quality PIPE investors also provide a strong positive signal to prospective public investors, about one-third of PIPE investors receive discounts of 10% or more relative to the IPO share price. Gahng et al. (2021) find that PIPE investors provided a median of 24.6% of total cash delivered to a target at the time of merger. (See Table 8.2 for SPAC characteristics.)

Private companies merge with SPACs to go public for a variety of reasons. Underwriters typically have criteria in terms of revenues, market capitalization, profitability and so on, for which companies they take public in a traditional IPO. Many companies that do not meet those criteria have no other way to become public other than through a SPAC.

Table 8.2 Overview of SPAC Characteristics

	Median	25th Percentile	75th Percentile
IPO proceeds (USD mn)	220	141	328
Redemptions (% IPO proceeds)	73	18	95
Total cash delivered to target in merger (USD mn)	151.6	26	353
Cash to target (% IPO proceeds)	71.5	16	121
Public SPAC investors (% total cash delivered)	64.2	28	99
Third party PIPE (% total cash delivered)	24.6	0	43
Sponsor PIPE (% total cash delivered)	0	0	11
Target post-merger market cap (USD mn)	501.6	321	955
Post-merger shares (%) held by all SPAC shareholders (including sponsor)	34.5	24	50
Post-merger shares (%) held by sponsor	11.7	6	15

Source: Michael D. Klausner and Michael Ohlrogge, A Sober Look at SPACs, *SSRN Electronic Journal*

In addition, going public via a SPAC only requires negotiations with a single entity, unlike in a traditional IPO where road shows and pricing meetings typically involve a large number of new institutional investors. SPACs also have the potential to enable companies to go public faster than by more traditional methods.

Finally, a point of friction for companies during a book-building process of a typical IPO is that valuation and share prices are often locked in. What is not locked in is the amount of capital that will be raised.

SPACs are not without substantial challenges and costs to some of their stakeholders. While it is suggested that their personal commitments align sponsors to the performance of a company more closely than underwriters have been in a traditional IPO, sponsors risk losing everything if no merger ends up going through. Their chief incentive is therefore a commitment to finding any deal, even if mediocre. Because of the promote, even a losing deal could generate substantial upside for a sponsor. Klausner and Ohlrogge (2020)[15] find that the dilution experienced by most SPACs – 50.4% of its IPO proceeds – is staggering and is borne almost entirely by non-redeeming IPO shareholders and PIPE investors. The post-merger public market performance of SPACs has also been disappointing in the time periods that followed. Gahng et al. (2021)[16] find that in the three months after a merger, the median SPAC return was –14.5%, or a performance of –32.5% against returns anticipated for a company three months after an IPO. Twelve months after SPAC mergers had gone through successfully, their median return to shareholders joining at the merger was –65.3%. (See Table 8.3 for SPAC returns.)

The merger of Luminar demonstrates how SPACs can facilitate going public.[17] Austin Russell founded Luminar Technologies, an autonomous vehicle sensor and software company, at the age of 17. Russell spent his teenage years researching optics and photonics at Beckman Laser Institute at the University of California Irvine, where he became fascinated with building laser LiDAR systems used in self-driving cars. In 2012, he incorporated the company, graduated high school and later matriculated at Stanford University to study physics. However, he dropped out after six months to work on his business full-time after he was awarded the prestigious Thiel Fellowship, a $100 000 grant from Peter Thiel given to students to drop out of college.

Luminar Technologies spent its first five years researching and building out its intellectual property. In May 2013, Russell recruited Jason Eichenholz, an experienced serial entrepreneur of various photonics technologies. To finance their ambitious operation, however, Russell soon turned to professional capital. He first raised funds from the 1517 Fund, a venture capital firm backed by Peter Thiel. Over time, hedge funds, automotive corporate venture capital funds and other venture funds joined in. In September 2020, Luminar raised $184 million in a round led by Alec Gores. While still private, Luminar Technologies raised over $434 million in capital. By the time of the SPAC merger on 3 December 2020, Luminar Technologies had over 350 employees, 88 issued patents and 80 pending patents in the US or abroad.

Gores Metropoulos, Inc., the SPAC with which Luminar ultimately merged, went public via an IPO in February 2019, raising $400 million in

Table 8.3 Post-Merger SPAC Returns (2019–20 Merger Cohort)

	Three-Month			Six-Month			Twelve-Month		
	All	HQ	Non-HQ	All	HQ	Non-HQ	All	HQ	Non-HQ
Mean return	-2.9%	31.5%	-38.8%	-12.3%	15.8%	-37.6%	-34.9%	-6.0%	-57.3%
Median return	-14.5%	-4.6%	-46.9%	-23.8%	-15.9%	-43.0%	-65.3%	-34.6%	-66.3%
Mean return (excess over IPO index)	-13.1%	25.1%	-53.0%	-33.0%	0.4%	-63.1%	-47.1%	-11.8%	-74.6%
Median return (excess over IPO index)	-32.8%	7.1%	-52.1%	-43.2%	-31.0%	-56.3%	-56.5%	-54.8%	-89.9%
Mean return (excess over Russell 2000)	-1.3%	37.5%	-41.9%	-10.9%	22.5%	-41.0%	-21.5%	9.7%	-45.7%
Median return (excess over Russell 2000)	-16.1%	16.9%	-47.2%	-17.5%	-2.4%	-57.0%	-44.9%	-36.3%	-55.0%
N SPACs	47	24	23	38	18	20	16	7	9

Source: Michael D. Klausner and Michael Ohlrogge, A Sober Look at SPACs, *SSRN Electronic Journal*

proceeds. The SPAC's sponsors were teams led by Alec Gores and Dean Metropoulos. Gores was a private equity investor who built his career making prominent leveraged buyouts of non-core businesses from Fortune 500 companies. Metropoulos, too, was a private equity investor who focused on buy-build transactions in the consumer brands sector. The two had collaborated before in 2016 when Gores had led the merger of his SPAC with Hostess Brands which had been privately owned by Metropoulos. Media reports attributed the subsequent explosion of interest in and growth of SPACs to the success that came from that merger.

In late 2020, Gores Metropoulos, Inc. announced that they had found an appropriate target. The merger included $400 million in cash in a reverse merger with Luminar Technologies at a market capitalization of $3.4 billion. This valuation included a contemporaneous financing round of $170 million which was also led by Gores and existing Luminar Technologies investors. Shortly after that merger, the company was valued at more than $10 billion with a share price over $40 per share. As of the beginning of 2022, however, the stock price has declined to roughly $15.

Strategic sales

There are several advantages to a strategic sale relative to other common PE exits. First, a strategic buyer will often realize synergies from the deal. These synergies could be elimination of overhead, synergies in selling, economies of scale and so on. As a result, a strategic acquirer can often offer a higher price than a public offering or a financial acquirer.

Second, a strategic sale usually offers a complete exit from the investment at a known price or value. As we have seen, this is not the case with a traditional IPO or SPAC. Usually strategic sales are all-cash deals. In some cases, however, the acquirer will offer some or all of the consideration in the acquirer's shares. In this case, the PE manager ends up with shares in a larger, typically public company. Those shares can usually be sold relatively easily and quickly compared to shares in an IPO or SPAC, but they do subject the PE seller to some price risk.

Offsetting these advantages are a few disadvantages. In many strategic sales, the acquirer replaces the top management team and creates synergies by firing employees. For some management teams, who are often significant (albeit typically minority) shareholders, this will be unattractive.

As a result, those management teams may be less than enthusiastic in the sales process.

Another downside to strategic sales is that they carry a degree of competitive risk. Potential acquirers need access to the firm's accounting information and other confidential records in order to formulate a bid. While some firms may show genuine interest, others may simply feign interest in order to understand any competitive advantages the firm has. Nondisclosure agreements can mitigate this concern, but cannot eliminate it entirely.

A final disadvantage is that strategic sales can be slow and/or risky to consummate. When one competitor seeks to acquire another, there can be antitrust concerns. In the case where these concerns are important, review of the proposed acquisition by the federal government can slow the closing of the deal or kill it entirely.

The sale of CelTel, a large sub-Saharan mobile telecommunications provider to MTC, the Kuwaiti mobile operator, demonstrates the value that can be achieved through strategic sales by private equity investors. CelTel was founded in March 1998 by Mo Ibrahim, a former British Telecomm engineer. Over the course of six years, Ibrahim raised over $413 million in private equity to build his company. Lead investors included Bessemer Venture Partners, Zephyr Asset Management and CVC International. In 2004, CelTel operated in 13 companies and was considering going public when they were approached by both MTN, a spinout of South Africa's phone company, and MTC. In the bidding process, CelTel ultimately accepted MTC's offer for $3.4 billion in cash. The sale of CelTel illustrates that synergy value can be an important driver of achieving high returns. Similarly, the ability to have multiple bidders was critical to the ultimate sale price for CelTel.

Financial sale

Like a strategic sale, a financial sale has the benefit of providing a complete exit of the investment. Unlike a strategic sale, however, antitrust concerns are not an issue; so, assuming the new PE firm has lined up the financing, financial sales can be relatively quick. This can be particularly important for PE firms that need to exit their investments relatively soon and in the form of cash, particularly deals in funds nearing the end of their life. Financial sales also eliminate the issue of competitive risk while often permitting the firm's current managers to retain their jobs. The importance of financial sales as an exit has grown considerably over the past decades as the private equity industry has continued to grow. Many portfolio companies are "traded up" from smaller PE managers to larger PE managers over the course of several buyouts.

The main possible downside of a financial sale is the price. Because a financial acquirer is unlikely to realize synergies, it may be unable to offer as high a price as a strategic buyer, holding all else equal. Additionally, because financial buyers typically rely on significant levels of debt, there is a possibility that their financing will fall through and scuttle the deal. In recent years, however, the amount of capital in the PE industry has grown substantially. It has become increasingly common for smaller private equity firms to sell their portfolio companies to larger PE managers.

Rockwood's purchase of Hanson Manufacturing which we discussed in Chapter 5 provides a useful illustration. Brett Keith and Owen Colligan purchased Hanson Manufacturing for $10.5 million in October 2000. Keith and Colligan were able to implement a large number of operational changes, performed several bolt-on acquisitions which were financed by debt and grew sales from $21 million in 2000 to more than $55 million in 2003. In 2004, Behrman Capital, a middle-market PE firm, bid for and purchased Hanson for $93 million. Rockwood had paid down the existing debt to $6 million at the time of the transaction. The deal grew equity value from $1 million at the time of the purchase in 2000 to $87 million at the time of sale to Behrman.

More recently, private equity funds have begun exiting investments via a different kind of sale called a continuation fund/vehicle. Continuation vehicles are private equity funds set up to invest in a portfolio company that the PE firm and LPs would like to exit, but the PE firms still believes is attractive to own. The challenge with continuation funds is managing the conflict of interest that PE firms face when they are both the seller and the buyer.

Leveraged dividend recapitalizations

A common and misunderstood form of partial exit is the leveraged dividend recapitalization. In a leveraged dividend recap, the portfolio company issues new debt to raise cash that is then paid out in the form of a special dividend to existing shareholders.[18] As with other exit strategies, leveraged dividend recaps have advantages and disadvantages.

One benefit is that recaps can provide a significant return to private equity investors; PE firms can often receive close to their full equity check back. While this reduces the downside risk of the investment, recaps allow PE firms to retain the upside as their share of the equity remains unaffected. Moreover, unlike other forms of exit, the PE firms retain control of the firm in the case of a recap. Recaps also can be done quickly. They are private transactions that require only the permission of the existing lenders and a willing lender of the new debt. It is worth noting that the lender of the new debt must believe the loan will be a profitable one.

However, a potential disadvantage is that, by increasing the debt level, recaps increase the risk of the remaining equity in the firm. Because recaps are not a full exit and PE firms continue to hold a substantial fraction of the equity, their stake, while smaller following the recap, is riskier. While this is a consideration, it is important to recognize that companies typically consider recaps only when they have paid down a meaningful portion of the debt in the original buyout or when the company's operating performance has improved meaningfully. Accordingly, after the debt in the recap is issued, the company will typically have less debt than it had in the original buyout and, rarely, will have more.

For example, in 2010, Oaktree Capital took out EUR 195 million from Nodenia International AG, a German packaging company, through a dividend funded by cash on hand and a bond issue. This represented more than Oaktree's entire original investment. Similarly, in September 2010, SK Capital took out $922 million from Ascend Performance Materials. It should be noted that SK Capital put only $50 million into Ascend in June 2009.

Another example of the ability to provide returns through leveraged dividend recapitalizations is Providence Private Equity Partners (PEP) portfolio company, World Triathlon Corporation (WTC), that PEP purchased in 2008 for $85 million. WTC owned the Ironman brand and aggressively grew races over the next several years. In June 2014, WTC borrowed $240 million ($220 million through a five-year term loan and $20 million via a revolving line of credit). WTC used $220 million of the financing to pay a dividend to PEP, which gave PEP more than a two times return on their initial investment. By taking money off the table, PEP was able to continue to build WTC and in August 2015, PEP announced it was selling WTC to Wanda, a Chinese sports conglomerate, for $650

Table 8.4   Fraction of PE Portfolio Targeted at Various Types of Exits

	Mean	Median	Low AUM	High AUM	Low IRR	High IRR	Old	Young	Local	Global
IPO	18.8	11.7	10.9	26.4	23.7	18.9	20.6	17.2	12.1	27.7
Strategic sale	51.0	50.0	57.3	44.8	46.3	51.4	44.2	56.7	57.5	42.3
Financial sale	29.5	30.0	31.8	27.3	29.6	28.1	33.6	26.0	30.4	28.3
Other	0.7	0.0	0.0	1.5	0.5	1.6	1.6	0.0	0.0	1.7
Number of responses	63	63	31	32	22	23	29	34	36	27

Source: Gompers, Kaplan and Muhkarlyamov (2016)

million including the assumption of debt. The deal represented a more than four times return for PEP over a seven-year holding period.

Factors influencing private equity exits

GKM (2016) provides some insights into what PE managers target and consider when setting an exit strategy. Table 8.4 indicates that PE investors expect to exit roughly one-half of their deals through a sale to a strategic buyer, i.e., to an operating company in a similar or related industry. In almost 30% of deals, they expect to sell to a financial buyer, i.e., to another private equity investor. In fewer than 20% of deals do PE investors expect to exit through an IPO. These percentages are consistent with, in fact almost identical to, the exit results reported in Kaplan and Stromberg (2009)[19] who report that 53% of deals with known exits are to strategic buyers, 30% are to financial buyers and 17% are through IPOs.

Not surprisingly, there is a significant difference between larger and smaller PE investors. Larger PE investors expect to exit through an IPO more than 26% of the time, while smaller PE investors expect to do so less than 11% of the time. For the largest deals, it is less likely that there is a strategic buyer large enough to sell to.

Table 8.5 presents the ranking of factors that PE investors consider in deciding when to exit. Achieving the expected operational plan and capital market conditions are the most important and are ranked roughly equally. They are important for more than 90% of the PE investors. As with capital structure decisions, this suggests that PE investors put roughly equal weight on fundamentals and on market timing.

Management's opinion, competitive considerations and hitting a return target are the next most important considerations and are ranked roughly equally. They are considered by more than 75% of the PE investors. Considering management's opinion is consistent with a cooperative/advisory relationship between PE investors and management. The requirement to hit a return target is potentially suggestive of an agency problem between the PE investors and their limited partners. (See Tables 8.6 to 8.11 and Figure 8.2.)

Table 8.5 Ranking of Factors That Affect Exit Timing

	Mean	Median	Low AUM	High AUM	Low IRR	High IRR	Old	Young	Local	Global
Achieve operational plan set out to achieve	5.5	6.0	5.4	5.5	5.8	5.3	5.3	5.6	5.5	5.4
Capital market conditions	5.3	5.5	5.4	5.2	5.3	5.3	5.4	5.2	5.0	5.7
Competitive considerations	3.5	4.0	3.5	3.5	3.2	3.1	3.4	3.5	3.9	2.9
Hit IRR or RCI target	4.0	4.0	3.9	4.2	4.2	4.6	3.8	4.3	3.9	4.3
LPs pressure to return capital	1.8	1.5	1.5	2.0	1.9	1.8	1.4	2.1	1.6	1.9
Management's opinion	3.7	4.0	3.4	4.1	3.8	3.7	4.3	3.2	3.8	3.7
Other	0.7	0.0	0.7	0.7	0.7	0.7	0.6	0.7	0.5	0.9
Number of responses	64	64	32	32	23	23	30	34	37	27

Source: Gompers, Kaplan and Muhkarlyamov (2016)

Table 8.6 PE Buyout Capital-Backed Exits

	No. of Exits	Exit Value (USD bn)	Average Exit Size (USD mn)
2009	683	113.4	446.4
2010	1 317	265.1	425.6
2011	1 633	365.6	523
2012	1 759	307.5	438
2013	1 928	313.2	401
2014	2 202	512	551.8
2015	2 371	452.2	480.6
2016	2 351	406.2	494.1
2017	2 487	417.1	489.6
2018	2 586	407.7	462.2
2019	2 104	447	703.9
Overall	21 421	4 007	187.1

Source: Preqin

Table 8.7 Private Equity IPOs

Year	No. of Exits	Exit Value (USD bn)	Average Exit Size (USD mn)
2009	114	31.6	400.1
2010	213	58.4	345.6
2011	227	99.6	553.6
2012	233	64.5	379.3
2013	327	94.2	395.7
2014	361	120.2	424.7
2015	367	118.4	438.6
2016	293	78.1	371.7
2017	377	136.5	464.2
2018	253	76.8	374.6
2019	198	139.4	805.8
Overall	2 963	1 017.6	343.4

Source: Preqin

Table 8.8   Strategic Sales

Year	No. of Exits	Exit Value (USD bn)	Average Exit Size (USD mn)
2009	68	18.7	813.3
2010	103	3.3	300.2
2011	146	22.5	1 021.5
2012	177	16.4	746.8
2013	181	15.5	535.5
2014	243	21.5	551.7
2015	236	43.1	1 268.8
2016	304	23	589.3
2017	327	28.6	818.3
2018	430	23.1	642.7
2019	316	79.2	2 083.5
Overall	2 531	295	116.6

Source: Preqin

Table 8.9   Financial Sales

Year	No. of Exits	Exit Value (USD bn)	Average Exit Size (USD mn)
2009	155	16.1	341.6
2010	377	92.7	597.8
2011	513	101.6	518.2
2012	570	105.5	546.8
2013	559	101.6	493.2
2014	704	125.3	519.8
2015	785	111.2	439.5
2016	802	120.1	517.6
2017	810	124.3	594.9
2018	868	149.5	622.8
Overall	6 898	1 176.7	170.6

Source: Preqin

Table 8.10 Management Purchases

Year	No. of Exits	Exit Value (USD bn)	Average Exit Size (USD mn)
2009	34	0.1	88.1
2010	37	0.4	73.6
2011	54	1.7	113.4
2012	71	3.1	195.4
2013	74	2.2	114.2
2014	72	5.8	278.5
2015	73	1.7	90.5
2016	70	2.3	188.7
2017	53	1.4	232.5
2018	66	4	232.8
2019	57	5.6	376.3
Overall	661	28.4	42.9

Source: Preqin

Table 8.11 Trade Sales

Year	No. of Exits	Exit Value (USD bn)	Average Exit Size (USD mn)
2009	363	67.6	493.7
2010	685	140.7	406.8
2011	859	245	628.2
2012	927	173.9	436.9
2013	1 011	172.6	426.3
2014	1 122	345.5	672.2
2015	1 190	292.4	572.3
2016	1 136	265.7	593
2017	1 135	229	562.6
2018	1 201	243.9	502.9
2019	976	281.6	818.5
Overall	10 605	2458	231.8

Source: Preqin

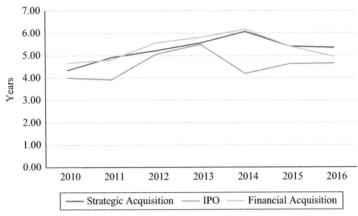

Source: Preqin

Figure 8.2 Median Hold-Times by Exit Type

Statistics on private equity exits

Tables 8.12 and 8.13 present pre-GFC data while Tables 8.16 and 8.17 present more recent data on private equity exits. Contrary to criticism of the private equity industry of flipping, i.e., exiting soon after the LBO occurs, the upper panel of Table 8.12 shows that PE firms held their investments for extended periods of time. For leveraged buyouts between 1970 and 2007 with an exit observed by the end of 2007, the PE firm holds its investment for an average of 49 months. Moreover, only 2.7% of LBOs are exited within 12 months of the LBO and less than 40% are exited within five years.

The lower panel of Table 8.12 shows that exits of private equity investments take the form of IPOs, strategic sales and financial sales. Among investments that had an exit by the end of 2007, 13% took the form of an IPO, 39% were strategic sales and 24% were sales to financial buyers. Interestingly, although LBOs result in significant increases in debt levels, confirmed bankruptcies represent only 6% of exits.

Just as exits vary over time, they also vary somewhat by geographies. Table 8.13 shows that relative to the US and Canada, exits in the UK and Europe are less likely to occur via IPO and more likely to occur via a

Table 8.12 Statistics on Private Equity Exits by Year of Buyout

	Total	1970-84	1985-89	1990-94	1995-99	2000-2	2003-5	2006-7
Time to Exit								
Mean (months)	49	87	80	61	54	43	24	9
Median (months)	42	63	72	52	50	43	24	10
Exit with 12 months	2.7%	1.6%	2.0%	3.9%	3.1%	2.5%	2.7%	2.0%
Exit with 24 months	10.7%	13.5%	11.3%	13.8%	12.4%	7.5%	11.0%	
Exit with 60 months	38.7%	46.0%	39.2%	52.1%	39.2%	33.3%		
Type of Exit								
IPO	13%	28%	25%	22%	11%	8%	10%	1%
Strategic sale	39%	32%	34%	38%	39%	39%	41%	38%
Financial sale	24%	6%	13%	17%	24%	30%	30%	22%
Sale to LBO-backed firm	5%	2%	3%	3%	5%	5%	6%	14%
Bankruptcy	6%	7%	6%	5%	8%	6%	4%	3%
Other/unknown	13%	25%	19%	15%	13%	12%	9%	22%

Source: Per Stromberg, 2008, The New Demography of Private Equity, *Globalization of Alternative Investment Working Papers Volume 1, The Global Economic Impact of Private Equity Report 2008*, World Economic Forum, Geneva

Table 8.13   Statistics on Private Equity Exits by Geography (1970–2002)

	US and Canada	UK	Europe	Rest of the World
IPO	15%	11%	10%	19%
Strategic sale	38%	42%	36%	42%
Financial sale	20%	22%	34%	17%
Sale to LBO-backed firm	6%	3%	3%	2%
Bankruptcy	9%	8%	3%	2%
Other/unknown	12%	14%	14%	18%

Source: Per Stromberg, 2008, The New Demography of Private Equity, *Globalization of Alternative Investment Working Papers Volume 1, The Global Economic Impact of Private Equity Report 2008*, World Economic Forum, Geneva

Table 8.14   Median PE-Backed Exit Multiples by Type

	Strategic Sale	IPO	Financial Sale
2010	7.36	7.35	8.62
2011	8.08	6.61	8.04
2012	7.89	5.82	8.37
2013	6.50	6.96	9.79
2014	8.53	7.25	8.09
2015	8.67	7.83	8.19
2016	9.17	7.74	9.43

Source: Pitchbook

Table 8.15   PE-Backed IPOs Hitting Range

	Above Range	Within Range	Below Range
2010	6.15%	64.62%	29.23%
2011	22.73%	54.55%	22.73%
2012	4.55%	65.91%	29.55%
2013	17.86%	63.10%	19.05%
2014	3.51%	72.81%	23.68%
2015	9.23%	72.31%	18.46%
2016	3.85%	76.92%	19.23%

Source: Pitchbook

Table 8.16 US Private Equity Exits

	Number of Transactions				Total Exit Value of Transactions			
	Strategic Sale	IPO	Financial Sale	Total	Strategic Sale	IPO	Financial Sale	Total
2006	389	71	309	769	81.51	40.49	67.92	189.92
2007	505	60	376	941	115.10	40.53	97.44	253.07
2008	388	16	229	633	78.28	5.79	34.71	118.78
2009	273	30	138	441	48.93	31.28	14.64	94.85
2010	470	48	328	846	107.16	30.09	68.34	205.60
2011	517	41	362	920	110.10	77.07	61.34	248.51
2012	594	43	492	1129	148.78	28.95	109.93	287.66
2013	548	68	444	1060	125.75	105.23	96.93	327.91
2014	681	69	575	1325	173.73	85.94	157.52	417.19
2015	702	45	616	1363	240.68	44.83	130.82	416.32
2016	669	39	565	1273	190.55	35.05	142.55	368.15
2017	636	48	623	1307	195.87	39.05	173.63	408.54
2018	571	46	623	1240	215.78	47.26	179.00	442.04
2019	358	23	523	904	111.33	33.16	146.62	291.11
	51%	4%	44%		48%	16%	36%	

Source: Pitchbook

Table 8.17 Europe: PE Exit Activity

	Exit Value (€bn)	No. of Exits Closed	Total Value of Transactions by Type		
			Strategic Sale	IPO	Financial Sale
2008	€116.11	710	€49.32	€8.83	€57.96
2009	43.84	513	€28.72	€0.37	€14.75
2010	139.46	737	€42.24	€51.46	€45.76
2011	205.15	971	€93.47	€48.42	€63.26
2012	136.27	863	€71.95	€10.84	€53.48
2013	191.10	1064	€72.52	€43.72	€74.86
2014	250.25	1172	€110.05	€44.65	€95.55
2015	299.00	1385	€133.31	€42.76	€122.93
2016	261.42	1262	€137.71	€25.10	€98.61
2017	309.42	1327	€136.06	€34.17	€139.18
2018	259.79	1182	€109.56	€23.17	€127.06
2019	€170.67	798	€73.57	€20.35	€76.74
			44%	15%	41%

Source: Pitchbook

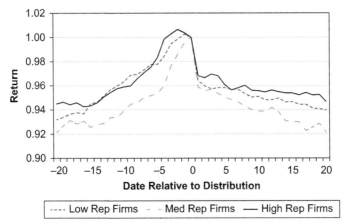

Source: T. Dore, P.A. Gompers and A. Metrick, 2012, Reputation and Contractual Flexibility: Evidence from Venture Capital Distribution Pricing Policies, Harvard Business School Working Paper

Figure 8.3 Return around Distribution Date, by PE Firm Reputation

strategic or financial sale. Interestingly, LBOs in the rest of the world are more likely to have exits via IPO. (See also Tables 8.14 and 8.15.)

Tables 8.16 and 8.17 look at the three primary forms of exit from 2006 to 2019 for US and European deals. In the US, the number of exits is dominated by strategic sales and sales to financial buyers, at 52% and 44% of deals. Strategic sales represent 48% of total value while sales to financial buyers represent 36%. Only 5% of the deals exited by IPO, but those deals accounted for 16% of exit value. In Europe, the percentages for value are very similar with 44% by strategic sale, 41% by financial buyers and 15% by IPO. (See Figure 8.3.)

Notes

1   General partners generally have the option to extend the fund for an additional three years with the consent of the limited partners. In practice, the median fund life is 15 years.
2   See Jay R. Ritter, IPO Statistics, https://site.warrington.ufl.edu/ritter/files/IPO-Statistics.pdf.
3   Joseph Bartlett, 1995, *Equity Finance: Venture Capital, Buyout, Restructurings, and Reorganizations* (John Wiley: New York).
4   It is important to note that the underwriter can release any of the securities subject to the lockup agreements at any time without notice. Alon Brav and Paul A. Gompers, 2003, The Role of Lockups in Initial Public Offerings, *Review of Financial Studies* 16, 1–29 find that early release was used in approximately 16% of the IPOs in their sample.
5   Alon Brav and Paul A. Gompers, 2003, The Role of Lockups in Initial Public Offerings, *Review of Financial Studies* 16, 1–29; Laura Casares Field and Gordon Hanka, 2001, The Expiration of IPO Share Lockups, *Journal of Finance* 56, 471–500.
6   Paul A. Gompers and Josh Lerner, 2002, Venture Capital Distributions: Short-Run and Long-Run Reactions, *Journal of Finance* 53, 2161–83.
7   Distributions are typically declared after the market closes. The recording distribution price is typically the closing price on the distribution day. Actual receipt of certificates and the ability to sell the shares may take several days.
8   The price quoted in cases where the PE firm transfers the shares is dictated by the agreement between the general partners and limited partners of the fund. It is often the closing price on the day that the shares are transferred, although an average closing price of the previous one or two weeks is also common. See Timothy E. Dore, Paul Gompers and Andrew Metrick, 2011, Reputation and Contractual Flexibility: Evidence from Venture Capital Distribution Pricing Policies, Harvard Business School Working Paper.

9   Paul A. Gompers and Josh Lerner, 2002, Venture Capital Distributions: Short-Run and Long-Run Reactions, *Journal of Finance* 53, 2161–83.
10 Jay Ritter, 1988, Initial Public Offerings, *Journal of Applied Corporate Finance* 1, 37–45.
11 See Paul Gompers and Natee Amornsiripanitch, 2015, Globant: Going Public, Harvard Business School Case 9-215-021.
12 Minmo Gahng, Jay R. Ritter and Donghang Zhang, July 2021 SPACs, University of Florida Working Paper.
13 Michael D Klausner and Michael Ohlrogge, 2020, A Sober Look at SPACs, *SSRN Electronic Journal*.
14 Michael D Klausner and Michael Ohlrogge, 2020, A Sober Look at SPACs, *SSRN Electronic Journal*.
15 Michael D Klausner and Michael Ohlrogge, 2020, A Sober Look at SPACs, *SSRN Electronic Journal*.
16 Minmo Gahng, Jay Ritter and Donghang Zhang, 2021, SPACs, University of Florida Working Paper.
17 This discussion is based largely on Paul Gompers, Shai Bernstein, Matt Wozny and Alex Gachanja, 2021, Luminar and the Rise of SPACs, Harvard Business School Case Number 221-099.
18 Unleveraged dividend recaps are also possible, where the firm issues a special dividend using cash on hand. However, due to the fact that only cash on hand is paid out, unleveraged dividend recaps are much smaller than leveraged dividend recaps.
19 Steven N. Kaplan and Per Stromberg, 2009, Leveraged Buyouts and Private Equity, *Journal of Economic Perspectives* 23, 121–46.

9 Raising a private equity fund

In this chapter, we examine the process by which private equity firms raise funds for investing. The vast majority of PE funds are organized as limited partnerships. The specific compensation and restrictions governed by these agreements are critical for the alignment of incentives between PE managers and their investors. This chapter starts by looking at the organization history within private equity, then examines issues related to fund governance.

A brief history of private equity investing[1]

The ancestors of modern private equity firms in the US developed in the late nineteenth and early twentieth centuries. Wealthy families which had made their fortunes during the early days of the Industrial Revolution began to look for ways to invest in private, potentially high-return undertakings. The earliest investors in growth-oriented private firms were wealthy family offices. This includes famous New York families like the Vanderbilts, Whitneys, Morgans and Rockefellers who provided private capital to grow companies in the railroad, steel, oil and banking industries. The market for private equity remained largely unorganized and fragmented throughout the late nineteenth and early twentieth centuries. The first impetus to organize investing into professional organizations came from these same wealthy Americans. In the 1930s and 1940s, members of the Rockefeller, Bessemer and Whitney families hired professional managers to seek out investment in promising private growth companies.

The earliest private equity firms were organized in the Northeast, primarily in Boston and New York. The earliest firms to invest capital into private firms were focused on early-stage, venture capital investments. The first modern venture capital firm was formed in 1946, when MIT president Karl Compton, Massachusetts Investors Trust chairman Merrill Griswold, Federal Reserve Bank of Boston president Ralph Flanders and Harvard Business School professor General Georges F. Doriot started American Research and Development (ARD). ARD and other early venture capital funds were typically structured as closed-end funds. Closed-end funds raised capital by selling shares to public investors, then used that capital to finance private companies. The closed-end structure proved problematic because raising additional capital for investments was always beholden to the fund's stock price. Once a closed-end fund had invested all the capital it had raised, it needed to issue new shares in a secondary offering in order to continue to have capital to invest. If the fund's share price was severely depressed, raising additional capital was very expensive or impossible. For much of its public existence, ARD's stock price was severely depressed and raising follow-on capital proved difficult.

In the late 1950s, a new fund structure arose which facilitated both the alignment of incentives and the ability to raise fund-specific dedicated capital, the limited partnership. The first venture capital limited partnership, Draper, Gaither and Anderson, was formed in 1958. Unlike closed-end funds, partnerships were exempt from securities regulations, including the exacting disclosure requirements of the Investment Company Act of 1940. The set of the investors from which the funds could raise capital, however, was much more restricted. The interests in a given partnership could only be held by a limited number of institutions and high net-worth individual investors.

The Draper partnership and its imitators followed the template of other limited partnerships common at the time: for example, those that had been formed to develop real-estate projects and explore oil fields. In such cases, the partnerships had a predetermined, finite life (usually 10 years, though extensions were often allowed). Thus, unlike closed-end funds, which often had indefinite lives, the partnerships were required to return the capital to investors within a set period. From the days of the first limited partnerships, the general partners of the fund could choose to return capital to their limited partners either by liquidating their ownership stake and returning cash or by distributing pro-rata shares of portfolio companies to investors.

The increase in institutional money had a dramatic impact on the process of private equity investing which facilitated the rise of the limited partnership as the dominant organizational form. A seminal event in the emergence of the private equity industry was the formation of Kohlberg Kravis and Roberts and Co. (KKR) in 1976 by three former Bear Stearns investment bankers. Most of KKR's early investments were financed by deal-specific limited partnerships including their first investment, a $25.6 million buyout of A.J. Industries, Inc.[2] Many of the early private equity firms focused on leveraged buyouts of both public and private companies. These leveraged buyout funds were often structured on a deal-by-deal basis.

Over time, limited partnerships moved to a co-mingled fund structure in which multiple investments would be pooled within a single limited partnership. Since 1980, most of the capital committed to private equity has been raised through limited partnerships. Most PE organizations raise partnerships (funds) every two to five years. The typical PE fund makes between 10 and 20 investments over its lifespan. In a private equity limited partnership, the PE managers are general partners and control the fund's activities. The investors, typically pension funds, insurance companies, endowments, family offices and sovereign wealth funds, serve as limited partners. Investors can monitor the fund's progress, but cannot become involved in the fund's day-to-day management if they are to retain limited liability. Compensation is, therefore, the most important contractual mechanism for aligning the incentives of the PE managers and their investors. We explore the nature of that compensation below.

The limited partnership agreement explicitly specifies the terms that govern the PE managers' compensation over the entire 10- to 13-year life of the fund. A model limited partnership term sheet published by the Institutional Limited Partners' Association (ILPA) can be found here: https://ilpa.org/wp-content/uploads/2020/07/ILPA-Model-LPA-Term-Sheet-WOF-Version.pdf. It is rare that these terms are renegotiated. The specified compensation has a simple form: the PE managers typically receive an annual fixed fee, usually between 1% and 2%, based on committed capital during the investment period and invested capital thereafter, plus variable compensation that is a specified fraction of the fund's profits (usually 20%). The simplicity and specificity of the contracts provide a readily assessable benchmark for the alignment of incentives.

Limited partnerships terms and conditions

In addition to the compensation structure described below, additional controls are often enumerated in the limited partnership. Because the investors are generally restricted from active decision making in day-to-day activities of the fund, these covenants serve to protect investors by restricting various activities or requiring others. The model term sheet from the ILPA provides a template, but many variants of each covenant are found in the partnership agreements. Generally speaking, the more worried limited partners are about potential conflicts, the more restrictive the agreement is. Prior research has shown that more restrictions are typically placed on newer PE firms and PE firms that tend to make more opaque investments.[3] LPs are concerned that relatively new GPs might seek to exploit the lack of active oversight. Many of these restrictions can be grouped into broad buckets.

The first set of restrictions in the ILPA's term sheet focuses on the fund's investment policy. The fund's broad investment strategy is laid out in the section on Investment Policy. More specific fund investment restrictions are then enumerated under the section Investment Restrictions. A common theme among the investment restrictions is to limit increasing volatility in the portfolio. To control for this potential, one common restriction is restricting the amount of investment in any one portfolio company. These provisions are intended to ensure a reasonably diversified portfolio. The general partners typically do not receive a share of profits until the limited partners have received the return of their investment. The PE managers' share of profits can be thought of as a call option: the general partners may gain disproportionately from increasing volatility of the portfolio at the expense of diversification. Putting all the investments in a small number of companies (or just one) would increase the overall riskiness of the portfolio and would serve to primarily benefit the general partner. This is one reason that private equity funds moved away from the single investment limited partnership model of early LBO funds towards a diversified fund approach. These limitations are frequently expressed as a maximum percentage of capital invested in the fund (committed capital) that can be invested in any one firm.

Other restrictions focus on other elements that lower the concentration of risk in the portfolio. As the model term sheet shows, this includes limitations on the amount invested in any one industry or in any one region. Similarly, these investment restrictions will also include classes of investments that the LP wants to avoid, including hostile tender offers or investments in other PE funds that charge a carried interest as well.

Finally, an increasing emphasis among LPs is to enforce certain ESG investment standards. A recent analysis of 8810 PE firms found that 703 are signatories to the PRI ESG investment policies. These 703 represent roughly $2.15 trillion in assets.[4] While it is too soon to know what the impact of the move towards ESG investing is, it is clear that many LPs look for transparency on the issue.

Generally speaking, as outlined in the ILPA term sheet, exceptions to these restrictions are possible with the approval of the Advisory Committee. Advisory Committees are common for PE funds and are generally made up of the largest investors in the fund. Exceptions to investment limits, extensions to the fund life, etc., typically require a formal approval of the committee.

A second covenant class limits the use of debt at the fund level (not the company level). As option holders, general partners may be tempted to increase the variance of their portfolio's returns by leveraging the fund. As discussed above, increasing the riskiness of the portfolio would increase the value of their call option at investors' expense. Partnership agreements often limit the ability of PE managers to borrow funds themselves or to guarantee the debt of their portfolio companies (which might be seen as equivalent to direct borrowing). Partnership agreements may limit debt to a set percentage of committed capital or assets, and, as the model term sheet illustrates, also restrict the maturity of the debt to ensure that all borrowing is short-term.[5]

An additional class of covenants relates to reinvestment of profits. For several reasons, PE managers may reinvest capital gains rather than distributing the profits to the limited partners. First, many partnerships receive fees on the basis of either the value of assets under management or adjusted committed capital (capital less any distributions). Distributing profits will reduce these fees. Second, reinvested capital gains may yield further profits for the general (as well as the limited) partners.[6] The reinvestment of profits may require approval of the advisory board or the limited partners. Alternatively, such reinvestment may be prohibited after a certain date, or after a certain percent of the committed capital is invested.

A number of classes of restrictions curb the activities of the general partners that may conflict with fund activity or seek to suspend the fund if key members of the GP depart. The first of these limits the ability of the general partners to invest personal funds in firms that fall within the scope of the fund's investment mandate. These restrictions are generally under the Exclusivity section of the LP agreement. If general partners invest in selected firms, they may devote excessive time to these firms and may not terminate funding if the firms encounter difficulties. Similarly, they may choose to invest their own funds in the most promising opportunities. In addition, the PE managers may be required to seek permission from the advisory board or limited partners. An alternative approach employed in some agreements is to require the PE managers to invest a set dollar amount or percentage in every investment made by the fund.

A second restriction addresses the reverse problem: the sale of partnership interests by general partners. Rather than seeking to increase their personal exposure to selected investments, general partners may sell their share of the fund's profits to other investors. While the general partnership interests are not totally comparable with the limited partners' stakes (for instance, the general partners will typically only receive distributions after the return of the limited partners' capital), these may still be attractive investments. Limited partners may worry that such a sale will reduce the general partners' incentives to monitor their investments. Partnership agreements may prohibit the sale of general partnership interests outright, or else require that these sales be approved by a majority (or super-majority) of the limited partners.

A third area for restrictions on the general partners is fundraising. The raising of an additional fund will raise the management fees that general partners receive and may reduce the attention that PE managers pay to existing funds. Partnership agreements may prohibit fundraising by general partners until a set percentage of the portfolio has been invested or until a given date. Alternatively, fundraising may be restricted to a fund of certain size or focus. For instance, the private equity organization may be allowed to raise a buyout fund, which would presumably be managed by other general partners.

Some partnership agreements restrict general partners' outside activities. Because outside activities are likely to reduce the attention paid to investments, PE managers may be required to spend "substantially all" (or some other fraction) of their time managing the investments of the partnership. Alternatively, the general partners' involvement in businesses, not in the private equity fund's portfolio, may be restricted. These limitations are often confined to the first years of the partnership, or until a set percent of the fund's capital is invested, when the need for attention by the general partners is presumed to be the largest.

An additional area of concern relates to concerns that LPs have about who manages the investments within the PE fund. Generally, the investment team's track record is marketed to investors and certain key individuals are considered to be particularly important. These important individuals are generally governed by a Key Person clause which can throw a fund into suspension if a certain number of these Key People leave the firm. Similarly, LPs may be concerned about the addition of new members to the GP. By hiring less experienced general partners, PE managers may reduce the burden on themselves. The quality of the oversight provided, however, is likely to be lower. As a result, many funds require that the addition of new general partners be approved by either the advisory board or a set percentage of the limited partners.

While many issues involving the behavior of the general partners are addressed through partnership agreements, several others typically are not. One area that is almost never discussed in the sample is the vesting schedule of general partnership interests. If general partners leave a private equity organization early in the life of the fund, they may forfeit all or some of their share of the profits. If PE managers do not receive their entire partnership interest immediately, they are less likely to leave soon after the fund is formed. A second issue is the division of profits among the general partners. In some funds, most profits accrue to the senior general partners, even if the younger partners provide the bulk of the day-to-day management, deal sourcing and analysis and oversight. While these issues are addressed in agreements between the general partners, they are rarely discussed in the contract between the general and limited partners.

Compensation in private equity funds

Management fees

Compensation in private equity provides a way to align the incentives. Considerable research and common sense have argued that value is

reduced or destroyed when corporate decision makers have little economic stake in the outcome of the companies they manage. Private
equity has been seen as an organizational form that entails high-powered
incentives for PE managers to maximize returns. While the advent of
mega-funds in the PE industry has renewed debate about whether PE
managers truly care about maximizing returns, it is still the case that
total compensation is highly dependent upon investment performance.

PE limited partnerships typically explicitly define compensation in two
specific components. The first component is a fixed management fee
which is outlined in the model term sheet under the section entitled
"Management Fee." The fee is typically a percentage of capital commitments made by the limited partners. While LBO funds in the 1980s often
had fees based upon NAV, today nearly 97% of funds have fees that are
based upon total commitments.[7] Thus, even though GPs draw capital
down over a number of years (typically called "paid in capital"), LPs pay
on a fixed fee based upon the total amount that they will pay in over
the life of the fund. Early PE funds looked to the precedent set by venture capital limited partnerships which typically charged 2.5% on committed capital.[8] While fixed fees in PE funds tend to be slightly lower, a
paper looking at fees in the 2000s found that 11 of 144 funds charged
greater than 2%, 59 charged exactly 2% and 74 of 144 charged less than
2%.[9] More recently, Figure 9.1 shows that management fees in buyout
funds tend to be lower than fees in growth funds; 47.5% of funds have
fees between 1.76% and 2%. Another 45.8% have fees between 1.26% and
1.5%. Over half of growth equity PE funds have fees between 1.51% and
1.75% with 23.6% having fees higher than 1.76%.

These fees typically decrease as the fund passes its investment period.
As discussed earlier, PE funds typically have a 10-year life. Investments
are made in the first two to five years. There are a variety of ways that
fees decline over the remaining life of the fund. Sometimes, there are
explicit step downs at various fund anniversaries. The ILPA model term
sheet defines fee reductions in terms of two benchmarks. First, once the
fund fully invests its capital in underlying companies, the fee is reduced
to a given percentage of the capital that has been committed by LPs less
the cost basis of the investments in the funds that have been liquidated.
Similarly, if the PE firm raises a new fund, the fee is also reduced accordingly. These provisions are meant to prevent PE investors from layering
fees from multiple funds in such a way that the GP is certain to make

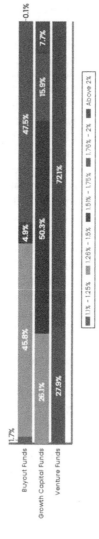

Source: MJ Hudson Private Equity Fund Terms 2019/2020

Figure 9.1   Distribution of Management Fees for Private Equity Funds in 2019

meaningful income without having to generate attractive returns for investors.

Because there are many ways in which management fees are structured, it is interesting to understand how large they are in practice. To do this, research often computes the net present value (at the time of the partnership's closing) of the fixed fees that are specified in the contractual agreement.[10] To gauge how important these management fees are, they are typically expressed as a percent of the committed capital. Because the management fees are relatively certain, it is typical to use a relatively low discount rate (on the order of 5–10%) to calculate the fee NPV.

The research on PE compensation has shown that the NPV of the base compensation (as a percentage of committed capital) is generally lower for older and larger PE firms when expressed as a percentage of committed capital. Although this ratio depends upon how fees change over the life of the fund, the ratio of the NPV of management fees per $100 of committed capital generally falls between $10 and $11 over the life of the fund.[11] Because there are economies of scale in PE investing (i.e., funds are able to grow the amount of capital per partner by doing larger investments), the range of management fees per partner per $100 of committed capital ranges averages $18.47, but ranges from a lower quartile of $6.85 to an upper quartile of $24.33. With an average of six partners and an average fund size of $1238 million, a typical fund generates between $13 million and $48 million in management fee per partner.[12]

Transaction and monitoring fees can also be a source of considerable value to PE investors. Metrick and Yasuda (2010) estimated these fees to be roughly $4 per $100 of committed capital over the life of a fund. More recently, Phalippou et al. (2018) estimate that these fees have been roughly 6% of the total equity invested by PE funds and represent nearly 3.6% of the EBITDA of the underlying portfolio companies.[13] While up to 70% of the fees are offset by reductions in management fees, these portfolio company fees are still an important form of compensation to GPs.

Carried interest

A second source of compensation for PE investors is the carried interest, i.e., the percentage of profits that they are paid. How much and when the profits are paid is defined under the section entitled "Distributions/

Waterfall." Distributions are paid to investors upon the realization of exits. These distributions can be in cash (if the investments are sold or public stock is liquidated) or they can be publicly traded shares. Research on PE compensation demonstrates that virtually all PE funds pay a carried interest of 20%.[14]

There are two different methods to determine the timing of the payout of the carried interest. They are known as return of capital (or European waterfall) and deal-by-deal (or American waterfall). In the European waterfall, PE investors do not receive carry until the LPs have received distributions exceeding the fund's total invested capital. In the American waterfall, PE investors receive carry on any distribution as long as the value of the fund's realized portfolio is sufficiently greater than the capital invested in realized deals. As their names suggest and Figure 9.2 shows, approximately 90% of European PE funds utilized a European waterfall while 60% and 80% of North American-based PE funds utilize an American waterfall.[15]

Most private equity funds also have a hurdle rate or preferred return that further affects the payment of carry. (See "Preferred Return" section of the ILPA model term sheet.) As Figure 9.3 shows, the most common hurdle rate is 8%, although some debt-focused PE funds have a hurdle rate of 6% and some funds, 22.6% in 2019, do not have a hurdle rate.

In a European waterfall, the carry is paid as long as the net return or IRR to the LPs on the entire fund exceeds the hurdle rate. The carry is not 20% of the profits above the hurdle rate. For example, if after paying the carry equal to 20% of the profits, the LPs have a net IRR greater than 8%, then the PE investors receive the entire carry of 20% of the profits. In an American waterfall, the PE investors receive 20% of the profits on each exited deal as long as the IRR to the LPs for all deals exited to that point exceeds 8% after the carry is paid.

From a GP's perspective, an American waterfall is preferred because the GP receives the carry sooner. Hence, from a time value of money perspective, it is more valuable. The American waterfall, however, can lead to circumstances in which GPs receive a greater portion of the fund's profits than they are ultimately entitled to receive. This occurs when early realizations are very successful, but later realizations perform poorly. The General Partner Clawback section of the model term sheet outlines the

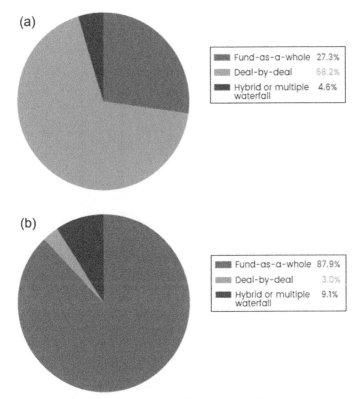

(a)

▨	Fund-as-a-whole	27.3%
▨	Deal-by-deal	68.2%
▨	Hybrid or multiple waterfall	4.6%

(b)

▨	Fund-as-a-whole	87.9%
▨	Deal-by-deal	3.0%
▨	Hybrid or multiple waterfall	9.1%

Source: MJ Hudson Private Equity Fund Terms 2019/2020

Figure 9.2 Waterfall Structure for 2019 PE Funds. (a) US-Managed Funds, (b) European-Managed Funds

manner in which total distributions are evaluated at the end of the fund in circumstances in which GPs have received a greater portion of the payout.

Figure 9.4 presents the distribution of the percentage of profits allocated to the general partners after any provision for the return of invested capital or of invested capital plus a preferred return. The carry ranges from 0.7% to 45%, but between 84.7% and 87.5% of the funds have a 20% share of the profits. The consistency of the percentage of profits is similar to compensation in a number of other professions (like real estate or various types of litigation) in which fees cluster on a particular percentage.

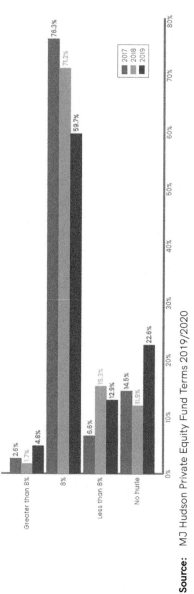

Source: MJ Hudson Private Equity Fund Terms 2019/2020

Figure 9.3   Hurdle Rate on Private Equity Funds 2017–19

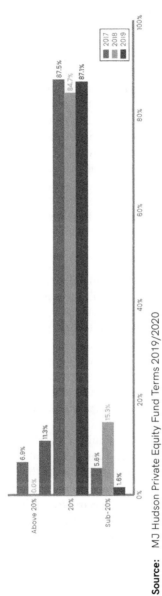

Source: MJ Hudson Private Equity Fund Terms 2019/2020

Figure 9.4   Carried Interest Percentage in Private Equity Funds Raised 2017–19

What we know about PE compensation

Research on compensation has often looked at the alignment of incentives between managers and investors. Many scholars and pundits have lamented the relatively weak incentives that corporate managers have to perform. Most of the research on PE fund compensation has generally highlighted the close alignment of incentives between LPs and GPs. Relative to the work that has been done on covenants and restrictions in PE limited partnerships, a significant amount of research has examined the role of compensation in PE limited partnerships as well as its evolution. Early work on PE compensation showed that young, smaller PE firms generally had higher management fees relative to older and larger firms.[16] Carried interest percentage was also highly concentrated at 20% with more than 80% of the partnerships allocating 20% of the profits to the GPs.

As discussed in Chapter 3, gross of fees as well as net of fees, PE firms have generated positive risk-adjusted returns. One question that naturally arises is whether higher performing managers increase their fees and, if they do, do they take greater compensation by increasing management fees, carried interest or some other aspect of compensation. In general, the time series pattern of PE compensation shows that total GP compensation rises when the fundraising environment is robust. When LP interest in investing in PE funds is high, some (or perhaps all) of the surplus is extracted by GPs by raising fees.[17] This result raises the question of what are net returns to LPs and how do those net returns vary with GP compensation. In the aggregate, funds that charge higher fees earn high gross investment returns such that, on a net return basis, there is no relationship between GP compensation and net returns.[18]

Another question is whether this result implies that there is little incentive to generate positive net returns for investors. If all of the value created by PE investors in portfolio companies is taken up by higher compensation, then perhaps the incentive alignment is not as high as one would hope. Another way to examine this issue is to assess other incentives that GPs have. Given that PE firms raise funds every three to five years, there is a powerful incentive to deliver attractive net returns to LPs. LPs care about what they receive and, hence, evaluate managers based upon what they are returned on a net of fee basis. The implicit incentive effects of generating positive net returns to LPs have been shown to be as significant as the carried interest percentage.[19] The limited lifetime of PE limited partnerships imposes powerful discipline on GPs to continually prove themselves.

Conclusion

This chapter has examined how PE managers raise capital. The PE limited partnership has evolved as the primary vehicle by which PE investors raise, invest and return money. The governance and compensation within private equity limited partnerships are critical for aligning incentives in an opaque investment class. Understanding the control levers that investors can utilize to prevent perverse behavior as well as the role that compensation plays are central to the themes discussed. The value-add activities that we discussed in earlier chapters (namely operational, governance and financial engineering) are directly related to the rise of the limited partnership as the dominant fund structure.

Notes

1   This section is largely based on Paul A. Gompers, 1994, A History of Venture Capital, *Journal of Business History* 23, 1–24.
2   Peter Lattman, 2009, KKR – a Q&A with Pioneers in M&A, *Wall Street Journal*.
3   Paul Gompers and Josh Lerner, 1996, The Use of Covenants: An Empirical Analysis of Venture Partnership Agreements, *Journal of Law and Economics* 39, 463–98.
4   Ken Pucker and Sakis Kotsantonis, 2020, Private Equity Makes ESG Promises. But Their Impact Is Often Superficial, *Institutional Investor*.
5   A related provision – found in virtually all partnership agreements – is that the limited partners will avoid unrelated business taxable income. Tax-exempt institutions must pay taxes on UBTI, which is defined as the gross income from any unrelated business that the institution regularly carries out.
6   Another reason why PE managers may wish to reinvest profits is that such investments are unlikely to be mature at the end of the fund's stated life. The presence of investments that are too immature to liquidate is a frequently invoked reason for extending the partnership's life beyond the typical contractual limit of 10 years. In these cases, the PE managers will continue to generate fees from the limited partners (though often on a reduced basis).
7   MJ Hudson Private Equity Fund Terms 2019/2020.

8   Paul Gompers and Josh Lerner, 1998, An Analysis of Compensation in Venture Capital Limited Partnerships, *Journal of Financial Economics* 51, 3–44.

9   Andrew Metrick and Ayako Yasuda, 2010, The Economics of Private Equity Funds, *Review of Financial Studies* 23, 2303–42.

10 Gompers and Lerner (1998) were the first authors to take an NPV approach to compare fixed fees. Subsequent research has generally tended to follow their methodology to compare management fees.

11 See Metrick and Yasuda (2010).

12 See Metrick and Yasuda (2010). Clearly, there is significant overhead and additional staff in PE firms. Hence, this level of management fee does not flow directly to partners.

13 Ludovic Phalippou, Christian Rauch and March Umber, 2018, Private Equity Portfolio Company Fees, *Journal of Financial Economics* 129, 559–85.

14 See Gompers and Lerner (1998), Metrick and Yasuda (2010) and D.T. Robinson and B.A. Sensoy, 2013, Do Private Equity Fund Managers Earn Their Fees? Compensation, Ownership, and Cash Flow Performance, *Review of Financial Studies* 26, 2760–97.

15 MJ Hudson Private Equity Fund Terms 2019/2020.

16 Gompers and Lerner (1998).

17 David T. Robinson and Berk A. Sensoy, 2013, Do Private Equity Fund Managers Earn Their Fees? Compensation, Ownership, and Cash Flow Performance, *Review of Financial Studies* 26, 2760–97.

18 David T. Robinson and Berk A. Sensoy, 2013, Do Private Equity Fund Managers Earn Their Fees? Compensation, Ownership, and Cash Flow Performance, *Review of Financial Studies* 26, 2760–97.

19 Ji-Woong Chung, Berk A. Sensoy, Léa Stern and Michael S. Weisbach, 2012, Pay for Performance from Future Fund Flows: The Case of Private Equity, *Review of Financial Studies* 25, 3259–330.

10   Managing the private equity firm

Private equity (PE) firms have a wide range of organizational structures and strategies. As discussed in prior chapters, PE firms have increasingly focused on how to improve the underlying performance of their portfolio companies through financial, governance and operational engineering. This emphasis is reflected in the staffing and compensation structures that PE firms employ. What does the team structure look like? What are their past experiences and skills? How are employees compensated? All of these factors are critically important for executing an investment strategy and aligning incentives.

In this chapter, we dive into how PE firms manage their business. We start by understanding staffing structures in PE firms. What are the various tiers of employees? What are their roles in the deal process? We then examine the background of PE professionals. We look at the resumes of PE professionals to understand who gets hired and promoted in PE firms. We also look at various models for recruiting talent in PE. These different models reflect the particular skill sets that are required to execute one or more of the levers of value creation. Finally, we provide a description of compensation structures and levels for PE professionals. The nature and level of compensation is an important tool for aligning the incentives of PE managers to create value for their investors.

Given the increasing size and competitiveness of the industry, private equity firms also have evolved their structures to account for the importance of specialization. PE firms often organize their staff around investment strategies. The most common approach is to organize around industry sectors, geographies and transaction types. These specializations are an important tool PE firms utilize to increase value and generate attractive returns.

Throughout this section, we will focus on seven private equity firms to illustrate how firms are organized and staffed. These seven PE firms represent a range of strategies and geographies. The strategies encompass all aspects of the private equity spectrum. From a size level, the firms range from large, mega-fund PE managers to middle-market and small PE firms. The firms also have distinct industry sectors in which they focus. The industry focus is related to how the firms staff and make decisions. Finally, the firms also have different strategies for how they intend to generate returns: proprietary deal sourcing/selection versus governance, operational or financial engineering. By examining these seven PE firms, one can get a better understanding of the relationship between a firm's capabilities, its staff and the execution of its strategy.

We examine two mega-fund PE firms, Bain Capital and KKR. While the exact definition can vary, typically, mega-funds are considered to be private equity vehicles which raise at least $5 billion. The firms generally manage over $20 billion in aggregate investment capital. Nearly a third of all capital raised and invested over the past decade has been managed by a small number of mega-fund PE managers.

We then profile three middle-market PE firms, Berkshire Partners, BC Partners and Vistria Capital. Firms that raise funds from several hundred million dollars up to $5 billion are typically considered to be middle market. Additionally, middle-market PE firms generally target transactions with enterprise values between $25 million and $1 billion. These firms can invest in buyouts of these middle-market companies or invest in growth equity situations.

Finally, we profile two small PE firms, Housatonic Partners and Alpine Investors. Smaller PE firms generally invest in small, owner-led companies. Deal sourcing and partnering with owner-managers are critical for these types of investors.

Private equity firm profiles

Bain Capital, founded in 1984, is a leading global private equity firm based in Boston. As of 2021, it had roughly $150 billion under management.[1] The primary focus of Bain Capital's private equity investment activity is sponsoring leveraged acquisitions and recapitalizations, including both growth capital and traditional buyouts across a variety of industries. In April 2021, Bain Capital raised $11.8 billion in commitments for their most recent private equity fund.

The founding of the firm can be traced to Bill Bain's, the then head of the consulting firm Bain & Company, offer to Mitt Romney to start a new company to invest in private equity. Romney, along with two other partners at Bain & Company, launched Bain Capital with no formal connection to the consulting firm in 1984. The founders leveraged their management consulting expertise and preserved the company's operational approach to managing. Through its consulting-based strategy, Bain Capital emphasizes people-intensive, data-driven diligence that focuses primarily on operational engineering. As we will see below, this is reflected in the large number of investment and operational staff who have prior consulting industry experience.

Bain Capital is organized around five industry verticals: consumer, financial and business services, healthcare, industrials and technology. The operations and investment professionals are typically associated with one of these industry segments based on their prior career experience.

KKR, the first or one of the first PE firms, was founded in 1976 by Jerome Kohlberg, Henry Kravis and George Roberts, former investment bankers at Bear Stearns. In 1984, KKR raised the first $1 billion PE fund.[2] KKR became a household name after its high-profile buyout of RJR-Nabisco in 1988 for an enterprise value of almost $30 billion, the largest PE deal up to that point in time. It would remain the large PE transaction in absolute value for more than 15 years and, even today, is by far the largest PE deal as a fraction of the value of the stock market. Today, it would be the equivalent of a $200+ billion deal.

KKR was also one of the first PE firms to expand geographically. In 1998, KKR opened its London Office, and in 2007 it opened offices in Hong Kong and Tokyo.[3] In an attempt to provide more services to its portfolio companies, KKR formed Capstone Consulting in 2000. Capstone is a wholly owned consulting firm that provides analysis and operational recommendations to portfolio companies. The Capstone team is engaged in the due diligence process and throughout the life of KKR's involvement in the portfolio company. Unlike Bain Capital, which integrates the consulting/operational team in the structure of the investment team, KKR employs their consulting team members through a separate firm.

Berkshire Partners, a Boston-based firm, is representative of a middle-market PE manager. The firm was founded in 1984 by Brad Bloom, Chris Clifford, Russ Epker, Carl Ferenbach and Richard Lubin when they raised $59 million for their first fund. The founders had worked together at Thomas H. Lee Partners, an early PE firm also formed in Boston, in 1974.

Berkshire Partners' stated investment strategy is to "partner with management teams who are building industry-leading companies with sustainable differentiation and have a track record of innovating."[4] This strategy is one focused on operational engineering as opposed to governance engineering and replacing management. The focus of Berkshire is typically growth equity investments as opposed to leveraged buyouts.[5] Berkshire has five industry verticals structured around business services and technology, communications, consumer, healthcare and industrials. The investment team is organized around these industry verticals. Fund II was raised in 1986 and had committed capital of $125 million. In the 1990s, Berkshire raised a series of funds from $168 million in 1992 for Fund III to $985 million in 1998 in Fund V. Fund size grew in the 2000s with their first billion-dollar fund, Fund VI at $1.7 billion in 2002. The largest fund that Berkshire Partners has raised to date was their 2016 Fund IX which had committed capital of $5.5 billion.

BC Partners is another upper middle-market firm, but one with its founding roots in Europe as opposed to North America. BC Partners was formed as a spinout of Barings Bank in 1996 as part of the restructuring which followed the bankruptcy of Barings. In 1996, BC Partners raised its first independent fund, a €450 million fund which they named BC Partners V. During the 2000s, fund size increased rapidly, with BC Partners VII being raised at €4.3 billion and BC Partners X at €10.4 billion. Their most recent fund, BC Partners XI, raised less, coming in at €4.9 billion.

BC Partners focuses on buyouts with a primary geographic concentration in Europe. The firm emphasizes deal sourcing and deal selection as important elements of its value creation strategy.[6] Among the value creation levers, BC Partners highlights governance engineering through "aligning with strong, incentivized management teams."[7]

Vistria Capital was founded with the formation of Fund I with $400 million in 2014 by Kip Kirkpatrick and Marty Nesbitt in Chicago with the intention of aligning the firm's investment strategy along two pillars: generating returns for investors as well as achieving a social return.[8] Increasingly, limited partners have become interested in measuring how their investment dollars are impacting society. Many limited partners have begun evaluating PE firms on the basis of their commitment to the environment, social and governance (ESG). Several organizations have begun the process of certifying investors as "ESG Compliant." This type of strategy is often labeled impact investing or double bottom line investing. Vistria is a relatively new PE firm that has tapped into this trend.

The firm lists its industry sectors as healthcare, education and financial services. In particular, it emphasizes how these sectors are likely to have "significant financial returns combined with positive social change for communities across America."[9] Vistria's two most recent funds have had more than $1 billion in committed capital. In January 2020, the firm closed Fund III with $1.1 billion and in June 2021 it raised Fund IV at $2.68 billion.

Alpine Investors is a middle-market private equity firm based in San Francisco with just over $7 billion of assets under management. The firm was founded in 2001 by Graham Weaver a year after graduating from Stanford Business School. Alpine targets companies with EBITDA between $1 and $50 million and enterprise values up to $500 million.[10]

The firm lists its areas of focus as software and services. The investment thesis of Alpine is to focus on management team quality with a heavy focus on recruiting and retaining top CEO talent. Hence, the focus of Alpine's value creation relies more on governance engineering than direct involvement in operational engineering. Like many PE firms in the latest cycle, their fund size has grown substantially recently. Alpine raised Fund I in 2001 with committed capital of $54 million. Fund II, raised in 2003, had $68 million in commitments. Three years later, Alpine III had committed capital of $125 million. In 2011, the firm raised $262 million in Fund IV. As recently as 2017, Alpine VI had only $532 million in commitments. Most recently, in September 2021 Alpine raised its eighth fund at $2.25 billion.

The final PE firm that we examine is Housatonic Partners. Housatonic was founded in 1994 by Will Thorndike, Michael Jackson and Eliot Wadsworth. The firm targets equity check sizes of between $10 and $50 million across a range of PE transaction types in the business services, technology and healthcare sectors.[11] While taking board seats in most of their companies, Housatonic generally does not become involved in the operations of their portfolio companies.[12] The firm manages $1.3 billion in committed capital and has invested in more than 100 companies since its founding.

Private equity firm staffing

As PE firms increase in AUM and scale, they tend to have many employees and specific roles for them. In this section, we outline the various roles in private equity firms, and then explore the staffing structures of the seven private equity firms that we consider in this chapter. While the discussion covers the typical structure, there are many different variations across firms on titles and roles that are beyond the scope of this book.

PE firms typically employ both investment and operating professionals although it is common for staff to wear both hats in smaller firms. Virtually all firms, from the smallest PE shops to the mega-funds, employ a tiered structure in which junior staff members support senior professionals. Generally, there are more junior professionals at each level than there are senior professionals. The most senior professionals in the firm are typically managing directors, or MDs. Some firms use the term partner or senior partner to refer to those most senior professionals. MDs and partners typically make the investment decisions as well as determining firm hiring, promotion and compensation. As we will see when we discuss compensation, they also typically are owners of the management company and receive a share of the residual profits of the firm.

Staffing under MDs and partners in PE resembles the structure used by investment banks. Typically, the entry level investment professionals are analysts. Analysts are part of the deal team and responsible for pulling together data, creating spreadsheets and presentations and generally providing low-level support to the deal team. Most analysts are recent college graduates who also have had two to three years of investment banking experience. Increasingly, PE firms also are hiring analysts directly out of college.

Most private equity firms have associates/senior associates who are primarily recent MBA graduates. Some PE firms also choose to promote their best analysts without requiring them to go to business school. Some of those firms provide in-house training in lieu of an MBA program. Associates are usually responsible for overseeing due diligence and financial modeling. If a firm has analysts, the associates typically manage their work product.

Next come the vice president positions, the most junior of senior staff members. Vice presidents often manage the day-to-day work on deals, supervising associates and analysts as they develop models and investment presentations/recommendation memoranda. Responsibility for the investment thesis and value creation is usually part of the vice president's role.

Above vice presidents are principals and directors. A major role for principals and directors is to generate deal flow. This can be by maintaining contact with deal brokers and investment bankers. It can also be through direct outreach to business owners, particularly for middle-market and smaller private equity firms. Finally, the most senior staff members are the partners, managing partners and managing directors. The exact use of particular titles may vary by firm, but these senior professionals are usually the face of the firm to investors. They maintain close relationships with the most important limited partners. They are also typically responsible for deal approval as well as staff promotions. And the largest portion of economics typically is allocated to this group of senior professionals.

Figure 10.1 looks at the typical years of PE experience by position.[13] On average, analysts have one year of PE experience. Associates/senior associates range in PE experience of up to five years with an average of two. Many associates/senior associates have prior experience in related finance positions like investment banking. Vice presidents have six years' PE experience on average while principals have worked in PE

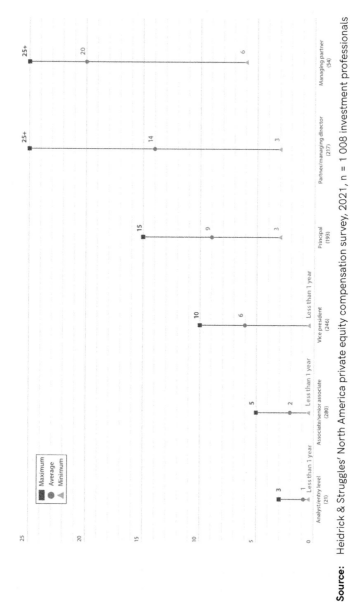

Source: Heidrick & Struggles' North America private equity compensation survey, 2021, n = 1 008 investment professionals

Figure 10.1   Years of Private Equity Experience by Level of Seniority

for an average of nine years. Finally, the most senior roles in PE, partner/ managing director and managing partner, have typically much longer experience at 14 and 20 years on average, respectively. The minimum amount of PE industry experience for these senior positions is two and three years. This indicates that some senior industry professionals have careers in other sectors before transitioning to investing.

Staffing and backgrounds in PE firms

In this section, we examine the staff structures in the seven private equity firms profiled above. In addition, we tabulate the prior career history of these employees, highlighting the education and employment history of those who work at each of the firms. There are important differences among private equity firms, and these differences appear to be embedded in the human capital of the PE managers.

We start with the two mega-fund PE firms, Bain Capital and KKR. Given their size, it is not surprising that they employ hundreds of people. In Table 10.1, we look only at the investment and operational professionals. There are many other employees critical to the success of the firm. This includes administrative, human resource, information technology and other areas. We focus on investment and operational employees because they are most directly linked to the investment strategies of the PE firms.

Given their size, mega-funds often appoint a senior professional to manage the firm's affairs. In the case of Bain Capital, that role is held by the chairman, of which the firm has two. KKR has a single president who serves a similar role. The most senior title at both Bain and KKR is managing director. Bain has 63 managing directors while KKR has 22 as part of the private equity team and nine in KKR Capstone. KKR has two additional senior professional levels: partner and director. On the PE investment side, KKR has 32 partners and 27 directors while KKR Capstone has two partners and 16 directors. Mid-level senior staff at Bain includes principals (32) as well as several different vice presidents (11 senior VPs, 14 executive VPs and 63 vice presidents). Principal is the largest category listed at KKR with the company having 44 principals on the investment team and 25 in KKR Capstone.

Table 10.1 Staffing Structures at Representative Private Equity Firms

Panel A: Mega-Fund Private Equity Firms

Mega-Funds

Bain Capital		KKR	
Chairman	2	President	1
Managing director	63	Managing director	22
Principal	32	Director	27
Executive vice president	14	Partner	32
Senior vice president	11	Principal	44
Vice president	63		
Operating partner	17	Partner	2
Senior advisor	6	Managing director	8
Senior executive	3	Director	16
		Principal	25
Total	211	Total	178

Panel B: Middle-Market Private Equity Firms

Middle-Market

Berkshire Partners		BC Partners		Vistria Capital	
Managing director	21	Managing director	10	Senior partner	4
Director principal	3	Director	5	Partner	7
Principal	11	Partner	17	Principal	2

Role		Role		Role	
Operating executive	2	Industrial partner	1	Vice president	6
Operating director	6	Principal	13	Senior associate	1
Vice president	4	Associate	19	Associate	4
Operating vice president	2	Analyst		Analyst	1
Senior advisor	4				
Advisory director	12				
Associate	19				
Total	84	Total	65	Total	25

Panel C: Small Private Equity Firms

Small

Housatonic Partners		Alpine Investment Partners	
Managing director	3	Partner	4
Partner	2	Director	1
VP	2	Principal	3
Director	1	Vice president	3
Associate	4	Senior associate	2
		Associate	4
		Analyst	5
		Investment professional	9
Total	12	Total	31

Source: Company Websites

There are several other positions at Bain Capital including 17 operating partners. Operating partners in private equity are typically former senior executives with a track record of successfully operating companies in industries targeted by the PE firm. Operating partners typically help with the due diligence for deals, serve on the board of directors of portfolio companies after they are purchased and sometimes serve as interim or permanent senior management of the portfolio companies.

Both Bain and KKR have senior advisors (Bain Capital having six and KKR having one). Senior advisors are generally not employees of the PE firm, but provide contacts for deals or advice during the due diligence process. Most are compensated with a retainer plus performance incentives. It should be noted that both Bain Capital and KKR employ analysts and associates, but these employees are typically not profiled on company websites or documents because most do not stay with the firm long term. This is true of most mega-fund PE firms, but as we will see below, middle-market and smaller PE firms do highlight more junior staff.

As shown in Panel B of Table 10.1, Berkshire Partners is typical of middle-market PE firms with a range of staff members. The most senior are the 21 managing directors. Below the MDs are principals (11) and directors (three). Below the senior staff are vice presidents (four on the investment team and two operating VPs). Like many middle-market PE firms, Berkshire makes use of a large number of associates to leverage the senior partners, having 19 as of late 2021.

Berkshire Partners, given its focus on operational engineering, also has a large number of professionals dedicated to assisting portfolio companies. Among those positions are advisory directors and operating executives. Berkshire defines advisory directors and operating executives as

> business executives or industry experts well known to Berkshire who participate in specific activities that arise in their areas of expertise, including deal origination, due diligence investigation, investment deliberation, and portfolio company advisory services. Advisory Directors are independent advisors that provide consulting services to Berkshire or its portfolio companies at varying levels of engagement.[14]

Berkshire has 12 advisory directors and two operating executives. The significant number of operating staff leads to a large number of professionals being associated with Berkshire relative to the other middle-market

PE firms which we profile. In total, we identified 80 investment staff members.

The heritage of BC Partners emerging from Baring's Bank can be seen in the heavy focus on investment professionals as opposed to pure operating staff members. The only partner directly allocated to operating activities is their industrial partner which aligns with a greater focus on governance and financial engineering in particular. BC Partners has 10 managing directors, five directors and 17 partners. Among junior staff members, they have 13 principals and 19 associates. The total staff size on the investment team that we could collect was 65 professionals.

Vistria, a relatively new PE firm, has a smaller staffing structure than either Berkshire or BC Partners. The most senior professionals in Vistria are senior partners and partners. There are four senior partners including the co-founders and seven partners. Vistria has a similar number of lower-tier senior professionals, two principals and six vice presidents. There are fewer junior staff as well, with one senior associate, four associates and one analyst employed at Vistria. This staffing structure comports with Vistria's strategy of adding value through high-level advice and contacts, focusing on helping to provide guidance with staffing and strategic relationships, as well as streamlining operations.[15]

Finally, we turn to staffing at small private equity firms. Housatonic illustrates a small PE firm focused on entrepreneur-led companies. Its investment philosophy is to back "exceptional entrepreneurs to build lasting companies that re-define their categories."[16] At the senior level there are three managing directors, one director and two partners. They are supported by two vice presidents and four associates.

Alpine Investors, a small PE firm in San Francisco that has recently grown, demonstrates a PE firm in transition from being a smaller manager to more of a middle-market one. There are only a few senior professionals (four partners and one director). The middle tier of staff members is substantially larger than Housatonic Partners. Alpine has one principal, three vice presidents and two senior associates. The firm also has a large number of junior team members, four associates and five analysts. Given the team nature of PE, most firms do not scale by adding substantially at the senior level. Like Alpine, they add middle and junior tier staff that can grow with the firm.

Educational and work backgrounds of private equity professionals

In this section, we examine the education and work histories of employees in the firms we have profiled in this section. These summaries provide insights into how firms match investment strategy with human capital. Little research has explored these differences and how these differences affect the types of investments a PE firm makes, the sources of value creation they pursue and the ultimate returns that the PE firms generate.

Our summary of backgrounds is taken from data we obtained from EMSI/Burning Glass (EMSI). EMSI gathers data from online resume sites and standardizes the information. Names of employers, titles, educational institution names and degrees are standardized to allow easier data gathering and analysis. We collected resumes for individuals who worked for any of our seven PE firms summarized in Table 10.1. Our analysis looks at junior staff (associates, senior associates and vice presidents) and senior staff (principals, partners, directors, managing directors and managing partners). In our analysis of junior staff members, we include everyone who was ever a junior staff member, even if they ultimately get promoted to a senior position in the firm, if they leave the firm or if they are still at the firm in a junior position.

In Panel A of Table 10.2, we look at Bain Capital employees. As is true of all our PE firms, they are heavily male dominated; 85.5% of senior employees and 66.4% of junior employees are male. In terms of professional background, 26.9% of junior employees had a consulting background prior to coming to Bain while 37.6% of senior employees had consulting experience. This is a high percentage relative to other large PE firms. Another large fraction of senior employees were CEOs/founders prior to joining Bain Capital (9.2%) while 15.0% had investment banking experience.

Educational background at Bain is also different from other mega firms. Senior employees are likely to have an MBA (66.9%) and that MBA is likely to be from an elite MBA program (classified as Harvard, Stanford, Wharton, University of Chicago and Northwestern). Elite or top-tier MBA adds Dartmouth, MIT and Columbia. Similarly, a high proportion of the senior (53.2%) and junior staff (40.7%) went to an elite undergraduate

Table 10.2   Educational and Employment Background of PE Firm Employees

Panel A: Bain Capital

Characteristic	Junior Employees (All)	Senior Employees
	Mean	Mean
Prior consulting experience	26.9%	37.6%
Prior CEO/founder experience	5.1%	9.2%
Prior IB/big bank experience	17.5%	15.0%
Prior finance experience (broad)	49.9%	43.4%
Male	66.4%	85.5%
Has MBA	28.0%	66.9%
Has elite MBA	21.4%	50.7%
Has elite or top-tier MBA	23.3%	54.9%
Elite undergraduate degree	40.7%	53.2%
Non-US undergraduate degree	5.5%	4.9%
Total	475	173

Panel B: KKR

Characteristic	Junior Employees (All)	Senior Employees
	Mean	Mean
Prior consulting experience	13.5%	16.0%
Prior CEO/founder experience	3.2%	1.9%
Prior IB/big bank experience	32.1%	38.8%
Prior finance experience (broad)	63.9%	66.0%
Male	65.8%	70.4%
Has MBA	15.7%	29.8%
Has elite MBA	10.8%	18.2%
Has elite or top-tier MBA	11.5%	21.6%
Elite undergraduate degree	33.6%	33.3%
Non-US undergraduate degree	10.6%	8.4%
Total	504	430

(Continued)

Table 10.2 (Continued)

Panel C: Berkshire Partners

Characteristic	Junior Employees (All)	Senior Employees
	Mean	Mean
Prior consulting experience	35.0%	37.8%
Prior CEO/founder experience	5.0%	2.2%
Prior IB/big bank experience	31.7%	17.8%
Prior finance experience (broad)	50.0%	57.8%
Male	79.7%	81.4%
Has MBA	44.9%	91.4%
Has elite MBA	42.9%	91.4%
Has elite or top-tier MBA	42.9%	91.4%
Elite undergraduate degree	51.2%	59.3%
Non-US undergraduate degree	6.1%	0.0%
Total	60	45

Panel D: BC Partners (US-Based Employees Only)

Characteristic	Junior Employees	Senior Employees
	Mean	Mean
Prior consulting experience	0.0%	16.7%
Prior CEO/founder experience	0.0%	5.6%
Prior IB/big bank experience	100.0%	77.8%
Prior finance experience (broad)	100.0%	88.9%
Male	87.5%	94.4%
Has MBA	0.0%	44.4%
Has elite MBA	0.0%	38.9%
Has elite or top-tier MBA	0.0%	38.9%
Elite undergraduate degree	87.5%	38.9%
Non-US undergraduate degree	0.0%	27.8%
Total	8	18

(Continued)

Table 10.2   (Continued)

Panel E: Vistria Capital

Characteristic	Junior Employees	Senior Employees
	Mean	Mean
Prior consulting experience	21.4%	17.6%
Prior CEO/founder experience	0.0%	11.8%
Prior IB/big bank experience	78.6%	47.1%
Prior finance experience (broad)	85.7%	94.1%
Male	71.4%	82.4%
Has MBA	35.7%	64.7%
Has elite MBA	35.7%	58.8%
Has elite or top-tier MBA	35.7%	58.8%
Elite undergraduate degree	35.7%	35.3%
Non-US undergraduate degree	7.1%	0.0%
Total	14	17

Panel F: Housatonic Partners

Characteristic	Junior Employees	Senior Employees
	Mean	Mean
Prior consulting experience	20.0%	42.9%
Prior CEO/founder experience	0.0%	14.3%
Prior IB/big bank experience	60.0%	28.6%
Prior finance experience (broad)	100.0%	100.0%
Male	100.0%	85.7%
Has MBA	20.0%	71.4%
Has elite MBA	20.0%	71.4%
Has elite or top-tier MBA	20.0%	71.4%
Elite undergraduate degree	40.0%	71.4%
Non-US undergraduate degree	0.0%	14.3%
Total	5	7

(*Continued*)

Table 10.2 (Continued)

Panel G: Alpine Investment Partners		
Characteristic	Junior Employees	Senior Employees
	Mean	Mean
Prior consulting experience	0.0%	0.0%
Prior CEO/founder experience	3.7%	22.2%
Prior IB/big bank experience	7.4%	0.0%
Prior finance experience (broad)	37.0%	44.4%
Male	63.0%	100.0%
Has MBA	0.0%	33.3%
Has elite MBA	0.0%	22.2%
Has elite or top-tier MBA	0.0%	33.3%
Elite undergraduate degree	92.6%	44.4%
Non-US undergraduate degree	0.0%	0.0%
Total	27	9

Source: Authors compiled from EMSI

program (defined as Ivy League, MIT, Stanford, University of Chicago, UC Berkeley, Duke and Northwestern).

Panel B of Table 10.2 shows a contrast between Bain Capital and KKR. KKR is slightly less male dominated with 70.4% of senior employees and 65.8% of junior employees being male. In terms of prior experience, KKR is more focused on finance with 38.8% of senior employees having an investment banking background and 66.0% having some form of finance experience prior to KKR. Junior staff finance backgrounds look very similar. On the other hand, relatively few senior or junior staff have consulting (16.0% and 13.5%) or prior CEO/founder experience (1.9% and 3.2%). This is consistent with the perception that KKR has a heavier focus on financial engineering than does Bain Capital. It also is consistent with KKR having an affiliated consulting firm in Capstone.

KKR is less reliant on MBAs. Only 29.8% of senior employees have an MBA and only 15.7% of junior employees have an MBA. Many of the mega-fund PE firms, like many investment banks, have invested in their internal training programs and, as such, a larger fraction of the junior staff do not go back to business school.

We also see a range of backgrounds for middle-market PE firms. Berkshire Partners has a higher percentage of junior and senior employees who are male than either KKR or Bain Capital with 81.4% of senior employees and 79.7% of junior employees. This is consistent with the work of Calder-Wang and Gompers (2021) who look at how more than 90% of senior investment professionals at small venture capital firms are male.[17] Given that middle-market PE firms are smaller than the megafund firms, it is more likely that homophily will lead to less diversity.

Berkshire Partners similarly has a high fraction of employees with consulting backgrounds, 37.8% and 35.0% for senior and junior staff respectively. A high percentage (57.8% for senior staff and 50% for junior staff) also have prior finance experience. What is perhaps more striking, however, is the heavy reliance on MBAs and especially elite MBAs. Of senior staff, 91.4% have an MBA from an elite school while 42.9% of junior employees have an elite MBA.

In Panel E, we tabulate the backgrounds of the US-based employees of BC Partners. Our data are limited to resumes of individuals in the US. At least for its US-based employees, BC Partners is heavily male, with 94.4% of senior employees and 87.5% of junior employees being male. The data show the clear link of BC Partners to its banking roots; 77.8% of senior employees have investment banking experience and 88.9% have prior broad finance employment. For junior employees it is 100%. The staffing matches the firm's strategy of focusing on financial engineering in its transactions. The firm also tends to rely less on MBAs; 38.9% of senior employees have an elite MBA and none of the junior employees.

Our final middle-market PE firm, Vistria Capital, has a more mixed staffing model. There is still a heavy reliance on finance experience; 47.1% of senior employees and 78.6% of junior employees have an investment banking background. When we look at a broader definition of finance experience, that number increases to 94.1% for senior employees and 85.7% for junior employees. Roughly a fifth of both senior and junior employees have some consulting experience. This brings both operational and financial skills to the deals that Vistria executes. Finally, Vistria has a moderate reliance on elite MBAs with 58.8% of senior employees holding an MBA from an elite program and 35.7% of junior employees.

Housatonic Partners and Alpine Investment Partners, as representative of small PE firms, offer contrasting approaches to staffing. One similarity is that both firms are heavily male, with 100% of all employees at Housatonic and 100% of senior professionals at Alpine being male. Housatonic is heavily dependent upon senior professionals with consulting backgrounds and elite MBAs; 42.9% of senior staff have consulting experience and 71.4% have an elite MBA. Interestingly, both senior and junior professionals at Housatonic have prior finance experience as well. This would seem to indicate that Housatonic wants professionals who can combine both operating and investing experience. This is consistent with Housatonic's stated investment strategy of taking board seats to advise management, but not becoming deeply involved in operations. At Alpine, none of the senior or junior staff have consulting backgrounds; 22.2% of senior employees have prior CEO or founder experience. Only 33.3% of Alpine's senior professionals have an MBA from a top program. Given that Alpine's focus is on finding quality management teams, it is likely the operational and deep finance experience may be less important.

Compensation structure and levels

In recent years, the interest among young professionals and MBA students in careers in PE has grown tremendously. One motivating factor is the perceived attractive compensation of PE professionals. Compensation in PE is complex and contains a number of pieces. There are a number of organizations that do compensation surveys. Each has slightly different methodologies and samples. For those interested in comparing surveys, the reference section lists several other PE compensation overviews. Here, we use data from Heidrick and Struggles 2021 North American Private Equity Compensation Survey. The survey received compensation data from 1011 PE investment professionals across a variety of fund sizes.

Like most professional positions, private equity cash compensation typically has two components: base salary and bonus. Second, incentive compensation also typically takes the form of a share of the carried interest. Carried interest compensation is expressed as a number of points of carry. One point of carry is 1% of the total carried interest that the firm is paid on a particular fund. For example, if a PE firm is paid 20% carried interest on a particular fund and an employee is allocated 10 points of carry, that represents 10% of the 20% or 2% of the profits on invested capital.

Carry is typically allocated primarily to senior-level staff in private equity firms. Ivashina and Lerner (2019) look at how various PE funds allocate carried interest in individual funds.[18] PE funds can have relatively "flat" carry allocation in which most senior professionals (directors and partners) receive similar allocations. Other firms have unequal distributions. In these funds, Ivashina and Lerner find that typically founders of the PE firm received substantially larger allocations of carry than other senior professionals. This unequal allocation comes with costs. The greater the unequal nature of carry, the higher the likelihood that senior professionals leave the PE firm. The departure of senior professionals is then associated with more difficulty fundraising afterwards.

The compensation survey from Heidrick and Struggles that we explore looks at all three elements of compensation in 2020 across various levels of seniority. In the compensation survey, carried interest is report as "carried dollars at work." It is simply the share of the carried interest (in percent, p) times the size of the fund (S), and the percent carry charged by the private equity manager. As an example, if a manager has 10 points of carry (out of 100) on a $1 billion fund that charges a 20% carry, she would have $20 million of carry dollars at work (10% × 20% × $1 000 000 000). This would also be her expected payout if the fund returns twice the invested capital. The survey expresses carry for all funds collectively for which the employee has a share.

Figure 10.2 tabulates compensation in 2020 for PE managing partners by firm AUM. For the smallest PE firms, those with AUM less than $500 million, average base cash compensation is just over $1 million and average cash bonus was $823 000. For the largest PE firms, managing partners had the lowest base compensation ($300 000), but the largest cash bonus ($3 million). This is likely due to these individuals owning a large share of the PE firm's management company. Management fees for a PE fund are paid to the management company which is owned typically by the PE firm's founders or most senior employees. The management company then pays all the expenses of the firm, e.g., salaries, rent, travel. Management fees in excess of these expenses are then paid out on an

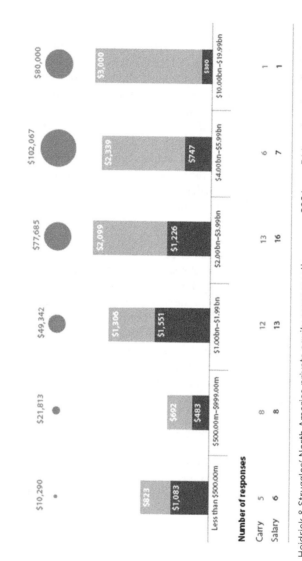

By AUM (USD, thousands)

■ Average base 2020 ■ Average bonus 2020 ● Average carry across all funds

	Less than $500.00m	$500.00m–$999.00m	$1.00bn–$1.99bn	$2.00bn–$3.99bn	$4.00bn–$5.99bn	$10.00bn–$19.99bn

Number of responses

	Less than $500.00m	$500.00m–$999.00m	$1.00bn–$1.99bn	$2.00bn–$3.99bn	$4.00bn–$5.99bn	$10.00bn–$19.99bn
Carry	5	8	12	13	6	1
Salary	6	8	13	16	7	1

Source: Heidrick & Struggles' North America private equity compensation survey, 2021, n = 51 investment professionals

Figure 10.2   Managing Partner Compensation in 2020 in Private Equity

annual basis to the owners of the management company. Hence, many of the most senior partners who own a large stake in the management company take relatively low salaries and receive a large share of the management company profits.

For most managing partners carried interest is by far the largest source of compensation. For the smallest PE firms, the managing partners' carry averaged $10.29 million. As discussed above, this is what they would expect to earn if all their funds earn a two times return on invested capital. Managing partners at large PE firms (those with more than $2 billion under management) have carry across all funds that is very large, ranging from $77.7 million for firms with $2.0 to $3.99 billion AUM to $102 million for PE firms with $4.0 to $5.99 billion.

The difference in compensation between a managing partner and partner/managing director is relatively small for small PE firms, but quite large for large PE firms as seen in Figure 10.3. Partners/managing directors for firms with less than $1 billion in capital have base cash salaries between $332 000 and $435 000. Cash bonus in 2020 averaged between $325 000 and $513 000 for this group. Carry across all funds was roughly $11 million. For large PE firms, those in excess of $4 billion in AUM, partner/managing director compensation was substantially below that of the managing partners. Base cash salary ranged from $435 000 to $885 000 and cash bonus averaged between $801 000 and $1.0 million. These levels, especially the bonus, are substantially below those of managing partners. As mentioned above, the difference is largely due to ownership of the management company. Carry, while larger for partners/managing directors at larger PE firms, was also substantially smaller than the carry of managing partners. For partners/managing directors of PE firms with $4.0 to $5.99 billion under management, carry averaged $27.2 million across all funds. For firms with greater than $10.0 billion under management, carry for partners/managing directors was between $36.9 and $40.2 million across all funds.

In Figure 10.4, the most junior senior professionals, principals, have substantially lower base cash salary and bonus than their senior colleagues. Base cash salary, depending upon the size of the PE firm, ranges between $250 000 and $350 000. Cash bonus at smaller PE firms is around $200 000 and at larger PE firms can be around $600 000. Principals begin to share in carry in a more meaningful way relative to their more junior

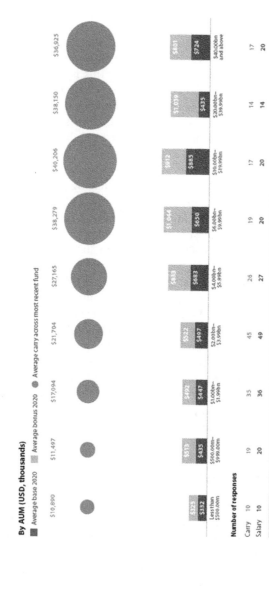

Source: Heidrick & Struggles' North America private equity compensation survey, 2021, n = 216 investment professionals

Figure 10.3   Partner/Managing Director Compensation in 2020 in Private Equity

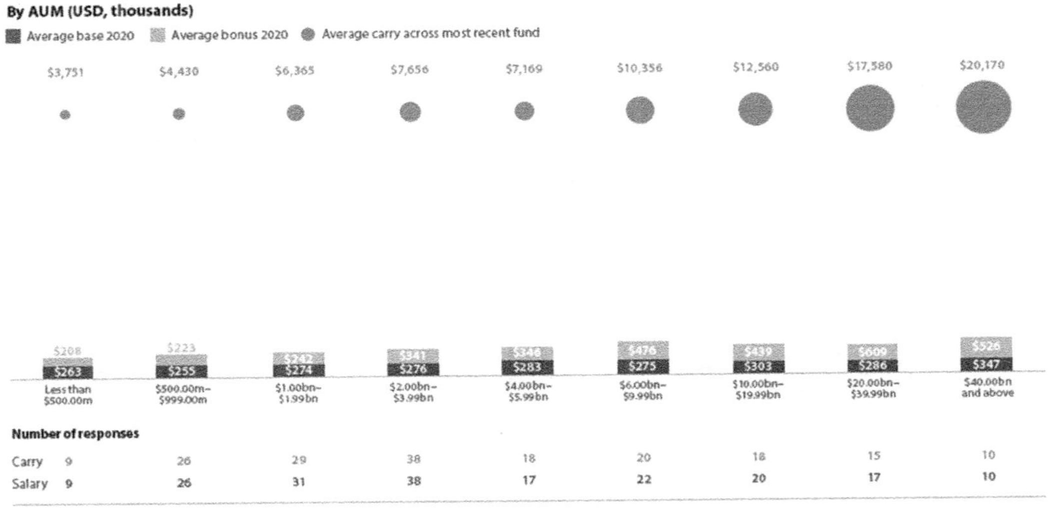

By AUM (USD, thousands)

Legend: ▪ Average base 2020   ▪ Average bonus 2020   ● Average carry across most recent fund

	Less than $500.00m	$500.00m–$999.00m	$1.00bn–$1.99bn	$2.00bn–$3.99bn	$4.00bn–$5.99bn	$6.00bn–$9.99bn	$10.00bn–$19.99bn	$20.00bn–$39.99bn	$40.00bn and above
Average base 2020	$208	$223	$242	$341	$348	$476	$439	$660	$926
Average bonus 2020	$263	$255	$274	$276	$283	$275	$303	$286	$347
Average carry	$3,751	$4,430	$6,365	$7,656	$7,169	$10,356	$12,560	$17,580	$20,170

Number of responses

	Less than $500.00m	$500.00m–$999.00m	$1.00bn–$1.99bn	$2.00bn–$3.99bn	$4.00bn–$5.99bn	$6.00bn–$9.99bn	$10.00bn–$19.99bn	$20.00bn–$39.99bn	$40.00bn and above
Carry	9	26	29	38	18	20	18	15	10
Salary	9	26	31	38	17	22	20	17	10

Source: Heidrick & Struggles' North America private equity compensation survey, 2021, n = 190 investment professionals

Figure 10.4   Principal Compensation in 2020 in Private Equity

colleagues. At small PE firms, carry at work is roughly $4 million while at larger firms it can be as high as $20 million on average. These carry figures are several-fold higher than the carry for vice presidents. As deal authority increases for principals, allocation of a share of profits and the alignment of incentives become more important.

For more junior professionals, the economics are generally substantially lower. Figure 10.5 looks at the 2020 compensation for vice presidents and Figure 10.6 shows associate/senior associate statistics. Base cash compensation for vice presidents is around $200 000 for all size PE firms while base cash salary for associates/senior associates is between $110 000 and $150 000. Cash bonus is usually close to or a little below the base salary numbers. As mentioned above, junior professionals get allocated relatively little carried interest. Given that junior professionals are primarily working at the direction of senior employees and have little deal authority, this makes sense.

The survey clearly shows that PE professionals are well compensated. The other important pattern is that compensation scales rapidly at more senior levels. This compensation increases in both cash compensation as well as incentive compensation as represented by carry allocation. Finally, managing partners, who are usually founders of the PE firms, receive a disproportionate share of the economics relative to other very senior professionals.

Conclusion

In this chapter we have explored how PE firms are staffed, recruited and compensated. Earlier chapters have been able to rely on extensive academic research to explore broader fund and investment issues including how firms add value to portfolio companies. Much less work has been done on the human capital that PE firms contain and how that human capital facilitates different strategies for value creation. We hope that this final chapter provides some insights into the tremendous heterogeneity that exists in the PE industry and how that can affect investment performance.

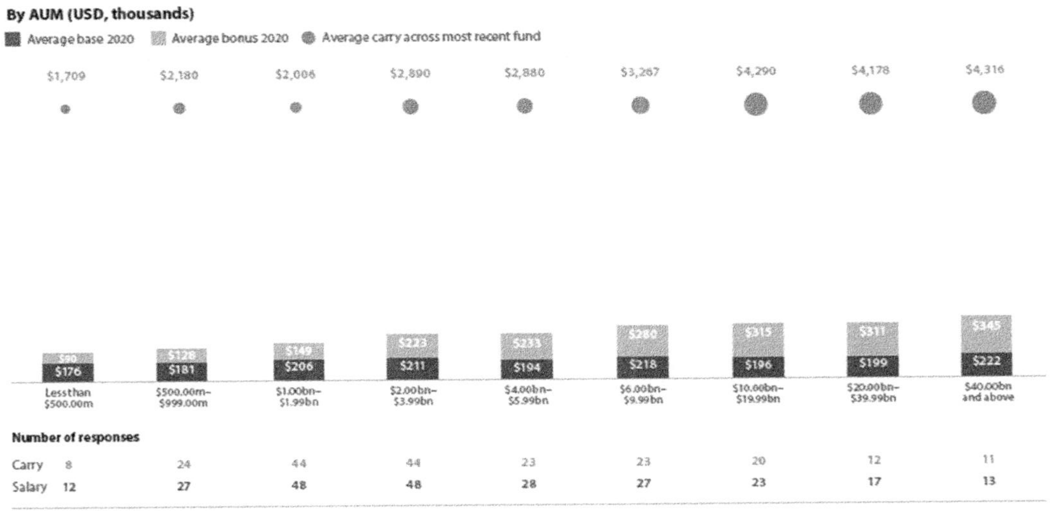

By AUM (USD, thousands)

■ Average base 2020   ▨ Average bonus 2020   ● Average carry across most recent fund

	Less than $500.00m	$500.00m–$999.00m	$1.00bn–$1.99bn	$2.00bn–$3.99bn	$4.00bn–$5.99bn	$6.00bn–$9.99bn	$10.00bn–$19.99bn	$20.00bn–$39.99bn	$40.00bn and above
Average carry	$1,709	$2,180	$2,006	$2,890	$2,880	$3,267	$4,290	$4,178	$4,316
Average bonus	$396	$328	$349	$223	$233	$260	$315	$311	$345
Average base	$176	$181	$206	$211	$194	$218	$196	$199	$222

Number of responses

	Less than $500.00m	$500.00m–$999.00m	$1.00bn–$1.99bn	$2.00bn–$3.99bn	$4.00bn–$5.99bn	$6.00bn–$9.99bn	$10.00bn–$19.99bn	$20.00bn–$39.99bn	$40.00bn and above
Carry	8	24	44	44	23	23	20	12	11
Salary	12	27	48	48	28	27	23	17	13

Source: Heidrick & Struggles' North America private equity compensation survey, 2021, n = 243 investment professionals

Figure 10.5   Vice President Compensation in 2020 in Private Equity

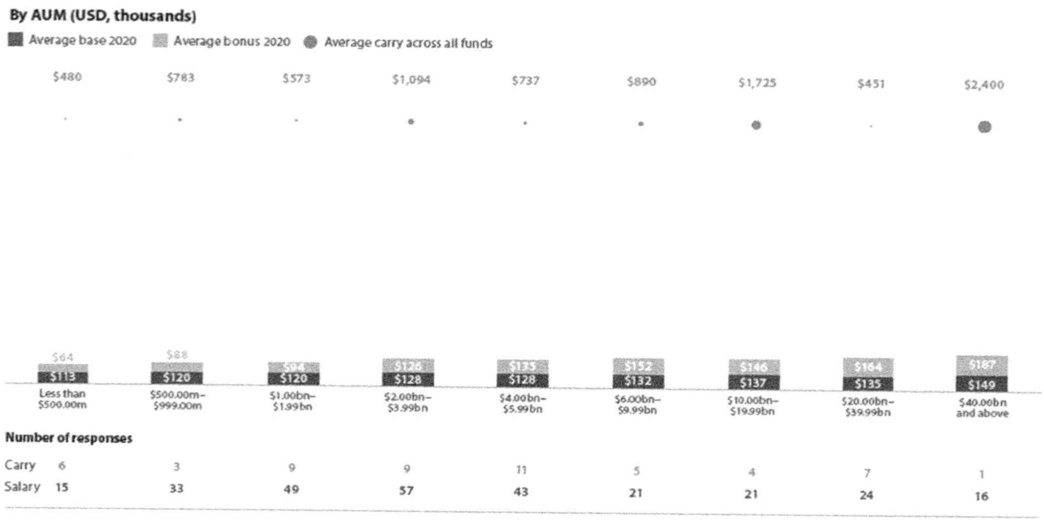

By AUM (USD, thousands)

Legend: ■ Average base 2020 ■ Average bonus 2020 ● Average carry across all funds

Average carry across all funds: $480, $783, $573, $1,094, $737, $890, $1,725, $451, $2,400

	Less than $500.00m	$500.00m–$999.00m	$1.00bn–$1.99bn	$2.00bn–$3.99bn	$4.00bn–$5.99bn	$6.00bn–$9.99bn	$10.00bn–$19.99bn	$20.00bn–$39.99bn	$40.00bn and above
Average base 2020	$64	$88		$124	$133	$132	$146	$164	$187
Average bonus 2020	$113	$120	$120	$128	$128	$132	$137	$135	$149

Number of responses

Carry	6	3	9	9	11	5	4	7	1
Salary	15	33	49	57	43	21	21	24	16

Source: Heidrick & Struggles' North America private equity compensation survey, 2021, n = 279 investment professionals

Figure 10.6 Associate/Senior Associate Compensation in 2020 in Private Equity

Notes

1   This discussion is based largely on Paul A. Gompers and Kristin Mugford, Bain Capital and Outback Steakhouse, Harvard Business School Case Number 212-087.
2   KKR website: www.kkr.com/businesses/private-equity accessed on 4 January 2022.
3   KKR website: www.kkr.com/businesses/private-equity accessed on 4 January 2022.
4   Berkshire Partners website: https://berkshirepartners.com/private-equity/sector-focus/ accessed on 7 January 2022.
5   Berkshire Partners website: https://berkshirepartners.com/private-equity/sector-focus/ accessed on 7 January 2022.
6   BC Partners website: www.bcpartners.com/private-equity-strategy, accessed on 6 January 2022.
7   BC Partners website: www.bcpartners.com/private-equity-strategy, accessed on 6 January 2022.
8   Vistria website: www.vistria.com/philosophy/ accessed on 6 January 2022.
9   Vistria website: www.vistria.com/philosophy/ accessed on 6 January 2022.
10 Alpine website: www.alpineinvestors.com/ accessed on 6 January 2022.
11 Housatonic website: https://housatonicpartners.com/companies/ accessed on 7 January 2022.
12 Housatonic website: https://housatonicpartners.com/companies/ accessed on 7 January 2022.
13 Heidrick and Struggles' North American Private Equity Compensation Survey, 2021.
14 Berkshire Partners website: https://berkshirepartners.com/team/michael-grebe/?rl=advisory-directors accessed on 9 January 2022.
15 Vistria website: www.vistria.com/platform/ accessed on 10 January 2022.
16 Housatonic Partners website: https://housatonicpartners.com/ accessed on 10 January 2022.
17 Sophie Calder-Wang and Paul A. Gompers, 2021, And the Children Shall Lead: Gender Diversity and Performance in Venture Capital, *Journal of Financial Economics* 142, 1–22.
18 Victoria Ivashina and Josh Lerner, 2019, Pay Now or Pay Later? The Economics within the Private Equity Partnership, *Journal of Financial Economics* 131, 61–87.

Index

Titles in the **Elgar Advanced Introductions** series include: